QTS

Teaching Science in Primary Schools

A Handbook of Lesson Plans, Knowledge and Teaching Methods

Graham Peacock

Letts

EDUCATIONAL

Aldine Place
London
W12 8AW

Tel: 020 8740 2266
Fax: 020 8743 8451
e-mail: mail@lettsed.co.uk

A CIP catalogue record is available from the British Library

ISBN 1-85805-351-X
Copyright Graham Peacock © 1999

Reprinted 2000

Designed and edited by Topics – The Creative Partnership, Exeter
Illustrations by Neil Annat and Clive Wakfer

Printed and bound in Great Britain by Ashford Colour Press Ltd

Contents

About the series

The Letts QTS Series offers support for all those preparing to become teachers and working towards Qualified Teacher Status (QTS). The content, teaching approaches and practical ideas are useful for trainee teachers, teacher tutors and mentors, and teacher educators in higher education.

The Letts QTS Series addresses the new standards for QTS and the content of the Initial Teacher Training National Curriculum (ITTNC). These are central to the improvement of standards in schools. The series is specifically designed to help all trainee teachers cover the content of the ITTNC and achieve the national standards in order to be awarded QTS.

The short series handbook *QTS: A Practical Introduction* gives trainees an overview of the QTS requirements and a more detailed interpretation of each standard.

The other books in the Letts QTS Series offer trainees the chance to audit their knowledge of the content of the subjects in the ITTNC, pinpoint areas of further work, and use support materials to develop their knowledge.

With the exception of information and communications technology (ICT), which is covered in a single, integrated volume, books in the Letts QTS Series address separately the needs of trainees preparing to teach in the primary or the secondary phase of schooling. For each type of trainee there are two books per subject:

Book 1 addresses trainees' subject knowledge at their own level by offering a systematic and comprehensive guide to the subject knowledge requirements of the ITTNC. Trainees can check their own knowledge of the subject against that specified in the ITTNC. Section one provides a comprehensive **audit** of this subject knowledge and understanding, with helpful **feedback** and follow-up set out in section two. Having identified areas of subject knowledge for attention, and pinpointed some of the subject's **key ideas**, trainees can then use the materials to map out their **personal learning plan**.

Book 2 for each subject is a handbook of **lesson plans**, **knowledge** and **methods**. This provides details of carefully selected lessons which illustrate effective teaching. It shows how lesson planning and classroom teaching draw on a high level of subject knowledge. It demonstrates how carefully integrated whole-class teaching and group and individual work can be designed to ensure that pupils make progress in their learning.

The Letts QTS Series aims to break down the requirements of QTS into manageable units so that trainees can evaluate and improve their knowledge of each subject. The books in the series are written in a straightforward way by authors who are all experienced teachers, teacher educators, researchers, writers and specialists in their subject areas.

About this book

Intended for both trainee and practising teachers, this book introduces the knowledge base and teaching approaches relevant to primary science. It includes a survey of some of the relevant skills in and uses of information and communications technology (ICT), summaries of the key ideas associated with the teaching and learning activities suggested, and an explanation of the common alternative constructs (misconceptions) that pupils bring to their work in science, so that trainee teachers in particular can be ready to meet the needs of the children who hold them. It also details a progression of learning activities at Key Stages 1 and 2, with lesson plans and other styles of working proposed.

The first three chapters introduce a range of ideas, approaches and issues in the teaching of primary science:

- **How do children learn science?** is a brief outline of two theories about how children learn scientific ideas.

- **Investigation skills in primary science** covers the planning and carrying out of investigations, focusing mainly on the handling of information and interpretation of data. It includes a useful list of starting points for investigations in primary science. A section on information and communications technology gives ideas about how to use ICT – including spreadsheets, databases and other computer applications – to help pupils in their learning about science.

- **Assessment in primary science** suggests a range of straightforward approaches and strategies, emphasizing that assessment is a means of helping children develop and not an end in itself.

The rest of the book is full of easy-to-use, practical ideas to support teaching and learning in primary science. Each chapter focuses on one subject area, and has the following common features:

- **Key ideas** summarizes the concepts and content that teachers will need to know to teach the area confidently.

- **Common misconceptions** alerts teachers to some of the more widely held misconceptions that some children may have. This section could, perhaps, be more appropriately called 'alternative constructs' or 'children's ideas'. However this book uses, where possible, the language of the ITTNC.

- A range of learning and teaching activities is suggested for each key stage. This section is divided into activities for Key Stage 1, early Key Stage 2 (2a) and later Key Stage 2 (2b). Each activity is accompanied by a few sentences of background information for teachers.

- A **teaching strategy** is proposed, featuring a particular approach developed in more detail, such as a series of lessons, a circus of activities, assessment activities, demonstrations or workcards. Although the criteria for choosing a strategy should be based on its appropriateness to subject area, many of the approaches suggested are transferable to a variety of contexts.

How do children learn science?

Knowledge
Learning
Attitudes, interests, skills

Motivation

Scientific and
mathematical skills

What is a concept?

The moving Earth

A mental picture of
the Earth in space

Not just knowledge

Although the emphasis in this book is on knowledge, when children encounter science they also learn other equally important things. They develop attitudes, interests and skills. The primary years are important for the formation of attitudes towards science, for challenging stereotypes about scientists and for enabling children to build confidence in their own abilities to do science. Teachers can help by providing scientific activities that are relevant to children's lives, by acting as role models and by encouraging pupils to see themselves as scientists.

Many skills can be learnt through science, via the planning and carrying out of investigations, for instance, or the use of equipment. Some, such as working collaboratively and systematically on practical tasks, have wider application. Equally, skills learnt in other subjects, such as graphing or measuring in maths, can be applied in science investigations. However children may need to be encouraged to transfer their skills in this way.

> The primary years are important to attitude formation.

> Teaching and practising skills enables pupils to gain greater competence and independence as they progress.

More than facts

It may seem that science is defined by the huge number of ideas it describes and that to be a good scientist only requires the learning of scientific facts. However, science is not just a catalogue of facts. More important than any individual piece of knowledge is the sense we make of the ideas of science. A concept is a mental construct that holds ideas together and may help to explain a particular phenomenon. For instance, we can learn the following isolated pieces of information:

- The sun rises in the east.
- The sun moves across the sky and sets in the west.
- It is night in Australia when it is day in Britain.
- The moon sets in the west.
- The stars rise in the east and set in the west.

All these ideas are linked to the scientific concept of a rotating Earth. With the strong mental picture of a rotating Earth, the individual pieces of information hold together to make coherent sense. However, it is also possible to know all these facts and yet have a completely different, and scientifically incorrect, concept. For instance, many children, and not a

> Great scientists make leaps of understanding that pull together already known facts to create a new and more convincing picture of the world.

few adults, still believe that the Earth stays still whilst the stars, sun and moon rotate about the Earth.

Classification concepts

A further example may help to illustrate the distinction between facts and the concepts that link them. Children and adults may know these facts:

- A cod is a fish.
- A cow is a mammal.
- A bat is a mammal.
- A frog is an amphibian.

All correctly describe vertebrates, but the facts alone do not necessarily form a concept. The concept of what constitutes a mammal or an amphibian has to be generalized from the characteristics of animals in the group. For instance, if the learner knows the distinguishing features of a mammal (hair, produces milk, has warm blood) she can apply this generalization to new animals, thereby extending and developing the concept.

Increasingly powerful concepts

At a higher level, the relatedness of the five vertebrate groups is an even more powerful concept with greater explanatory range. We may know for instance that reptiles lay leathery eggs on land whereas amphibians lay eggs in water. This is a useful distinction, but becomes a powerful concept when coupled with the insight that reptiles were descended from the more primitive amphibians.

Empty vessels?

Telling children a list of scientific facts is one view of how science is taught and learnt. This view of learning could be caricatured as simply opening up the learner's head and pouring in learning. However, most educationalists feel that this relatively simple view of how people learn is unlikely to be true. Learning is now seen as an active processing of information and ideas in which new links are formed.

Factual recall, as opposed to conceptual understanding, can easily be quantified and so it is the most common skill that is tested. For example, if you ask a child what is needed to light a bulb you may well elicit the correct answer 'a complete circuit'. But does this show that the child has a robust and powerful concept of what is happening in a circuit? To find out whether this is indeed the case requires careful questioning and observation. Testing factual recall is always easier than testing conceptual understanding.

Is practical work enough?

I hear and I forget. I see and I remember. I do and I get more confused.

In its original wording this old adage suggests that by doing a learner gains understanding. However, this rather cosy idea is only, at best,

---

Facts about animals

The concept of a mammal

Concepts help us deal with new experience.

Reptiles evolved from amphibians.

Can we teach facts alone?

Surface learning

A new proverb for teachers

When asked whether a worm is an animal, many junior children say it is not.

Many children are confused about whether or not people are animals.

Birds evolved from reptiles at the time of the dinosaurs.

The original ends 'I do and I understand'.

partly true. We understand things not simply by carrying out practical work but by reflecting on the experience it yields in the light of our previous knowledge. The role of a teacher is vital in getting learners to make sense of what they have seen and done.

Teachers help learners to understand.

For instance, we have all observed the difference between dropping a piece of tissue and a heavier item, like a stone. This is practical experience, but for the majority of us it does not lead to an understanding of gravity or air resistance. This is hardly surprising because the ideas connected with these two areas of science are quite difficult to work out from first principles. In many ways they are counter-intuitive. That is, they are not common-sense ideas.

Aspects of air resistance are counter-intuitive.

See pages 133–43 for more about gravity and air resistance.

Constructivism: An influential theory of learning

Introduction

A definition

Constructivism is a theory of learning that suggests that learners bring their existing knowledge to bear on new situations, extending and developing their ideas and knowledge in the light of new experiences. Most important, constructivism suggests, the learner must be involved in this process in an active way. Ultimately learners construct their new view of the world for themselves.

Constructivism is the most pervasive theory at present.

Constructivism suggests that the learner has personal mental frameworks that connect pieces of knowledge and otherwise isolated ideas and experiences. Children actively seek patterns in experiences long before they enter formal education and in many instances young children have well-developed conceptual frameworks that can be at variance with those held by scientists. These misconceptions are often highly resistant to change since they appear to explain much of what the child sees. For instance, the misconception that the Earth is stationary whilst the moon and sun are in motion around it nevertheless explains all the observations that a child is likely to make.

Misconceptions are resistant to change.

Many teachers feel that misconceptions should be called 'alternative constructs'.

Even when the word constructivism is not actually used by writers, the underlying ideas pervade much writing about learning in science. The National Curriculum Council (the forerunner of SCAA and QCA) used constructivist arguments in its advice to teachers, suggesting that the way a child's understanding develops depends both on existing ideas and on the process by which those ideas are used and tested in new situations.

Testing ideas in new situations

The National Curriculum Council (NCC) begat the School Curriculum and Assessment Authority (SCAA) which begat the Qualifications and Curriculum Authority (QCA).

Listen to children's ideas.

The NCC also emphasized the need to listen carefully to pupils' existing ideas, suggesting that existing understandings should not be viewed as wrong since they may fit the child's view of the situation. The NCC suggested that listening carefully to what children have to say on a subject helps teachers to identify the children's existing understanding.

A few key texts on constructivism

Driver was a productive and influential writer.

One of the seminal texts about constructivism was written by Driver (1983). She described how pupils, like scientists, view the world

See *Further Reading* on page 178.

through the lens of their preconceptions, and that many have difficulty in exchanging their preconceived ideas for the ideas presented in science lessons.

There is a large body of writing about the different meanings attached by people to scientific words. Even apparently simple classifying words such as 'animal' can present problems in understanding. An account of this, and much more, can be found in Osborne and Freyberg (1985).

The SPACE project (Russell *et al.* 1990) was an attempt to examine children's concepts in some detail and includes volumes dealing with most areas of primary science. Wynne Harlen, a highly influential primary science writer, was involved in the SPACE project. She has written extensively about how children learn scientific concepts, and you will find a description and analysis of constructivism in Harlen (1995). Ollerenshaw and Ritchie (1997) explain in detail how their version of constructivism applies to teaching science to young children.

Nuffield Primary Science (Collins, 1995) is a pupils' scheme which is firmly based on constructivist ideas.

Constructivism in practice

Many writers describe what constructivism means in practice. It is often expressed in a step-by-step approach that involves:

- finding out what the children already know

- asking the children to explain what they already understand

- working out how to teach the children so they can move on from their present understanding to a more scientifically correct one

- organizing active learning (This does not necessarily mean that the children will be physically moving around but it does mean that children will be actively trying to understand new knowledge for themselves.)

- discussing and applying new ideas.

The word 'elicitation' is often used to describe the process of finding out what children already know.

The limits of constructivism

With its emphasis on understanding scientific ideas through experience, a naive view of constructivism might suggest that learners could be expected to work out complex principles for themselves, such as the germ theory of disease or the structure of chromosomes. This is, of course, unlikely. Each of these theories is the product of generations of scientists building up a shared view of the world that transcends any one individual's view.

Science is a collaborative undertaking, and even geographically isolated scientists build on the published work of others.

It follows from this that teachers have a duty to do more than simply organize learning events from which children acquire a personal understanding of how the world works. Teachers are responsible for introducing the dominant notions of the culture of science, which learners are unlikely to understand by independent experience and thinking. In this context, teachers might be thought of as providing a scaffolding of ideas to help learners reach further than they would if operating alone. The pupil relies on the scaffolding for as long as it takes to reach secure mastery of the ideas and internalize them.

'Scaffolding' is a term associated with the Russian psychologist Lev Vygotsky.

Is it an animal?

Harlen is a highly influential figure.

Features of constructivist teaching

The meaning of 'active learning'

Can learners work out complex theories for themselves?

Introduction to the culture of science

Role of language

Another aspect of learning to which constructivism pays relatively little attention is the role of language, and particularly the cultural elements of language. In addition to the internal dialogue with which individuals attempt to construct meaning for themselves, we need to acknowledge the cultural aspects of building up a shared understanding through language. Vygotsky argued that children use language for problem solving and that the greater the complexity of the problem the greater the reliance placed on language, with correspondingly less emphasis placed on practical action.

Hodson (1998) is an accessible introduction to Vygotsky's work and its relationship to constructivist ideas.

Investigation skills in primary science

Planning

Asking questions

Practice in asking questions

Children need practice in asking questions. For instance, if you are doing work on rocks, ask the children to suggest things they want to find out about rocks. If you are doing investigations involving minibeasts, get the children to write a list of things they would like to know about minibeasts. Afterwards put the children in small groups to decide which were the best questions. Discuss the questions with the class and say which ones it would be possible to investigate practically.

What questions are practicable?

How we find some answers

The processes by which children can find out answers to their questions are also worth considering. For instance, they could answer 'How do ants breed?' by using a book or CD-ROM, 'What minibeasts are there in the flowerbed outside the classroom?' by investigation and 'Which minibeasts do gardeners find useful?' by asking a local gardener.

> Children may surprise you with the range of questions they suggest.

Predicting

What is a prediction?

A prediction can simply be what children say they expect will happen. Prediction is a very useful skill, partly because it helps children plan what they will do in the course of an investigation, but also because it encourages them to draw upon their scientific knowledge. Take care not to make predicting a chore. The routine requirement of having to make a written prediction before starting an experiment could become very tedious for all concerned.

Hypothesis

Distinction between prediction and hypothesis

To make a hypothesis, children must explicitly base their prediction on a theory or concept. A hypothesis must be phrased in a way that allows it to be tested and then either confirmed or falsified. 'I think the car will roll further off the ramp if it is loaded with plasticine' is a prediction. A hypothesis would be: 'I think that if we add heavy lumps of plasticine to this car it will roll further off the ramp because it has more energy.'

Incidentally, this idea makes an interesting experiment, but the results may not be the ones you would expect.

> A hypothesis could be viewed simply as a prediction with 'because' at the end.

Changing factors

Change one factor at a time.

Factors are also known as variables. Children should be taught how to change one factor whilst leaving the others the same. So in a test to see which of several balls bounces highest the only thing to vary each time is the ball (the independent variable). All other factors, such as the height of drop, the surface dropped on, the method of measurement and the way in which the balls are dropped should remain the same. This control of variables constitutes a fair test.

This is the idealized version. Reality is less straightforward. For instance, if you wanted to investigate the effect of changing the size of a parachute canopy, you would need to keep all factors, apart from area of canopy, the same. However, by increasing the canopy's area you are also increasing the weight of the parachute. So the test is no longer fair. Similarly if you were to try to see what effect less light has on the growth of plants you would almost certainly change the air temperature surrounding the plants as a consequence of shielding or repositioning them. This would result in the change of two variables at the same time and, strictly speaking, make the test unfair.

Professional scientists spend much time and energy trying to disentangle the variables in their experiments and surveys. You only need to think about the confused messages we receive about diet and lifestyle to realize that researchers find it almost impossible to disentangle associations from cause and effect.

Fair tests are not easy to design.

Changing one factor can change another.

Is butter 'bad' for you?

> Some children think a test is fair if everyone in the group gets a chance to do the interesting part of the experiment!

> In practice, this will have little practical effect on work done in the primary classroom, but teachers should be aware of it as a possible source of error.

> Even the clear-cut health risks of smoking are disputed by some people.

Using planning templates

Many teachers find it helpful to use templates when getting children to plan their work. These help the children to focus on the step-by-step nature of an investigation. However, it would be tedious for children to be faced with a template every time they did any scientific work, and it is conceivable that slower children would spend longer filling in the template than doing any practical science. Teachers often find templates useful as a means of structuring their questioning of children prior to an investigation.

Templates vary according to the age of the children who are going to be using them. Here are two examples:

Templates provide a useful structure.

Key Stage 1 template (left)

Key Stage 2 template (right)

Our question:

What we are going to do:

What we think might happen:

What happened:

Our explanation:

Our question:

What we are going to do:

What we will change:

What we will measure:

What we think will happen:

We think this will happen because:

We will record what happens like this:

The results:

Our explanations:

Was the test fair?

> Write the children's ideas on 'post-it' notes and stick them on to the planning template.

> 'What we will change' is the independent variable. 'What we will measure' is the dependent variable.

Obtaining evidence

Measuring quantities

Measuring

Children need to be taught how to use basic measuring apparatus. At some stage they will need to measure the following quantities:

length   mass
time   weight and other forces
volume
temperature

Choosing the correct instrument

Give the children a simple task such as measuring a string (Key Stage 1) or measuring the air temperature in the classroom (Key Stage 2). Letting them choose the instrument will give you valuable information about their ability to select and use appropriate instruments.

> Weight is a force and should be measured with a spring balance.

Teaching how to use it

Children will need to be taught the correct way to handle and read measuring instruments. For instance, do not take it for granted that everyone will know which knob to press on a stopwatch to start it, stop it, reset it or change the mode.

> Untutored children may lift thermometers out of a liquid to read them.

Using computers

Computers can be used to gather information via a datalogger.

> See page 24.

Repeating measurements

By the time children reach Year 3 they should be beginning to repeat tests. They should do this because:

Why repeat measurements?

- the result of one test might be a fluke
- the final result is more accurate if some form of average can be calculated
- an anomalous measurement can be spotted by looking at the other results.

Calculating the mean

The mean is calculated by adding up a series of readings and dividing by the number of readings:

Making a tower with left hand	
Attempt	Speed (seconds)
1	15
2	14
3	10

Mean = 13 seconds

> Mean, median and mode are all ways of finding an average. The easiest method for young children is the median. Often this will be very similar to the mean.

The median

The median is the middle value in a series of readings:

Rolling a ball	
Test	Distance (cm)
1	76
2	60
3	74

Median = 74 cm

The mode

The mode is the most frequently occurring value in a series of readings:

Colour of eyes in the class	
Colour	Number of children
blue	12
brown	10
hazel	4

Mode = blue

Considering evidence

Discrete data

Types of data
Data can be either discrete or continuous.

Discrete data consists of separate items. They are usually measured in whole numbers and there are no decimal points or fractions. Examples of discrete data include:

- the performance of different toy cars on a ramp
- the number of bricks under the ramp
- the number of layers of insulation round a bottle
- the type of ball used in bouncing tests.

Continuous data

Continuous data is measured in quantities that can be any value between zero and the highest number recorded. Examples of continuous data include:

- the distance rolled by a car on a ramp
- the height of the ramp measured in centimetres
- the mass loaded on to one car
- the distance rolled by that car
- the mass of insulating material packed around a bottle
- the number of strokes from a pump used to inflate a football
- the height of the bounce of a ball.

> This distinction is important when you are considering the type of graph to use to display the data.

Overlapping sets

Venn and Carroll diagrams
Venn diagrams show sets of objects. Overlapping sets indicate that certain members of certain sets share common features.

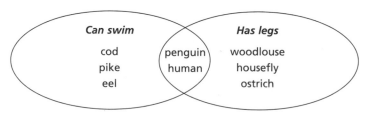

Carroll diagrams

Carroll diagrams show the relationship between two sets of data. Each data set has two mutually exclusive categories.

	Farm animal	Not farm animal
Has hair	cow sheep	lion giraffe
No hair	chicken	eagle snail

> Carroll diagrams are easier to handle if built up in several stages.

Dependent or
independent variable?

Dependent and independent variables

The independent variable is the value that we can systematically change in an investigation. Examples of independent variables are:

- the height from which a ball is dropped
- the area of a parachute canopy
- the weight attached to a piece of elastic to make it stretch
- the number of paperclips attached to a gyrocopter.

Continuous and discrete

Notice that the first three are also continuous variables whilst the last one is a discrete variable.

The dependent variable is the value that changes in response to the systematic changes made to the independent variable. Examples of dependent variables are:

- the height of the bounce of a ball
- the time taken for a parachute to fall
- the length of an elastic band when stretched by weights

Notice that all of these also happen to be continuous variables.

> This information is essential to understanding how to draw graph axes correctly. See below.

The *x* and *y* axes

Introduction to graphs

Graphs have two axes: the *x* axis and the *y* axis. The *x* axis shows the independent variable, the *y* axis shows the dependent variable.

In the graph below, force is the dependent variable and mass is the independent variable.

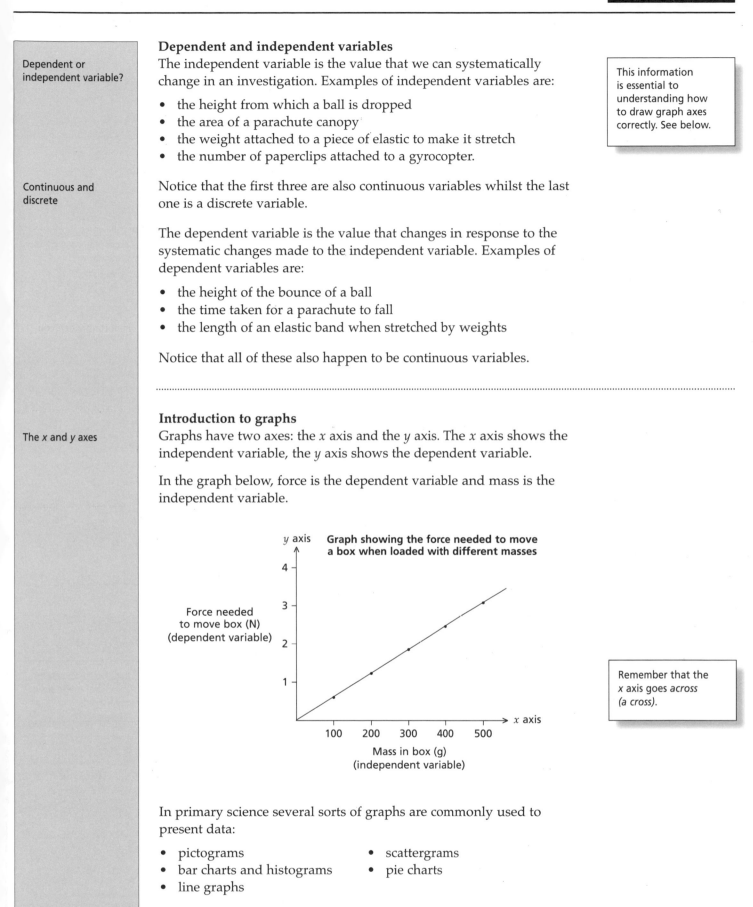

> Remember that the *x* axis goes *across* (a cross).

In primary science several sorts of graphs are commonly used to present data:

- pictograms
- bar charts and histograms
- line graphs
- scattergrams
- pie charts

Pictograms

These can be made in a variety of ways. Children can place a brick of the appropriate colour to show what colour of sweet they like.

Eye colour

Children can colour an eye on a square piece of paper and place it on a graph like this:

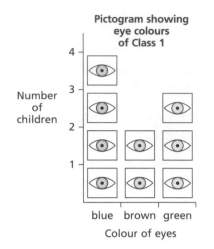

Pictogram showing eye colours of Class 1

Number of children

Colour of eyes

Graphs like this are interpreted with ease by young children who can talk or write about what they notice.

Hair colour and gender are two good categories for simple pictograms.

Bar charts and histograms

Easy bar charts

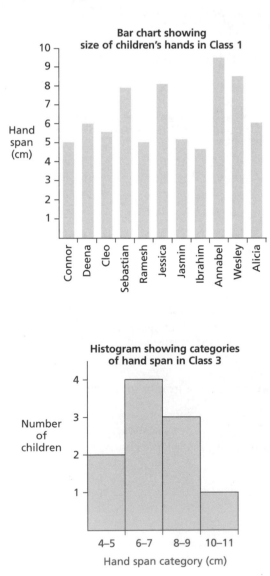

Bar chart showing size of children's hands in Class 1

Hand span (cm)

Connor, Deena, Cleo, Sebastian, Ramesh, Jessica, Jasmin, Ibrahim, Annabel, Wesley, Alicia

Bar charts can show individual items along the *x* axis.

Histogram showing categories of hand span in Class 3

Number of children

4–5   6–7   8–9   10–11

Hand span category (cm)

Bar charts are used more commonly than histograms in primary science since they are much easier to construct. They differ from histograms in these respects:

- Their bars are separate; in histograms the bars are touching.
- Their bars are the same width since only the height of each bar is significant; in histograms the area of the bar is significant.
- They deal only with discrete data; histograms deal with continuous data.
- Histograms often represent categories of readings.

Easy bar charts can be made in the classroom using strips of paper. First use the strips to measure the dependent variables that involve length (e.g. of a foot) or circumference (e.g. of a head), cutting them to size. Then make the strips into bar charts. For example, using different coloured strips for boys and girls, get each child to put one foot on a strip of paper. Cut the strips to length and mount them on a large sheet of graph paper.

This cut-and-glue method can be applied to many dependent variables which have dimensions that can be measured.

Line graphs

A line graph can be drawn when you have continuous data from both the dependent and independent variables in an investigation and there is a clear trend in the readings.

For instance, you could count the number of swings made by pendulums of different lengths over a period of 30 seconds. In this case the number of swings is dependent only upon the length of the pendulum. The line graph with length of string on the *x* axis and number of swings on the *y* axis will show a clear trend.

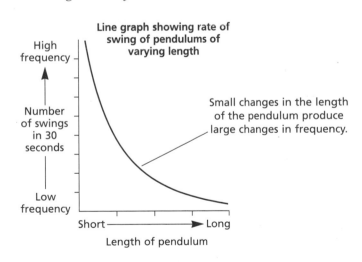

Line graph showing rate of swing of pendulums of varying length

High frequency

Number of swings in 30 seconds

Small changes in the length of the pendulum produce large changes in frequency.

Low frequency

Short — Long

Length of pendulum

If the children were to do this work you would want them to look at the trends shown in the graph. For instance, they would notice that a pendulum swings more slowly as its length increases, but that it is never stationary. Even if the pendulum were several miles long it would still swing. Similarly, if the pendulum were only several molecules long, in theory it would be possible to measure its very rapid swings. The line in the graph does not at any point cut either axis.

Differences between bar charts and histograms

Two sets of continuous data

Trends

Graphs help you imagine theoretical possibilities.

Histograms are rarely used in primary schools.

String or coloured wool can also be cut to length and mounted on the paper.

The length of the string is the independent variable here.

Taking a pulse before and after exercise gives the data for a good line graph.

Two related readings

Scattergrams

Scattergrams are useful when you have data that indicates a relationship between pairs of readings. For instance, the table below records the heights and hand spans of individual children. There is clearly a relationship between the two variables that is best shown using a scattergram.

Height	120	132	124	126	121	115	135
Span	11	13	11	12	10	8	14

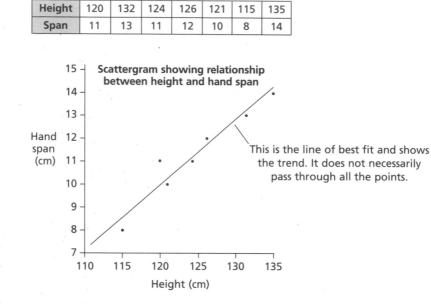

Scattergram showing relationship between height and hand span

This is the line of best fit and shows the trend. It does not necessarily pass through all the points.

A line of best fit can show the trend on a scattergram.

Opportunities to use scattergrams

Other examples of variables whose relationship can be measured by scattergrams include speed of child running 30 metres against leg length, size of arm length against height, and age against circumference of head. Like a line graph, a scattergram needs two sets of continuous variables.

Pie charts

Computers make pie charts easy.

Pie charts are quite complex to draw by hand since they involve tricky calculations involving angles and fractions. However, with the aid of computers pie charts are simple to produce.

Pie charts are useful when you have data that shows how one whole set subdivides. For instance, if you have been observing birds on the playground during a ten-minute period you could use the computer to draw a pie chart showing the relative abundance of types.

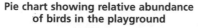

Pie chart showing relative abundance of birds in the playground

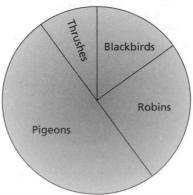

A pie chart can show you absolute numbers. In this case, if you know that a total of 20 sightings was made, the numbers of each bird seen would be:

5 robins   2 thrushes
3 backbirds   10 pigeons

Computers draw pie charts showing either percentages of the whole pie or the absolute numbers represented by each slice.

<table>
<tr><td>

Opportunities to use pie charts
</td><td>

Pie charts can be used to analyse a variety of data. For instance, they might be used to show the proportion of various minibeast types found in different locations in the school, the proportion of different plants found in a hoop during ecology investigations or the different types of fuel used by children to heat their food at home.
</td></tr>
</table>

Examples of productive investigations

Different levels for each key stage

Introduction

There are a great many contexts for good scientific investigations. A wide selection is presented in the later sections of this book. The ideas suggested below have been broken down into the different levels of approach required at Key Stages 1, 2a (Y3 and Y4) and 2b (Y5 and Y6). These are followed by a list of starting points for investigations for you to adapt to the age group you are teaching.

Growing seedlings

Which conditions are best?

Key Stage 1
Grow seedlings in a variety of conditions. Which grow? What conditions do seedlings grow in best? Draw a pictogram of the results.

> Seeds need only air and water to germinate, but seedlings must have light as well in order to photosynthesize.

Graph the results.

Key Stage 2a
Water five identical seedlings with different amounts of water. Which grows best? Graph the results with a bar chart.

List factors.

Key Stage 2b
List the factors that affect the growth of seedlings. Plan tests to investigate one of the factors. If one measurement is distance from a window it might be possible to draw a line graph of the results.

What do birds eat?

Bird cafe

Key Stage 1
Put out some food for the birds: bread, fat, nuts, chocolate, potatoes. Which one are they attracted to the most? Which food gets finished first? Present the results in the form of a menu for the birds.

Tally charts

Key Stage 2a
Survey the birds that come to the playground after morning play. Make a simple tally chart for each type of bird. Draw a bar chart.

Pigeon	III
Sparrow	II
Blackbird	⊬⊬⊬ I

> The children might make a connection between different foods and types of beak.

Using a spreadsheet

Key Stage 2b
Investigate which species of bird likes which sort of food out of the range offered. Draw up a table and enter a tally each time a species of bird eats a particular food. Enter the results on a spreadsheet (see page 22).

Habitats

Key Stage 1

Where do they live?

Look for minibeasts in different places in the school grounds, such as a lawn, a flowerbed and a rough grassy area. Draw a pictogram showing the number of individuals found in each.

The term 'habitat' means the place or kind of place where an organism lives.

Key Stage 2a

Which habitat has greatest diversity?

Where are most types of minibeast found? Tally the types found in each habitat and make a bar chart.

Key Stage 2b

Comparing habitats

Are there more tiny animals living in the lawn, flowerbed or rough grassy area? Collect data about the types and the numbers of individuals. Present the data on a spreadsheet. Print graphs based on data in the spreadsheet.

Dissolving powders

Key Stage 1

What dissolves?

Which types of powder – flour, bicarbonate of soda, sugar, salt, washing powder – dissolve in water? Present the results in the form of a tick table.

A solution is usually transparent but it can be coloured (e.g. coffee).

Key Stage 2a

Dissolving sugars

Which type of sugar – caster, brown, icing or granulated – dissolves the fastest? Present the results as a bar chart.

Key Stage 2b

Does temperature affect things?

What effect does the temperature of water have on the solubility of sugar? Use water at different temperatures and observe how rapidly granulated sugar dissolves in each case. Present the data in the form of a line graph.

Washing powders

Key Stage 1

Dolls' wash day

Wash dirty dolls' clothes with and without washing powder. Which gives the cleanest results? Display the washed items.

The way detergents work is explained on page 110.

Key Stage 2a

Does soaking help?

Does it help to soak the clothes before washing? Present the findings in the style of a TV consumer report, such as 'Watchdog'.

Key Stage 2b

Grease removal

Investigate whether washing powders really do remove grease at low temperatures.

Stretchy clothes

Key Stage 1

Which is stretchy?

Which out of a range of materials is most stretchy? Give children pre-cut pieces to test which stretches most. Display unifix blocks to show the length before and after.

Look at cloth through a strong lens to check if it is knitted or woven.

Key Stage 2a

Compare stockings.

Hang two stockings from a line. Plan an investigation into what happens when you put weights into the toe end of each stocking. Draw bar charts.

Which is most comfy?	*Key Stage 2b* Investigate which of three or four elastics would be best for the waistband of running shorts. It has to be strong and comfortable. Record as a series of cartoons showing what you did.

Bouncing balls

Best bouncer	*Key Stage 1* Out of a selection of balls, which bounces the highest?	When a ball hits the floor it behaves like a spring.
Does the type of floor have an effect?	*Key Stage 2a* Is the same ball always the highest bouncer on different types of floor? Display the results in a table.	
What happens when you pump it up?	*Key Stage 2b* How high does a flat football bounce? What happens to the height of bounce as you pump the ball up? Display the results as a line graph.	

Parachutes

Soft landing	*Key Stage 1* Investigate different ways in which a small, soft toy can be given a gentle landing if dropped from a height.	A parachute reduces the terminal velocity of the fall. For more information, see the companion volume in this series, *Science for Primary Teachers*, page 93.
Speed of fall	*Key Stage 2a* Investigate what happens to the speed of the fall when more mass is added to the parachute.	
List the factors.	*Key Stage 2b* List all the factors that affect the fall of a parachute, then choose some to investigate. Do parachutes perform differently with a hole in the canopy? Display the results as a series of questions and answers.	

Sun shadows

Changing shadows	*Key Stage 1* Look at how shadows change during the day. Use chalk to draw around shadows in the playground at different times of the day.	Use a compass to check that shadows point north at midday.
Shadow-length bar chart	*Key Stage 2a* Investigate the changing length of shadows during the day. Display the results as a bar chart.	
Changes in two line graphs	*Key Stage 2b* Investigate the changing length of shadows on two days two weeks apart. Compare the line graphs of the length of the shadows against the time of day on the two days.	

Other starting points

There are many starting points for investigations.	*Germinating seeds* – what conditions are needed? *Weather changes* – is there a connection between temperature and wind direction? *Absorbency* – which is the most absorbent tissue? *Waterproofing* – which material is best for making a pair of waterproof boots? *Evaporation* – under what conditions do things dry fastest?	Sentences beginning with the words 'what' or 'which' are likely to provide useful starting points.

Candles – how long will they burn under an inverted jar?
Cooling – which is the most effective insulation material?
Gyrocopters – do they fall more slowly with longer wings?
Bulbs – how can you make electric bulbs glow more dimly?
Magnets – which is the strongest magnet?
Shadows – are the shadows bigger when the torch is nearer the toy?
Sound – which is the most effective sound insulator?

Information and Communications Technology (ICT)

Introduction

Computers are an invaluable tool in the primary science classroom. This brief survey looks at several applications and gives examples of suitable programs (software) and the machines for which they are available (hardware). For those who want to find out more, specialist publications, such as Frost (1995), will give more detail.

> If you are inexperienced with computers, first become familiar with a word processor, then a simple branching database.

The applications summarized here are:

- spreadsheets
- graph drawing packages
- databases
- binary branching databases
- datalogging
- CD-ROM simulations
- word processing

The variety of computer applications

Spreadsheets

A spreadsheet is a matrix of cells that can perform calculations and be used to table results. Once it has been filled in you can sort the results and quickly draw a graph.

> *Excel* (Microsoft) is a spreadsheet for PCs and *Claris Works* (Claris) is designed for use on Apple Macs.

Setting up a spreadsheet

	A	B	C	D	E
1	size of wings	time of fall 1	time of fall 2	time of fall 3	average time
2	2 cm	3.1	3.3	3.2	3.2
3	4 cm	3.5	3.4	3.5	3.5
4	6 cm	3.8	3.7	3.9	3.8
5	8 cm	3.8	3.9	3.9	3.9

Spreadsheet containing data about the time taken for gyrocopters of different sizes to fall

In this example Year 5 children have taken three readings of the speed at which their gyrocopters fall. Their teacher has also shown them how to make the spreadsheet calculate the average of their results:

Finding the average

- In cell E5 enter the formula: = AVERAGE (B5:D5)
- Click on that cell and copy it
- Paste it into cells E2 to E4.

Now when the children enter their data the average is calculated automatically.

Using spreadsheets to draw a variety of graphs

A variety of graphs can be drawn by highlighting in a spreadsheet the cells you want to graph. For instance, by highlighting the relevant cells the list of averages can be graphed. On the other hand, if you highlight the entire table the bar chart will show every reading, allowing you to compare individual results.

Look at the graphs on screen. Discuss them one by one. Print the most informative one.

Opening and saving files

To make the spreadsheet available to all groups you should save it in your teacher's folder, then ask the children to open it from there. They should immediately SAVE AS to their own folder or their own floppy disk. This leaves the original file untouched.

> SAVE AS always leaves the original untouched.

Simply drawing graphs

Graph drawing packages
These programs range from the very simple, such as *Graph-IT* (NCET) for the BBC master computer and *Counter* (Black Cat) for the PC, to the more complex graphing packages associated with spreadsheets, such as *Excel* on the PC and *Claris Works* on the Apple Macintosh.

> *Graph-IT* is essentially a very simple spreadsheet.

Databases

File, field and record

A database is a computer program that allows you to enter information about a group of related items (a file), such as 'pets'. The file is made up from different categories (fields), for example 'number of legs'. Each individual pet will have an entry (record) that contains information in each field.

> See below for another example explaining these terms.

Pupils can use the database to search for records that match a certain description, such as 'all pets that live in the house and don't have fur'.

Do you really want to make a database?

Some teachers are a little sceptical about the use of databases with primary children. The process of gathering the data can be fairly time consuming and the way the data is used can sometimes be a little forced. Why do we need to know the name of a boy with brown hair and blue eyes whose favourite food is spaghetti? The techniques used to examine the data are more important than compiling the data in the first place. If all you want to do is draw graphs then use a graphing package or a spreadsheet.

Compiling a database

When compiling a database the best place to begin is with the class itself. First, decide what information is going to be collected. Keep it very simple at first. For example, younger children might ask:

name?   height?
boy or girl?   hair colour?

> *Datashow* (NCET) is the classic data-handling package for BBC computers.
>
> *Junior Pinpoint* (Longman) is a database for Archimedes computers.

Fields
Records
Files

These four categories are referred to as fields (e.g. boy or girl). A whole set of filled-in fields is a record (e.g. the record about Joanne or Sam). A whole set of records is a file (e.g. the file about Class 3).

Entering data

You need to be very precise about how the data is entered. Make sure that spaces and units such as cm or mm are used consistently.

Using the data

Once you have collected the data from each child in the class you can sort the information, graph it, and ask questions such as:

> Save all work regularly.

'How many boys have black hair?'
'How many girls are taller than 120 cm?'
'How many boys are taller than 120 cm?'

Other database opportunities

Databases could be used to record the types of trees in your school grounds, the minibeasts or pond animals you find, animals that are in danger of extinction, and types of motor cars and sea shells.

Branch forms a key.

Binary branching databases

These programs, also called dichotomous keys, build up to form an identification key. They can help the children identify things as diverse as fruit, people, animals, plants and types of powder.

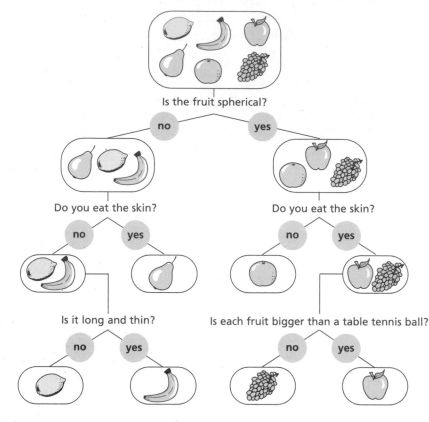

Branch (NCET) is an excellent program for BBC computers.

Window Tree (SITSS) for PCs is another example of a branching database.

When planning to use a branching database always begin away from the computer. Sort the materials or objects on paper first.

'Twenty Questions'

Play 'Twenty Questions'. The teacher thinks of one of the objects. The children ask questions that can only be answered 'yes' or 'no'.
Do this with a number of objects or materials.

Use the program.

Now start a branch file. The questions as they appear on screen guide the children through the process of building up the file and then using it. Branching databases make the children focus on classification skills.

Datalogging

What is 'datalogging'?

Datalogging simply involves plugging sensors into a small box attached to the computer. You then run a program that records readings from the sensors. These readings are plotted on a graph. The graph is built up in real time and is a very useful teaching tool.

'Real time' means the moment the data is produced.

Temperature, light and sound sensors are the three that you are most likely to use at first. Here are a few of the investigations you can perform using sensors:

Light

Using light sensors

- Which sunglasses let most light through?
- Which is the best fabric to make curtains from?
- What happens to the light readings as you move the sensor further away from a torch?
- Which source of light is brightest?
- Which road-safety reflective strip reflects most light?

Datalogging software draws a graph of readings from sensors.

Sound

Using sound sensors

- Which wind instrument is loudest?
- Which stringed instrument is loudest?
- Which material makes the most effective sound insulator?
- What happens to the sound level as you move away/towards a sound source?

Junior Insight (Longman) is a useful datalogging software program that handles most sensor kits.

Temperature

Using temperature sensors

- Which insulation material slows cooling most effectively?
- Do large volumes of water cool more slowly than small ones? (And how does this relate to large and small animals in the Arctic?)
- What happens to the temperature of icy water left in the classroom?
- What happens to the temperature in the classroom on a sunny day?

Dataloggers are useful because they produce such excellent, immediate results. However, they are expensive, and getting to know the program takes time. To maximize use of the datalogger ensure that all pupils know how it works by giving an initial demonstration of its use.

In the first instance, quickly demonstrate the use of a datalogger.

CD-ROM simulations

CD-ROMs (Compact Disc Read Only Memory) contain a huge amount of data on a single disc. They are surprisingly inexpensive and can support a range of work in science.

Many encyclopaedias have a high reading level.

Reference material such as *Eyewitness Encyclopaedia* (Dorling Kindersley), *Multimedia Encyclopaedia* (Hutchinson), Grolier Encyclopaedia and *Encarta* (Microsoft) are excellent sources of information for teachers and older children. However, you may need to discourage children from simply printing out pages full of barely digested information.

As teacher reference, these are excellent sources of information.

A good way to reinforce learning

Interactive programs, such as *Polar Lands* and *Electricity and Magnetism* (Two Can) are good ways to extend practical work. In the excellent *Electricity and Magnetism*, for instance, children can make circuits at the click of a mouse and see what happens when they make parallel and series circuits. They can easily see the effects of switches and resistors. Of course, this is no substitute for handling the real thing, but it is a superb addition to the children's range of experience.

The Way Things Work (Dorling Kindersley) is another first-class, fairly inexpensive and widely available CD-ROM.

Word processing

Children can use the computer simply as a typewriter to write about their science work. However, until such time as every child has a computer it is more productive to use the available equipment selectively.

Using a word processor

For instance, the teacher can write something using the word processor, save it and then ask the children to alter it, complete it or in some way improve it.

- Write a short piece about food chains.

> **FOOD CHAINS**
> Most food chains start with a green plant. They get energy from the sun. Herbivores eat the plants and use the materials to build up their own bodies. Carnivores eat the plant eaters and obtain raw materials to build their bodies and energy to move around. In this way even lions depend on plants for life.

Cloze procedure

Always back up.

- Remove some words to make a simple cloze procedure for the children to solve, or jumble up the sentences and ask the children to CUT AND PASTE them into a sensible order.
- Now save the file in the teacher's folder.
- Pairs of children open the file.
- Children immediately SAVE AS in their own folders.
- Children then complete their cloze, or reorder.
- Children SAVE again in their folder.

Back up the original version in case someone deletes it by mistake.

You can use a similar procedure when saving spreadsheets for children to complete.

Assessment in primary science

Introduction

Science can be assessed using a wide variety of methods. The combination of knowledge and skills can be assessed verbally, by observation, practically, and using children's drawing and writing.

Type of assessment	Strategy
Verbal	*Child could* • answer a single question • ask a question • make a verbal report • explain an event or procedure
Draw and/or label	• picture • diagram • map • graph or chart
Written	*Child could* • provide a written report • plan a test/devise a recording grid • write a short answer in response to a single question • complete a cloze procedure • complete a proforma • complete a written test/SAT • fill in a table • perform a calculation from data provided
Practical	*Child could* • weigh/measure an object • read a chart or thermometer • use a piece of equipment, such as a compass • demonstrate a technique, such as taking a pulse

Objectives

Set simple objectives

Good assessment starts with clear learning objectives. Learning objectives make explicit what you want the children to know, or what skills you want them to acquire, as a result of your teaching. Some examples of clear learning objectives are:

* The children will be able to carry out a fair test to see which is the most effective washing powder.
* The children will know that only iron and steel objects are attracted to magnets.

Make learning objectives clear.

Good examples

- The children will know that plants need light and water to grow.

Other verbs that can be used to phrase objectives include: identify, list, describe, distinguish between, contrast, compare and understand.

If objectives are limited and well defined they will be manageable to teach, clear for the children and more easily assessed by the teacher. Guard against the tendency to be too general:

Poor examples

- The children will learn how to perform an investigation.
- The children will learn about magnetism.

> Avoid being too general when setting your objectives.

Avoid objectives that are difficult to assess:

- The children will become better at science.
- The children will learn how to investigate.

Match method to objective

Assess against the objective.

Once you have refined your learning objective for a lesson you should decide how you will assess the children's learning against that objective. Usually it is more convenient to assess written or drawn responses. These can be kept as a portfolio of evidence for the individual child, the whole class and the school.

> Look back at your lesson objective when assessing.

File for each child

If time allows, obtain a short verbal response from each child. It is best to avoid assessment at the same time as teaching; teaching can be stressful enough as it is.

The table below shows three objectives and an assessment method that might be appropriate in each case.

OBJECTIVE (CRITERION)	ASSESSMENT METHOD (MODE)
The children will be able to carry out a fair test to see which is the most effective washing powder.	Examine written accounts. Did the children control the variables and make a fair test?
The children will know that only iron and steel objects are attracted to magnets.	Did the children fill in the table correctly and did they write a correct conclusion at the end of their written report?
The children will learn that plants need light and water to grow.	Short test at the end of the work on plants. Did the children include light and water in their list of things plants need to grow?

Records

Everyday records

You do not necessarily need a special book for everyday science records. The children's progress in science can be monitored in your general daily class records. A way of doing this using a simple table is shown on the facing page.

Name	1/6/98 **Washing powder test:** Did they make a fair test?	7/6/98 **Magnetic attraction:** Was the table filled in correctly and a valid conclusion given?	14/6/98 **Science test:** Score out of 9
Jane A	✓	✓	7
Rashid C	⊘	⊘	9
Kate G	⊘	⊘	8
Jim E	✗	✓	6

⊘ objective met   ✓ objective partially met   ✗ objective not met

Interpreting the records

Interpreting the table

As you can see from the table, in the washing powder test Rashid and Kate were assessed as having completed a fair test; Jane was assessed as having completed a partially successful test; Jim was assessed as not having met the objective.

Using the records for the whole class

There are two methods of using these formative records. For the class as a whole look at a column of assessment results for one objective. Did the majority of the children achieve what you intended? If so, then the level of that lesson was about right. If, on the other hand, only a few children achieved the objective then the activities were clearly aimed too high, or the lesson was poorly taught and you will need to rethink your approach. If all the children achieve your objectives all the time in science, then it is likely that you need to present more challenging objectives to the children and demand more of them.

> These everyday records provide data for completing summative records at the end of term or year.

Using the records for individuals

Formative records also indicate an individual's profile. Does this show few marks of achievement? If this is the case the child may need extra support. On the other hand, if the child easily achieves every objective they may need more challenging activities.

Assessment sheets devised by schools

Some schools have devised assessment sheets to accompany each unit of science they teach. They:

Guidelines for assessment

- listed the learning objectives for the unit of work
- wrote nine questions aimed at assessing whether the relevant concepts have been successfully learnt
- kept each set of questions to one side of A4
- included tables to complete and diagrams to label where possible.

> The sheets can also be used formatively, before the teaching of a particular unit of work begins.

Level of questions

Pitch the first three questions at a level of ability below average for the class, the next three for the average level and the last three for the level above average. The results should give an indication of the level at which each child is working.

Make it fun.

Ideally the assessment should take place just before the end of a unit so that there is time to take remedial action where necessary. Let the children feel they are completing a quiz rather than a test, to reduce unnecessary stress.

Summative records

Photocopy a small sample of each child's work and annotate it with comments. File the work along with test scores and scores from any assessment sheets that may have been devised and completed at the end of a unit of work. This will help you to assign a summative level to each child's work for each of the attainment targets. You should use the level descriptions to help you form this judgement.

Use the level descriptions.

Avoid the temptation to atomize the level descriptions. Does the child fit the description that is average for the class? If not, try the one above or below.

Planning for assessment

From time to time you should plan an activity specifically for assessment purposes. This will help you quantify the impressions you have gained from the more formative elements of your assessment. The activity could take one of the following forms:

Assessing prediction skills

- Ask the children to predict what will happen when the length of the wings of a gyrocopter is changed. Each child should hand in their prediction on a slip of paper with their name on it.

Assessing measuring skills

- As the class leaves the room at playtime, ask each child to read the temperature on a thermometer as they pass you, or to answer a question requiring a short answer. Children working at different levels of achievement can be asked differentiated questions.

Try to carry out quick, focused assessments on a regular basis.

Assessing conceptual understanding

- Put three sentences, only one of which describes a concept accurately, on the blackboard at the end of a lesson. Ask the children to copy the correct concept at the end of their recording for the day. For example:

  The moon and Earth orbit the sun separately.
  The sun orbits the moon and Earth.
  The moon orbits the Earth while the Earth orbits the sun.

Use SATs.

- Use the materials supplied by the government for SATs tests as a means of assessing the level of attainment for each child. Using this material also helps the children get used to this form of testing and the skills required to complete it successfully, such as using the correct vocabulary and working to a set time.

Based on a combination of strategies, assessment in primary science can be manageable and informative.

Use published materials.

Sciencecheck (Collins, 1998) is a series of four books containing accurately levelled paper-and-pencil assessment sheets. They provide a useful starting point for devising your own assessments or can be used as they are.

Humans and other animals

Key ideas

Humans are apes.

Mammals are warm-blooded.

Food gives energy.

Classifying humans

Human beings are animals. In terms of classification we are:

vertebrates – we have a backbone.
mammals – we have hair, feed our young on milk.
primates – we have fingernails and shoulder blades.
apes – we have no tail and we have a 'Y' shape pattern on our molars.
humans – we make intricate tools.

You can construct similar classifications for all living things.

Like all mammals we keep our body temperature above that of our surroundings. This means that we use large quantities of energy to keep warm. In fact, we use the majority of our food to keep warm. We also use food energy to power our life processes.

Food

Foodstuffs give us energy – even a lettuce leaf provides a little energy. The energy contained in food is measured in calories. Water, salt and vitamins are auxiliary foods that do not have any energy value. However, they are essential to good health and are contained in many foods.

All foods contain calories, even if in very small amounts. This means that all foods give us energy.

We digest food in the alimentary canal. Food is broken down into soluble substances by the gut. This soluble food passes through the gut into the bloodstream, which carries it to the cells of the body.

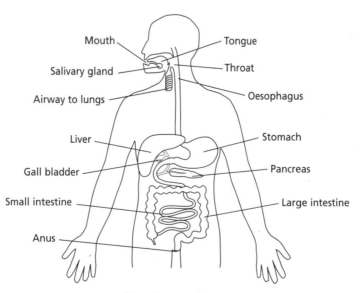

Mouth
Tongue
Salivary gland
Throat
Airway to lungs
Oesophagus
Liver
Stomach
Gall bladder
Pancreas
Small intestine
Large intestine
Anus

The main parts of the gut

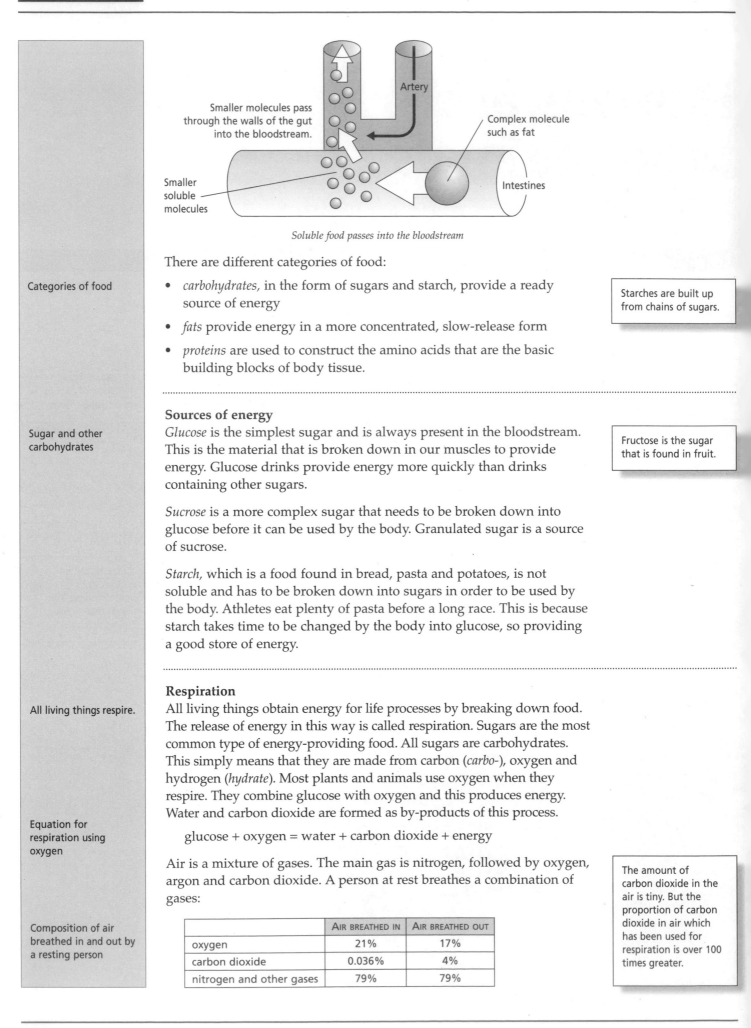

Soluble food passes into the bloodstream

Categories of food

There are different categories of food:

- *carbohydrates,* in the form of sugars and starch, provide a ready source of energy

- *fats* provide energy in a more concentrated, slow-release form

- *proteins* are used to construct the amino acids that are the basic building blocks of body tissue.

> Starches are built up from chains of sugars.

Sugar and other carbohydrates

Sources of energy

Glucose is the simplest sugar and is always present in the bloodstream. This is the material that is broken down in our muscles to provide energy. Glucose drinks provide energy more quickly than drinks containing other sugars.

Sucrose is a more complex sugar that needs to be broken down into glucose before it can be used by the body. Granulated sugar is a source of sucrose.

Starch, which is a food found in bread, pasta and potatoes, is not soluble and has to be broken down into sugars in order to be used by the body. Athletes eat plenty of pasta before a long race. This is because starch takes time to be changed by the body into glucose, so providing a good store of energy.

> Fructose is the sugar that is found in fruit.

All living things respire.

Respiration

All living things obtain energy for life processes by breaking down food. The release of energy in this way is called respiration. Sugars are the most common type of energy-providing food. All sugars are carbohydrates. This simply means that they are made from carbon (*carbo-*), oxygen and hydrogen (*hydrate*). Most plants and animals use oxygen when they respire. They combine glucose with oxygen and this produces energy. Water and carbon dioxide are formed as by-products of this process.

Equation for respiration using oxygen

glucose + oxygen = water + carbon dioxide + energy

Air is a mixture of gases. The main gas is nitrogen, followed by oxygen, argon and carbon dioxide. A person at rest breathes a combination of gases:

Composition of air breathed in and out by a resting person

	AIR BREATHED IN	AIR BREATHED OUT
oxygen	21%	17%
carbon dioxide	0.036%	4%
nitrogen and other gases	79%	79%

> The amount of carbon dioxide in the air is tiny. But the proportion of carbon dioxide in air which has been used for respiration is over 100 times greater.

We can respire without oxygen for short periods.

Some bacteria and yeast live without oxygen.

Exercise

If we run quickly for a long time, or take other vigorous exercise, our muscles need a great deal of oxygen. We cannot breathe quickly enough, nor can our blood be pumped fast enough, to supply the need for oxygen. When this happens the muscles have to break down glucose without using oxygen. This is a much less efficient way of using sugar but sometimes, say if you are being chased by a lion, it is essential! The resulting muscle cramp occurs because there is a build up of lactic acid in the muscles, a by-product of this biochemical process.

Many kinds of bacteria and yeast respire without oxygen. They carry out vital parts of the decay process and we use them to produce food and drink:

- Yeasts respire without air and are used to ferment beer and raise bread.
- Bacteria produce lactic acid and are used in making butter, yoghurt and silage.
- Bacteria produce methane gas when used to break down sewage. This gas can be used as an energy source.

See pages 75–82 for more information on micro-organisms.

Sensitivity to stimuli

Eyes show enormous variation

Smell

Vibration

Sound navigation

Touch

Sensitivity

All living things are sensitive to stimuli. Reaction to stimuli is one of the critical tests that indicate if an object is alive. Stimuli include light, sound, heat, pressure and chemicals in the environment. Animals, including humans, detect chemical stimuli through their senses of taste and smell.

Sensitivity to light is very common in plants and animals. The biggest eyes in the animal kingdom belong to the Atlantic Giant Squid, which has eyes measuring up to 40 cm in diameter. In contrast, many smaller animals have only tiny light detectors on their bodies. The single-celled organism called *Euglena* has a light-sensitive organ on its body that helps to guide it towards light so it can photosynthesize efficiently.

Bees are sensitive to ultraviolet light.

Many animals have a good sense of smell but that of moths is incredibly sensitive. The feathered antennae on the heads of moths are smell detectors; male Emperor moths can detect the smell emitted by a female at a distance of over 11 kilometres. In fact, most insects are responsive to an astonishing range of chemicals. Mosquitoes, for instance, home in on carbon dioxide concentrations, which betray the presence of a breathing animal.

Smell detects minute traces of chemical in the air.

Vibrations, which cause sound, can travel through air, water or the earth. Fish live in an environment that transmits sound very well. They do not need an ear opening as sound travels from the water and through their skulls with great ease. In contrast, bats produce sounds that travel through the air and are reflected back to their highly sensitive ears. They use sound to detect the position of their main source of food, flying insects.

Snakes detect vibrations through the earth and are virtually deaf to sounds that travel through the air.

We often think of our sense of touch in connection with detecting changes in texture. Fish have an astonishingly acute sense that detects changes in pressure. The lateral line on a fish is a system of sensory organs that detects changes in pressure, helping to explain how a shoal of fish can move in perfect unison.

Heat detection	The ability to detect heat is what prevents us from being burnt; we have efficient heat detectors located in our skin. We also make machines that are sensitive to heat. Military missiles, for instance, can home in on a jet plane's engines. A group of animals has been using a similar form of detection for millions of years: snakes have pits between their nostrils and eyes that are able to detect tiny amounts of heat, such as that given off by a warm-blooded animal.

Some blood-sucking insects also home in on heat radiation.

Reproduction

Asexual reproduction

All animals die, and if their species is not to become extinct they must reproduce. The range of reproductive methods used by animals is very wide. Many organisms reproduce on their own without any help from another individual. This type of reproduction is called asexual. Single-celled organisms such as *amoeba* reproduce simply by splitting in two. Bacteria also reproduce by division. In good conditions they can do this at the alarming rate of once every 20 minutes.

Asexual reproduction is rapid and does not waste energy.

Organisms such as the single-celled fungus, yeast, reproduce by budding. A small outgrowth develops and then splits away from the parent cell.

Sexual reproduction

Sexual reproduction of most fish and amphibians uses water as the means of bringing together separately released eggs and sperm. Reproduction of the horseshoe crab relies on a huge gathering of individuals at which enormous quantities of eggs and sperm are released simultaneously into the water. Some fish, such as the stickleback, build individual nests where the eggs are carefully laid and fertilized.

Sexual reproduction mixes genetic information from two individuals.

Some animals can fertilize themselves.

Hermaphrodites are organisms that have both male and female parts. Although there are advantages in not needing other individuals to reproduce, they try to avoid self-fertilization where possible. For instance, worms are hermaphroditic but prefer to copulate with other worms on moist soil at night. They glue themselves together with mucus and pass sperm to each other through their saddles. In this way eggs in both worms are fertilized by a second individual.

Hermaphrodites do it alone.

Sexual and asexual reproduction compared

Advantages of asexual reproduction

Advantages of sexual reproduction

Organisms tend to reproduce asexually when they have plenty of food and space. Asexual reproduction is much more efficient than sexual reproduction because only females are required. However, all the progeny of asexual reproduction are clones of their mothers. This means that if a new disease threatens, or a change occurs in the environment, for which the mother was poorly equipped, then her descendants may not thrive. On the other hand, sexual reproduction involves mixing the characteristics of two different parents and this introduces variation into the genetic code. Some of the progeny of sexual reproduction may be resistant to a new disease or able to cope with a changed environment.

Large, slow-growing animals need to keep ahead of rapidly evolving diseases.

Common misconceptions

What is an animal?

Is it an animal?

Children have a clear idea that cows and other hairy animals with four legs and a tail are animals. However, when considering whether a worm, spider or woodlouse is an animal they may be less sure.

Are humans animals?

Many children do not see humans as animals. They think of humans as being separate in some way from the rest of the animal kingdom. This may be the result of religious teaching.

Children also find the plethora of classification terms confusing: they may know the term 'mammal', for instance, but not that it is a subset of the group 'animal'. Additionally, some educationalists would argue that 'minibeasts' is an unnecessary term.

At primary level, organisms can be classified as either plants or animals.

List of resources

Resources for studying humans and other animals

- a variety of illustrations showing different parts of the body
- a variety of illustrations showing internal organs and the skeleton
- stopwatches
- measuring tapes
- scales (including bathroom scales)
- eyesight charts
- a variety of insects and other invertebrates
- pond dipping nets
- white trays
- low-power microscopes
- magnifying glasses

The best microscopes for children are binocular and magnify up to 20 times.

Summary of the programmes of study

Key Stage 1 Sc2: 1a–b, 2a–f

Children should be taught about the following:
- the external parts of the body
- the differences between things that are living and things that have never been alive
- animals, including humans, move, feed, grow, use their senses and reproduce
- humans need food and water to stay alive
- taking exercise and eating the right types of food helps keep humans healthy
- the role of drugs as medicines
- humans can produce babies and these babies grow into children and then into adults
- humans have senses that enable them to be aware of the world around them

Key Stage 2 Sc2: 1a–b, 2a–h

- life processes of nutrition, movement, growth and reproduction are common to animals, including humans
- the function of teeth and the importance of dental care
- food is needed for activity and growth
- a simple model of the structure of the heart and how it acts as a pump
- circulation of the blood
- the main functions of some of the organs in the human body (L5 description)
- the effect of exercise and rest on the pulse rate
- humans have skeletons and muscles
- the main stages of the human life cycle
- tobacco, alcohol and other drugs can have harmful effects

Key Stage 1 classroom activities

Characteristics of living things	**Living and not alive** • Get the children to draw a picture of a living thing. Ask them to say how they know it is alive. Discuss their ideas in detail – these will be very useful pointers to the children's existing ideas or misconceptions.

Living things show seven characteristics:

movement	reproduction
feeding	use of energy
excretion	sensitivity
growth	

> Children at this age will probably mention only two or three of these.

Living things die.

• Discuss with the children how they know that dead leaves, dead flowers, meat and fish are dead. This reverses the previous teaching point and will help to sharpen the children's ideas.

> The point at which a thing is dead is debatable: is a cut-off finger alive or dead?

Cells can live long after their donor has died.

Living cells taken from an animal can be cultured independently of their donor. Living skin grafts are taken from a donor and grown in laboratory conditions; the skin could be alive and growing long after the donor has died.

Minerals

Some things have never been alive.

• Show the children materials and objects that have come from the ground and never been alive. Talk about the things they know of that are dug from the ground and the uses to which they are put.

Minerals

Material that has never been alive is referred to as a mineral. Minerals can be dug out of the ground and include all metals and rocks. These are easy to understand. However, oil and coal are substances that originate in plant and animal matter, but they do not betray much evidence of their organic (living) past.

> Play a simplified version of 'Animal, Vegetable or Mineral?'

Food

Humans need food and water to stay alive.

• Ask the children to draw the contents of a rucksack for a two-day journey across a desert. Discuss with them what happens to people who have to go without food for more than a week.

> List the animals the children keep as pets. Map the food they feed to them.

Chemical energy

Food is chemical energy which living things convert into heat energy and movement energy. Our bodies are composed of 65% water. If we are deprived of water for more than a week, death is almost certain.

Good food is necessary for health.

• Ask the school cook to talk to the children about the sorts of food that are popular and unpopular in the school dining room. Graph the food that is popular with children in the class. Ask them which foods they think contribute to a healthy diet. Design healthy meals.

Diets can be healthy or unhealthy.

There is no such thing as unhealthy food. There are diets that are healthy and diets that are unhealthy. A healthy diet will include plenty of carbohydrate and some sugar for energy, proteins for building the body, fats for energy and vitamins for disease resistance and good skin.

Keeping healthy

- Ask the children to suggest exercise for granny or granddad and for someone in hospital with a broken leg.

When we exercise a muscle it gets larger and more efficient. This is just as true for heart muscles as it is for muscles in the arm. By making yourself breathless you are making your heart pump blood harder and making your lungs expand more. This makes the muscles that control blood circulation and breathing stronger.

- Discuss with the children how their parents ensure that medicines in their home are kept safely. Ask them to say what they would do if their younger brother or sister managed to open the medicine cabinet and ate some pills.

All medicines are drugs and many of them have powerful effects, some of them unintentional. Drugs have an effect when part of their chemical make-up finds a receptive site in the body. For instance, antihistamines block the receptors for histamine, which causes mucus to form. However, the same drug might also affect part of the brain, causing drowsiness.

Our bodies

- Play 'Simon says' with the children. Draw round an outline of the body. Name the parts.

Our left and right sides are symmetrical. This is a feature common to all vertebrates such as mammals. Other animals are radially symmetrical – anemones and jellyfish for instance.

- Ask a mother to bring in her new baby, and discuss with the children how to care for it. Talk with the class about the growth rate of the baby and how this is measured.

As living things develop they get heavier because they absorb substances in the form of food into their bodies. Changes happen to humans throughout their lives, with the most dramatic taking place with the onset of puberty.

Senses

- The children can experiment with:

    blindfold activities – comparing the speed of building a tower with and without the ability to see

    smell and taste – guessing the names of different safe substances

    feely bags – focusing in detail on the texture and hardness of an object or material.

We are familiar with our five senses, but other organisms have different senses or have developed the same ones to a higher degree. For example, pigeons have developed a magnetic sense, some snakes can detect heat with incredible precision, and bloodhounds and moths have a phenomenal sense of smell.

Sidebar labels (left margin):

Taking exercise keeps you healthy.

Medicines

Side-effects of medicines

Names of external body parts

Humans change as they get older.

Living things use their senses.

Sidebar notes (right margin):

Although children now appear to be eating fewer calories than previous generations, some are overweight, perhaps because of a lack of vigorous exercise.

Some children will have their own growth records going back several years. Use these to draw bar charts.

Key Stage 2a classroom activities

Human life processes

Other mammals

Functions of the teeth

Dental care is important.

Enamel

Acid attack

Food is necessary for growth.

The skeleton has a particular structure and function.

People are alive

- Suggest that the children draw a person then list as many signs as they can that tell them he or she is alive.

We have seen that living things show seven characteristics: movement, feeding, excretion, growth, reproduction, use of energy, sensitivity. Humans are animals and carry out life processes in a similar way to all other animals. The similarities are easiest to see in mammals, which are our closest relatives.

Teeth

- Ask the children to draw diagrams showing the different kinds of teeth. Suggest that they use their tongues to count the number of each kind of tooth they have. The children can eat an apple or a carrot and note which teeth are used to chop, rip and grind.

We have four types of teeth: *incisors* at the front to chop and slice our food; *canines* at the side to rip and tear food; *pre-molars* and *molars* to grind and pulp food.

> Collect some dental health information (and maybe some dental hygiene samples) from a local dentist.

- Obtain clean, discarded milk teeth. Leave some in acid solutions such as vinegar and cola. The children can compare these with teeth left in other, neutral solutions.

Tooth enamel is the hardest substance in the human body, but if teeth are not brushed regularly bacteria breed on the sugar and other foodstuffs that stick to it. They eventually form a layer called bacterial plaque. The acid produced by the bacteria breaks down the enamel of the teeth leading to decay. Sugary acid solutions such as cola are particularly damaging to teeth.

> Disclosing tablets cling to plaque, staining it a bright colour. Children can try to clean off the plaque but will find it difficult.

Food

- With the children work out how many calories there are in different packets of food.

The calorific value of food indicates the amount of chemical energy that the food will yield when it is digested. Calorific value is calculated by finding how much heat is generated when food is dried and burnt. Carrots do not produce much heat but (unfortunately) chocolate does.

Bones

- Discuss which bones protect different parts of the body. Look at types of joint. Display x-rays of broken bones and joints. Categorize the different joints in the body according to degree of movement.

The human skeleton is the framework on which the rest of the body is constructed. The bones are jointed together in three different ways:

> *hinge joints*, e.g. elbow and knee
> *ball and socket joints*, e.g. hip and shoulder
> *sliding joints*, e.g. the bones of the spine or wrists.

> Bones have three functions:
> - protecting body organs
> - providing a framework for the muscles to pull on
> - producing white blood cells.

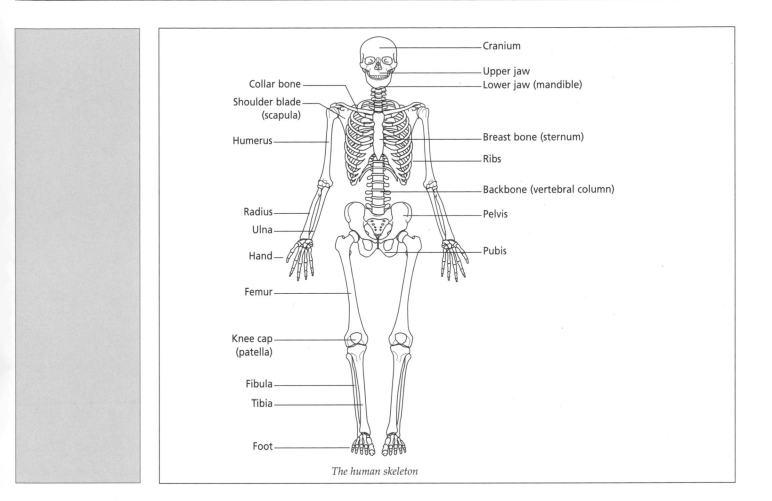

Cranium

Upper jaw

Lower jaw (mandible)

Collar bone

Shoulder blade (scapula)

Humerus

Breast bone (sternum)

Ribs

Backbone (vertebral column)

Radius

Pelvis

Ulna

Hand

Pubis

Femur

Knee cap (patella)

Fibula

Tibia

Foot

The human skeleton

Key Stage 2b classroom activities

Heart and pulse

Blood circulates in the body.

- Use a good quality stethoscope to listen to a heart pumping. Ask the children to work out how many beats the heart does in:

| a minute | a day |
| an hour | a lifetime |

A pump

Heart and lungs

The heart is a pump. It takes blood in from the veins and pumps it out through the arteries. The heart is in two halves; the blood enters the right side of the heart and is pumped to the lungs. The oxygenated blood is then pumped from the lungs to the left side of the heart from where it is circulated to the rest of the body. Each heartbeat is felt as a pulse.

> At this stage children only need to know about the function of the heart and the broad outline of its structure.

Exercise and rest affect pulse rate.

- Show the children how to take a pulse. If possible obtain an electronic pulse meter. Ask the children to exercise and see what effect it has on their pulse rates.

Waste production

When muscles are used in exercise they break down food more quickly than when at rest. Because of this extra respiration, more food and oxygen is required to power them. In addition more waste (e.g. carbon dioxide) is produced by the muscles, and this needs to be taken away. This means that the transport system – the blood – has to run more rapidly in order to bring extra supplies of energy and oxygen.

> For more information about activity and respiration, see the companion volume in this series, *Science for Primary Teachers*, page 57.

Each beat of the heart is felt as a single pulse. What you feel as a pulse is an expansion of an artery as the heart squeezes blood through your system.

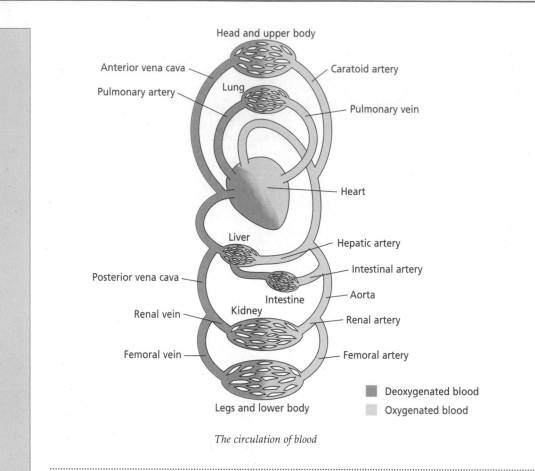

The circulation of blood

Human organs

Names of organs

- Draw a blank torso on the board and list the names of the body organs shown in the diagram below. Ask the children to copy the torso and draw in the organs in the positions they think are correct.

> Distinguish between the stomach, which is just below the ribs, and the whole of the abdomen, which contains several organs.

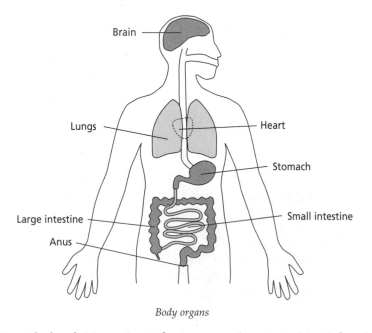

Body organs

Digestion

- Talk with the children about the journey of a piece of food through the body. Describe how it is chopped up in the mouth and chewed with saliva. It is then mixed with acid in the stomach. It passes through the intestines where nutritional value is taken out of it and water is removed. It is finally pushed out as waste.

Organs have a variety of functions.	• List the organs the children know. Discuss the function of each one: *brain* – thinking and control *lungs* – taking in oxygen and removing waste gas *heart* – pumping blood *stomach* – breaking up food and mixing it with digestive juices *intestines* – removing goodness from the food *kidneys* – removing waste products from the blood.

Tobacco and health

Harmful effects

• List health warnings that have appeared on cigarette packets. Ask the children to put them in order of effectiveness. Discuss ways in which children can be discouraged from smoking.

Tobacco smoke contains a wide range of chemicals. The tar in it clogs up the hairs in the lungs, causing dirt and germs to remain there longer than if the lungs were healthy. The nicotine in cigarette smoke is a drug to which the smoker can become addicted.

Reproduction

The start of the human life cycle

• Discuss reproduction in the context of the school's sex education policy.

Human conception occurs when sperm and egg cells combine either in a woman's body or in a laboratory dish.

The fused egg and sperm nuclei develop into an embryo. This does not look much like an adult human, but after two months the embryo has grown into a foetus, which does resemble the adult.

> Breeders of dogs, cats or farm animals can often give very interesting information about how they ensure the breeding success of their animals.

Teaching strategy: Key Stage 1 circus of activities

Helpers

Introduction
This circus of activities for infants focuses on the changes that happen as people grow. Extra adult helpers and older children from the school can add a great deal to the activities.

Ask each helper to work with the children in groups of about five for about 20 minutes. Each activity in the circus has a suggested recording idea to ensure that every group has something to do at the end of the activity.

> Children from older classes often like to help infants.

How am I different?

Parent with baby
Arrange for a parent bring into the classroom a baby and its toys, food and feeding equipment. What differences do the children notice between themselves, the adult and the baby? What can they do that the baby cannot do? What do we need to do to make sure that the baby is safe, healthy, happy and stimulated?

Recording
The children draw a picture of the baby. They write down its name and what it likes to do and what makes it cry.

What happens as you get older?	**Grandparent or older person** Ask a grandparent or older person to show the children pictures of themselves at different stages in their life: as a baby, toddler, young person, adult, older person. They could talk to the children about what they did at different ages.

Grandparent or older person

Ask a grandparent or older person to show the children pictures of themselves at different stages in their life: as a baby, toddler, young person, adult, older person. They could talk to the children about what they did at different ages.

Hands change dramatically.

Compare the hands of the older person with those of the children. What differences and similarities do the children notice?

Recording

The children list the differences between their hands and those of the older person or write about what the older person did as they grew up. Provide some A4 paper.

> The older person could bring photos of themselves at different ages.

Drawing a time-line

Adult helper

For each child, draw a time-line with points on it marking each year of the child's life. Talk with the children about what they could do when they were one year old, two years old, and so on.

Recording

The children add appropriate phrases and pictures to the time-line.

> Time-lines are frequently used in history lessons.

Measuring height and parts of the body

Adult helper

Measure the heights of the children individually on a large piece of paper pinned to the wall. The children can write their names next to their marks. Get the children to measure parts of their bodies, including hand span (on a piece of paper) and head circumference (using a piece of string cut to size and stuck on a prepared graph).

Recording

The children present the finished graphs and write about what each shows. Provide large sheets of paper, felt-tip pens, string, glue, strips of coloured paper and sheets of paper to glue the strips on to.

> Make the graphs by sticking the strips of paper or string directly on to the large sheets of paper.

Our teeth change.

Adult helper

Provide a very clean (or new) set of false teeth, mirrors, apple or carrot. Look at the teeth of the children. Talk about changes they have noticed in their teeth as they have got older. Get them to count their teeth and draw their teeth using a mirror. Discuss why babies don't have teeth.

Recording

Teeth observed

The children draw their teeth using a mirror. They write about the changes they have noticed about their teeth as they have got older.

> Clean hands are important.

How high can I jump?

Children from an older class

Ask five older children to help the infants. Provide chalk, measuring tapes, metre rules and a safe outside working area. Plan a series of games in which each infant works with an older child. They compare and record their performance in a series of activities: standing long jump, standing high jump against a wall (take the difference between the height of each child and the height jumped for each child), ball throwing.

Recording

Different jumps

In a list or simple table, record the performance of each child and compare the results.

> This method of working has great benefits both for the infants and their older helpers. If an older child is a low achiever, involvement like this can increase self-esteem.

Plants

Key ideas

Oxygen production

Plants are the basis of life
Plants provide all the food and oxygen animals need for life. Without plants, lifeforms on the planet would be restricted to the bacteria that can scratch a living from chemicals dissolved in water.

What plants need

Photosynthesis

Plants need only water, air and sunlight to grow. They grow best when there is an abundance of all three. All green plants produce their food by photosynthesis. This is the process by which leaves use sunlight energy to combine carbon dioxide and water to make simple sugar:

$$CO_2 + H_2O \rightarrow C_6H_{12}O_6$$

> Hydroponics is the soil-less method of growing plants.

Types of plants
The plant kingdom is divided into 12 main groups (bacteria and fungi are sometimes not included). Eight of these groups arc listed below:

Single cells

bacteria and blue-green algae – tiny, single-celled organisms. Most break down dead material and some can photosynthesize.

Agents of decay

fungi – single- or multi-cellular organisms that break down dead material. Many are useful but a few cause disease and even damage to houses.

Simple plants

algae – the simplest green plants, they range from single-celled diatoms to very long seaweeds.

> Many classification systems do not include fungi as plants since fungi and plants evolved separately for many hundreds of millions of years.

Combination organisms

lichens – a combination of a fungus and an alga growing together for mutual benefit.

Bryophytes

mosses and liverworts – resemble higher plants by having leaves and stems.

Spore producers

ferns – often have feathery fronds and always reproduce by means of spores.

Conifers

gymnosperms – these include coniferous trees that produce seeds on cones.

See page 44 for more on monocotyledons and dicotyledons.

Flowering plants

monocotyledons and dicotyledons are the two groups of flowering plants.

Flowering and non-flowering plants

Not all plants flower.

Not all plants have flowers. Many plants reproduce using spores. Spore producers include algae, mosses, liverworts and ferns. Cone-bearing

Groups of flowering plants

plants include coniferous trees, which produce seeds within female cones made of overlapping scales. These are fertilized by pollen produced from smaller male cones. Flowering plants are divided into two main groups: dicotyledons and monocotyledons.

Conifers are not flowering plants.

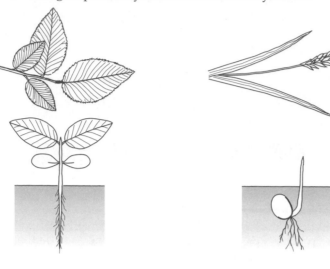

Seeds of dicotyledons contain an embryo with two seed leaves. Leaves are broad with branching veins.

Seeds of monocotyledons contain an embryo with one seed leaf. Leaves are narrow with parallel veins.

Dicotyledons and monocotyledons

Plant respiration

Plants respire.

As already mentioned, plants make food through photosynthesis, using sunlight to combine carbon dioxide with water to make sugar. However, they also respire with a chemical reaction very similar to that of respiring animals: sugar is combined with oxygen to liberate carbon dioxide. Plants produce more oxygen than carbon dioxide during the day.

At night plants produce only carbon dioxide.

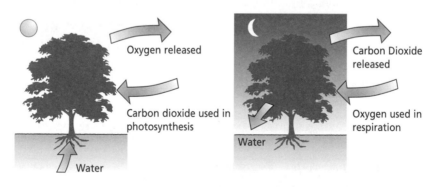

Oxygen released

Carbon dioxide used in photosynthesis

Water

Carbon Dioxide released

Oxygen used in respiration

Water

Photosynethesis and respiration

Plant reproduction

Plants reproduce using sexual and asexual methods.

Plants use a wide range of reproduction strategies. These include sexual and asexual methods.

Sexual reproduction employs mechanisms such as flowers that produce seeds, seed-producing cones, and spores. Seeds are tough bodies that are resistant to drying out whereas spores need a moist place to grow and develop sexually. All flowering plants and conifers produce seeds. Spores are produced by ferns, mosses, algae and liverworts.

Spores are the first stage in a complex sequence leading to fern reproduction.

Flowers

Fern reproduction

Flowers are the parts of flowering plants that produce seeds.

Asexual reproduction does not involve the fusing of male and female sex cells but the splitting of an individual to produce clones of itself. This is done by algae as well as many higher plants including some we grow as house plants. When a cutting of a plant is taken the reproduction is asexual.

For a detailed diagram of the principal parts of a flower, see page 50.

Stimuli

Plants move and respond to stimuli.

Gravity and light are the two main influences on a plant. A plant grows towards light and away from gravity. If a seed is germinated in a pot that is then tilted at an angle, the shoot and root will respond to this new position. Plants grow towards the light by adding extra growth on the side of the shoot in shadow.

In weightless conditions plants become confused.

Common misconceptions

Alive or not?

Plants do not seem to be alive at all.

Children may not share the biologists' view of what being alive means. Animals are obviously alive because they rush around and do things. Plants on the other hand hardly look alive at all. At first glance some, such as lichen and green slime on paths (algae), seem positively lifeless. Indeed many plants appear to have none of the seven attributes of life: they don't seem to feed, exchange gases, show sensitivity, excrete, grow, move, and they certainly don't seem to breed. It is little wonder that many children have difficulty in accepting the concept that plants are alive.

To counter this you need to look closely at plants and plant parts – flowers, seedlings, seeds and fast growing plants – that offer more for children to observe. Once it is clear that these show the signs of life then we can generalize to the wider world of plants. This is not the work of a lesson or two – it is the work of a whole curriculum in science.

Children need a wide experience of plants and plant types.

The function of flowers

Are flowers here just for us to enjoy?

Children have a very human-centred view of life and feel that all objects are in some way there for people to use and/or enjoy. Flowers are seen as having an aesthetic function rather than being exclusively the means for flowering plants to reproduce.

Many children find it difficult to accept that many plants never flower at all.

Flowering plants evolved 160 million years ago, which is very recently in geological terms.

Plant food

Plants make their own food.

Plants make food in their leaves via the process of photosynthesis. Many children and adults incorrectly think of fertilizer as plant food. This is true in the limited sense that the compounds in a fertilizer are taken up by a plant and contribute to its healthy growth.

Seeds

Seeds are simply the first stage of a plant.

Many children think that a seed starts with all the energy it needs to grow into a fully developed plant. They fail to recognize that most of the plant's mass will come from combining water, carbon dioxide and other compounds as it photosynthesizes and grows.

Grow some seedlings in the dark and discuss their early demise.

List of resources

<table>
<tr><td>Resources for studying plants</td><td>

• plant pots
• plant pot saucers
• compost
• variety of seeds
• plant labels
• roll of sticky labels
• dug-up weeds

</td><td>

• screw-topped plastic containers
• tweezers
• liquid plant fertilizer
• variety of cut flowers

</td><td>

Pots in module trays, used by professional growers, can be very neat and tidy.

</td></tr>
</table>

Summary of the programmes of study

Key Stage 1 Sc2: 1a, 3a–c

Key Stage 2 Sc2: 1b, 3a–d

Children should be taught about the following:
• the differences between things that are living and things that have never been alive
• plants need light and water to grow
• the names of the parts of flowering plants
• flowering plants produce seeds, which grow into new plants

• there are life processes including growth, nutrition and reproduction, common to plants
• plant growth is affected by the availability of light and water and by temperature
• plants need light to produce food for growth, and leaves are important to this process
• the root anchors the plant, and water and nutrients are taken in through the root and transported through the stem
• the life cycle of flowering plants, including pollination, seed production, seed dispersal and germination

Key Stage 1 classroom activities

Living things die.

Dead or alive?

The point at which plant material is dead is debatable. Is a cut flower or stem alive or dead?

A carrot top may look dead but given water and light will continue to grow.

• Look at some dead leaves, some dead flowers, some newly cut stems and a living pot plant. How do the children know some of these things are dead?

Plant cells can be cultured long after the parent from which they originally derive is dead. Individual plant cells can be grown in laboratory conditions. Many plants for commercial sale are now grown like this.

What is a plant?
- Look at a variety of weeds, tree leaves, and pot plants, then ask the children to suggest what features make a plant.

Plants have evolved over the last three billion years into a vast variety of types. They range from very simple blue-green algae that live only in boiling hot volcanic springs (some biologists do not regard these as plants) to huge and highly complex giant trees like Dawn Redwoods.

- Give the children examples of plants and animals to look at. Ask them to write down the differences they see.

Animals	Plants
Cannot produce their own food	Can make their own food
Have feeding structures such as a mouth and gut	Have no feeding structures
Do not make chlorophyll	Have chlorophyll
Do not have leaves	Have leaves
Do not have roots	Have roots
Can move around	Cannot move around
Have senses, such as ears	Have no sense receptors

Animal and plant cell structures are also quite different. For more information about this, see the companion volume in this series, *Science for Primary Teachers*, page 63.

Growing plants
- Germinate seeds in a variety of conditions. Ask the children to suggest places where they think the seeds will sprout quickly and places where they think that germination will be slow.

Seeds do not need light to germinate. Most seeds germinate more quickly if kept warm and damp. Some need a period of cold before they will germinate, to ensure that in nature they germinate after winter.

- Grow cress in half egg shells with and without water and light. Ask the children to suggest ways in which the conditions can be varied.

- Grow several bean seeds in model houses made out of shoe boxes, with chimneys or windows. The children will be fascinated when the shoots come straight up the chimney or out of the window seeking the light. Ask them to explain why this happens

All plants use sunlight and water to create food. Animals cannot do this and have to eat plants or other animals. Plants deprived of light or water will not grow.

Sow a handful of grass seed in a pan of compost. Children will be fascinated by the indoor lawn that results.

Parts of plants
- Dig up and carefully wash several large weeds to remove the soil from the roots. Ask the children to draw the weeds and label the parts.

Roots draw up water and trace minerals from the ground. These trace minerals are essential for healthy growth but are not plant food. Roots also anchor the plant in the soil.

Stems carry water from the roots to the leaves through an elaborate system of pipes called the vascular system.

Try to obtain weeds with long tap roots, such as dandelion, and those with fine fibrous roots, such as groundsell and daisy.

Types of plants

Plants and animals are different.

Food

Chlorophyll
Leaves
Roots
Movement
Senses

Seeds will germinate if kept warm and damp.

Plants need light and water.

Plants grow towards the light.

Roots
Trace minerals and water

Stems

Transpiration

The water and minerals carried through the stem are drawn upwards by the constant evaporation of water from the leaves. This process is called transpiration. In addition to evaporating water, the leaves make food by photosynthesis.

Seeds

Seeds
- Collect seeds and discuss with the children the way in which each type of seed is distributed. Burr seeds from plants like goosegrass are interesting when examined through a strong lens.

Life cycle of plants

The flower holds the reproductive organs of the plant. The male pollen fuses with the female egg cell (ovule) to form a seed. This seed carries genetic information from both parent plants.

Small seeds, like those of poppy and grass, are spread by wind. Animals help spread apple, burdock and oak seeds. Water spreads large floating seeds like the coconut.

> The seeds of fruit such as apple, pear, pepper and blackberry make interesting subjects for observational drawings.

Key Stage 2a classroom activities

Seed diary

Seeds
- Examine bean and pea seeds in detail. Get the children to weigh dry and soaked seeds. Grow seeds for a week. Draw diagrams and keep a diary.

Seed coat

Flowering plants produce seeds through the process of sexual reproduction. Seeds are covered in a coat called the testa.

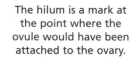

The hilum is a mark at the point where the ovule would have been attached to the ovary.

The plumule is the first bud. Formed inside the seed, it emerges as the plant's first shoot.

The radicle is the plant's first root, also formed inside the seed.

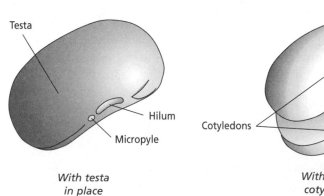

Testa

Hilum

Micropyle

Cotyledons

With testa in place

With testa removed and cotyledons opened out

Parts of a bean seed

- Investigate the conditions in which seeds will germinate. This can develop work begun at Key Stage 1. The children should be able to plan and carry out their work independently.

Seeds need warmth and water to germinate.

Seeds need warmth and water to germinate. Since the testa is waterproof, water enters the seed through a tiny hole called the micropyle. The seed coat splits and the root and stem emerge.

> Before seeds germinate they absorb very large quantities of water. They swell with great force and can sometimes spill out of the containers in which they are put for this investigation.

There are two main styles of emergence:

Both the root and the shoot emerge underground
from the seed coat.

Hypogeal germination

The root emerges underground. The stem
pushes the shoot and cotelydons into the air.

Epigeal germination

Growing material

- Compare the growth of seedlings sprouted in different material.
  The children could try pencil shavings, soil, shredded newspaper
  or compost.

Minerals

Seeds do not need light or special compost to germinate. Compost will
aid their subsequent growth because it contains the minerals needed by
plants.

> Older children could
> compare different
> types of seed compost
> and write up their
> results for *Which?*
> magazine.

Water for growth

Weeds

- Choose one type of weed common to your area. Dig up three plants
  of different sizes. Clean them and place each in a measuring cylinder.
  The children should try to work out ways of measuring which plant
  draws up most water. Make changes to the roots and leaves, e.g.
  shortening them. See what effect each change has on the amount of
  water drawn up.

Vascular system

The vascular system connects the roots with the leaves. If the leaf
surface area is reduced there is less evaporation of water so the pull of
water up the stem is reduced. If the root length is reduced there is less
root surface to draw up water.

> The vascular system
> consists of stem, roots
> and leaves, all of which
> are involved in the
> process of moving
> water from roots to
> leaves.

Different amounts of water

- Grow four pots of bean seedlings. Ask the children to investigate
  what happens when you give each pot a different amount of water.

Wilting plants

Plant cells need to be kept turgid to maintain stiffness. If the amount of
water in the cells falls below a critical level they become weaker and the
plant wilts. When the cells begin to dry out completely the plant is dying.

Suffocated roots

If a plant's roots are sitting in saturated soil they cannot take up oxygen
and so the plant suffocates.

Light for growth

Different amounts of light

- Grow four pots of beans. Put them in different amounts of light by
  placing them at different distances from a window.

Plants grow towards the light. They do this by producing a growth-promoting chemical on the side of the shoot in shadow. Extra growth here makes the plant stem tilt in the opposite direction, towards the light.

- Ask the children to measure and graph a seedling's growth every three days and to measure its mass at different stages of its growth.

A plant combines water and carbon dioxide to make the basic building blocks for its structure. An effect of taking in these substances is an increase in the plant's mass. Children are unlikely to understand easily where the extra mass of a plant comes from, but they will be able to observe that the plant gets heavier as it grows.

| Bending stem |
| Increase in size |

> Some plants can photosynthesize in low-light conditions. For instance, they can be found growing in caves near the artificial lighting provided for visitors.

Key Stage 2b classroom activities

Life processes

| Life processes common to plants and animals |

- Discuss the similarities between plants and animals. Which life processes do each carry out? Ask the children to use their knowledge of the seven life processes and work through them logically.

Check that all the seven life processes mentioned on page 36 apply to plants and animals. All plants have to respire in just the same way as animals. Respiration is the process of obtaining energy by combining oxygen and sugar to produce carbon dioxide and water. Plants respire all the time but at night or in low-light conditions, when they are not involved in photosynthesis, they release more carbon dioxide than they take in.

Flowers

| Flowers have male and female parts. |

- Show the children how to cut open a variety of flowers. Show them how to use powerful lenses and microscopes and to draw labelled diagrams.

> Many children believe that all plants have flowers. In fact many, such as mosses, ferns and algae, do not.

These are the principal parts of a flower:

| Principal parts of the flower |

petal	attracts insects to the flower
anther	produces pollen
filament	the stalk that holds the anther
stamen	the male parts in total
stigma	the sticky top of the carpel
style	the stalk that connects stigma and ovary
ovary	the seed container
ovule	the cell that develops into the seed.

The principal parts of a flower

Adaptation

Cacti

Daisies

Cacti adaptations

- Collect cacti and discuss with the children how cacti are adapted to life in deserts. Look at plants that commonly occur in gardens, like daisies and dandelions, and see what features they have that allow them to thrive in cut lawns.

For more on habitats, see page 65.

The main factors that shape plants are availability of light and availability of water. Plants like cacti are adapted to low water availability. They have thick leathery stems, which reduce water loss, and their leaves have been modified to form spines that also reduce water loss as well as prevent animals from eating them.

Teaching strategy: investigations for Key Stage 2a

Introduction

The experiments that follow highlight the skills of Sc1 set in the context of knowledge about plants.

Starting from a garden centre

A visit to a local garden centre makes a good starting point for classroom investigations. Arrange the visit with the nursery manager in advance. Explain that you want him or her to tell the children about the way that plants are propagated from seeds or cuttings, then grown and watered.

Many nurseries use information technology in their work, giving a useful starting point to classroom activity on databases, sensing equipment and computer control.

The investigations suggested here can be for:
- the class to do as a whole with teacher demonstration
- groups of children to carry out independently
- the whole class to do at the same time in groups.

The instructions are skeletal to allow children to design part of the investigation themselves. All the investigations take some time since they involve biological changes, so it may be sensible to have several running at the same time.

The instructions in italic are phrased as if the teacher is talking to her pupils.

Investigation 1

Select the seeds.

Keep careful records.

Control the conditions.

Subject:	WHICH SEEDS GERMINATE FIRST?
Objective:	The children will be able to keep a careful record of results.

What you need:	• about four or five different types of seeds such as
	    seeds from packets
	    seeds from fruits such as apples and oranges
	    big seeds such as avocado
	    weed seeds such as dandelion
	• small plant pots
	• saucers made from foil
	• compost

What to do:	*Label each pot with the sort of seed you will grow in it. Write down the number of each kind of seed you sow.* *Plant the seeds. Keep the pots damp (but not wet) and in a light place.* *Keep a careful note of when the first sprouts show.*

Use as wide a variety of seeds as you can.

Use lolly sticks as labels.

	WHICH SEEDS GERMINATE FIRST? *(continued)*

Recording:	*Draw a table showing:*
	    name of seed
	    number of seeds planted
	    number of days before the first seed sprouted
	    number of seeds that germinated
	
	Which seeds germinated first?

Assessment:	Has the child used her records when writing her report about speed of germination?
Extension:	*Compare the germination of the same type of seed from packets with different 'best before' dates. Do newer seeds germinate more reliably than older ones?*

Draw up a table with the children.

Investigation 2

Subject:	WHICH IS THE BEST GROWING MATERIAL?
Objective:	The children will learn to plan a fair test.
What you need:	• six pots • a variety of different materials to grow the seeds in – for example, sand, soil, ripped-up tissue paper, ripped-up paper, pencil shavings, cut-up knitting wool, small nails • about 30 small seeds such as lettuce or cress
What to do:	*Decide these things: what material to sow your seeds into, which seeds you will grow, which things you will keep the same and what you will measure.* *Sow the seeds and look at them regularly.*
Recording:	*Write about what you did. Say how you made your test fair. Write a report about which is the best material to grow seedlings in.*
Assessment:	Does the child's account show she understands how to carry out a fair test?

Fair test

What to measure

Decide on the criteria for the best compost.

> Make sure that the material is finely shredded.

> Alter the growing medium only. Help the children to keep all the other variables controlled.

Investigation 3

Subject:	DO BEANS GROW QUICKER THAN PEAS?
Objective:	The children will learn to take an accurate series of measurements and present them in a graph.
What you need:	• several bean seedlings • the same number of pea seedlings
What to do:	*Decide how to make the test a fair one. Which variables will be kept the same? The only independent variable in this investigation is the type of seed.* *Every day or two measure the growth of each seedling.*
Recording:	*Record your results in a table that shows the height of peas and the day they were measured.* *Draw a bar chart showing the growth of the plants. Use your graph to help you explain which type of plant grew most quickly.*
Assessment:	Does the child use the graph to present his results and support his conclusion?

Which variable will be the same?

Measure the dependent variable.

Conclusion

> Soak all the seeds – they will germinate more quickly.

> The dependent variable is likely to be the height of the seedling.

> A line graph could be drawn by more able or older children.

Investigation 4

Subject:	HOW MUCH WATER PASSES THROUGH A PLANT?
Objective:	The children will learn to keep some experimental factors constant.
What you need:	• three or four different weeds carefully dug up with roots intact (make sure they are of different types or different sizes)
What to do:	*Put the plants in measuring cylinders filled up with water. Look at the plants. Which do you think will take most water out of the cylinder? How could we find out?* *Think of a way to stop the water evaporating from the surface of the cylinder.* *How could we make the test fair?*
Recording:	*Fill in a table to show how much water was taken out of each container by the plants.* *Write about the things you tried to keep the same in each of your tests.*
Assessment:	Did the child list the factors she tried to keep the same in her investigation?

Transpiration

Measuring cylinders

Devise the investigation.

Evaluate the investigation.

Wash the roots carefully.

You could use plastic or foil to make a partial seal.

Using measuring cylinders makes it easy to calculate the amount of water that evaporates.

Variation and classification

Kingdoms of living things

Variety

Plants and animals show astonishing variety. Only a fraction of species have been described and categorized. Ecologists working in rain forests routinely collect animals that have never been seen by scientists before.

Living things are divided into kingdoms. Although some authorities believe that living things can be divided into two main groups – plants and animals – others think that it is better to divide them into six main kingdoms: virus, bacterium, protist, fungus, plant and animal.

There are over 30 million species on the planet. The greatest diversity of living things occurs in the forests.

Summary diagram

Every living thing within a kingdom probably shared a common ancestor.

This diagram is extremely useful reference.

The main classifications of living things

Minibeasts

There is a plethora of small invertebrates (minibeasts). These include flatworms, ringed worms, molluscs and arthropods.

In the school grounds you are most likely to come across earthworms, which are a type of ringed worm (annelid). Earthworms eat decaying vegetable material. You may also see flatworms in ponds.

> Earthworms feed mainly at night but can easily be found in compost heaps.

The molluscs you are most likely to find are the gastropods: snails and slugs. Both move by means of a muscular foot. They have a distinct head with eyes on stalks. Slugs are similar to snails but lack a shell. They feed by scraping away at vegetable material with a rasping tongue called a radula.

About 80% of all animal species are arthropods. They consist of the following groups:

crustaceans	woodlice and crabs
arachnids	spiders and scorpions
myriapods	centipedes and millipedes
insects	beetles and flies.

> The number of legs is an important characteristic for distinguishing types of minibeast.

Arthropods have an exoskeleton, which is like a suit of armour. The muscles move limbs by pulling on the inside of the exoskeleton.

> Arthropods have an exoskeleton made of a material similar to that found in fingernails.

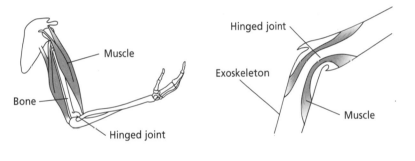

Human joint and muscles   *Arthropod joint and muscles*

Keys

Use of keys is an important feature of work on variation and classification. There are two basic types of key:

- binary keys laid out like a branching diagram where at each branch there are two choices

- keys where the options are numbered.

This is how a branching key sorts a dog, frog, ladybird and worm:

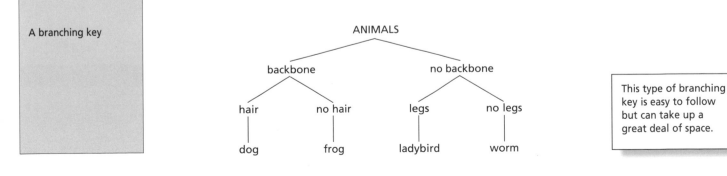

> This type of branching key is easy to follow but can take up a great deal of space.

A numbered key	A numbered key sorts a dog, frog, ladybird and worm like this:

A numbered key sorts a dog, frog, ladybird and worm like this:

| 1 | backbone | go to 2 |
| | no backbone | go to 3 |

| 2 | hair | dog |
| | no hair | frog |

| 3 | legs | ladybird |
| | no legs | worm |

> Most guides to natural history, such as *A Field Guide to the Trees of Britain and Northern Europe* (Mitchell, A., 1974, Collins) use this type of key.

Advantages and disadvantages

Binary branching keys are easy to follow and easy to construct but they take up a lot of space. Numbered keys are more compact but their brevity makes them difficult to follow.

Common misconceptions

Plant or animal?

| cow | grass | boy |
| spider | elephant | worm |

A simple test

When shown pictures of these living things and asked the question 'Is it an animal?' children frequently do not categorize the organisms correctly.

Are humans animals?

Humans are not seen as animals by the majority of children at age seven. At age nine most children do not think that spiders or worms are animals. About 4% of primary teachers and about 10% of teacher trainees are reported as having the same problem. One possible reason for this confusion is that the term minibeast has been coined to cover small invertebrates. However, though children know about mammals some do not think of them as a subset of animals.

> Even some adults get worm and spider wrong.

Cows are definitely animals.

The animal about which there is usually no confusion is the cow: if it has four legs, a tail and hair then most people have no problem in recognizing the organism as an animal.

List of resources

Resources for studying classification and variation

- petri dishes
- pooters (to collect small creatures)
- aquaria
- dropper pipettes
- short-handled, fine-mesh pond nets
- white plastic trays
- identification books, such as *The Clue Book of* ... series
- magnifying glass on stand
- microscope with × 20 maximum magnification
- minispectors
- trowel

> Pooters are designed to suck up tiny creatures.

Summary of the programmes of study

Key Stage 1 Sc2: 4a–b

Children should be taught about the following:
- recognizing similarities and differences between themselves and other pupils

Key Stage 2 Sc2: 4a

- living things can be grouped according to observable similarities and differences

- locally occurring animals and plants can be identified and assigned to groups, using keys

Key Stage 1 classroom activities

Similarities and differences

Differences between people

- Ask the children to draw a picture of a friend. Show all the pictures. Talk about which human features in the drawings are similar and which are different.

Identical twins

Every person is unique. Humans are extremely good at distinguishing an individual from his or her face. Identical twins, being physical clones, can look astoundingly alike but, even so, individual twins will acquire scratches and scars that distinguish them from each other.

Identical twins are clones of each other since they are the product of the same egg and sperm.

Non-identical twins

Non-identical twins are as unlike each other as normal brothers and sisters because they are the product of different eggs and different sperm.

> During the early nineteenth century a prevalent scientific idea was that people passed on characteristics they had acquired during their lives.

Groups of characteristics

Who looks like me?

- Ask the children to suggest things they have in common with some, but not all, of the children in the class. They might suggest:

Groups

hair colour	birth month
eye colour	right- or left-handedness
sex	

Get into groups in the classroom

Ask them to get into groups sharing these characteristics. Count the number in each group. Talk about areas of uncertainty.

Venn diagrams show sets of objects that share characteristics.

Measuring bodies

There are similarities between people.

- Ask the class what they could measure about their bodies (you will need be sensitive to individuals who feel they are different in some way). Measure hand span, size of head, length of leg or arm. Record the measurements in a simple table.

> Measure and record the features of individuals.

Normal distribution

People, like all living things, show considerable variation in their physical characteristics. Many characteristics, ranging from weight to hand span, show a normal distribution. A normal distribution is characterized by a bell-shaped graph, with most individuals falling under the highest part of the line.

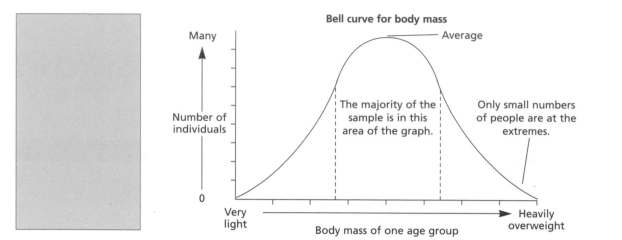

Bell curve for body mass

Key Stage 2a classroom activities

Living things can be sorted into plants and animals.

Plants and animals

- The children draw up a table with three columns. In the first two columns they list living things that they know are either plants or animals. In the third column they write the names of those they are uncertain about.

Make sets of plants and animals based on locally occurring organisms.

In general plants move little and have no feeding organs apart from leaves. They have roots, which animals do not have. However, animals like mussels and corals (which children can encounter on nature trips and in wildlife films) have structures that are not unlike those of plants and an immobile lifestyle that might lead children to think of them as plant-like. In fact, sea animals like this are sedentary rather than rooted like plants. This is because their food is brought to them on currents – so there is no need for them to waste energy going to get it.

Hunting

Leaf shapes

- Go to the local park with the children in autumn. Look for the following:

a wide leaf	a heavy leaf
a long leaf	a leaf with black spots
a brightly coloured leaf	a pointed leaf

Leaves can be sorted according to observable characteristics.

Draw the children's attention to the distinction between compound and simple leaves. Back in the classroom draw the leaves and use squared paper to measure their area. Put similar leaves in sets. Use a branching key to sort them.

Branching keys are described on page 55.

Different trees have evolved different leaves to enhance their chances of survival. Chestnut leaves are large to maximize their light-gathering potential whereas pine needles reduce the water loss from a tree adapted to drier conditions. Holly leaves are prickly to prevent animals eating them.

The main difference that can be used to sort leaves is:

simple: e.g. oak leaf

compound: e.g. chestnut. Each leaf is made up from leaflets.

See page 62 for more information about simple and compound leaves.

Twenty questions

- Ask the children to answer 'yes' or 'no' to questions; this is the basis of binary keys. Asking questions like this and listening to the answers is an important skill.

> TEACHER: I am thinking of an animal.
> CHILD 1: Does it have four legs?
> TEACHER: No.
> CHILD 2: Does it fly?
> TEACHER: Yes ...

The children have twenty questions to guess the correct animal.

This is a good way to identify living things.

> Play the game with a variety of animals and plants. It is an excellent way to fill the odd spare moment.

Differences between animals

- Present the children with pairs of animals to compare. Preferably use stuffed animals, live pets or pictures.

As you would expect, animals from different species often vary greatly in appearance. For instance, penguins and peacocks, although both birds, are different species and exhibit considerable differences.

These differences can be tabulated. For example:

Compare two similar living things.

> Writing prose comparisons is more demanding than listing comparisons in a table format.

EAGLE	OSTRICH
large wings	tiny wings
short legs	long legs

Tabulate the differences.

Key Stage 2b classroom activities

Non-flowering plants

- With the children go on a short walk around the local area looking at the plants, especially those growing on walls and in cracks in paving. Try to find examples of mosses and algae (green slime on paving and in ponds). If you are in a particularly diverse area you might also find ferns, fungi and lichens. Draw the children's attention to these as plants that never flower. They reproduce using spores.

A brief walk
Cracks in paving

Spore producers

> Choose a time when many local plants are in flower.

The distinction between flowering and non-flowering plants is important:

FLOWERING PLANTS	NON-FLOWERING PLANTS
oak tree	moss
dandelion	lichen
grass	pond weed
dock	

> Take samples of mosses in particular and look at them through a microscope. They look like wonderful miniature forests.

Keys to common flowers

- Collect a range of flowers with the children. Draw them, press them for later identification, describe them, put them into sets.

Use simple plant identification books to enable children to name the flowers.

Simple keys can be made to group common flowers.

Many plant identification books emphasize the style of the petals when naming flowers.

Cabbage-type flowers

Four-petalled flowers belong to the cabbage family. Examples include wallflowers and cabbage.

Pea-type flowers

Petals that are fused together often belong to the pea family. Examples include sweet peas and clover.

Daisy-type flowers

Flowers with many individual florets belong to the daisy family. Examples include daisies, dandelions and chrysanthemums.

Cow-parsley-type flowers

Flowers that are arranged in a group on the ends of stalks are the *umbelliferae*. These include cow parsley and carrot.

As a rule of thumb you can collect flowers if you are on private land, have permission, and the flower is common.

Use simple identification books to help the children name some of the flowers.

Wallflower

Four-petalled flower

Sweet pea

Pea-type flower

Dandelion

Cow parsley

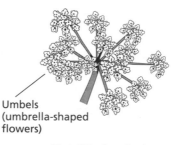

Florets (tiny flowers)

Umbels (umbrella-shaped flowers)

Daisy-type flowerhead

Umbellifer flowerhead

Classifying animals

- Draw two columns on the board and add these headings: 'animals with bones' and 'animals without bones'.

Research using secondary sources

- Ask the children to research information using the school library, CD-ROM disks and other sources. They could search out which is the smallest animal with an internal skeleton/backbone and which is the largest animal without a skeleton.

Big invertebrates

The largest invertebrates are found in the sea. These include giant organisms such as jellyfish and squid. On land, without the upthrust from water (see page 144 on floating forces), massive invertebrates cannot support themselves and are crushed by their own weight. The largest land invertebrates are worms (annelids), large insects like dragonflies, and snails (molluscs).

The smallest animals with bony skeletons are humming birds and pygmy shrews. The smallest vertebrates you are likely to find locally will be mice and blue tits.

Backbones evolved once.

The vertebral column or backbone evolved only once, and all animals with backbones are related to a common ancestor. All animals with backbones also have a bony skeleton.

Classifying vertebrates

Write down in sets the names of three animals: two from one vertebrate group and one from another. Get the children to spot the odd one out in each group.

The five vertebrate groups

- Teach the children that there are five main vertebrate groups:

fish:	scaly skin, gills, live in water. Cold-blooded
amphibians:	soft moist skin, lay eggs in water. Cold-blooded
reptiles:	dry scaly skin, lay eggs in leathery cases on land. Cold-blooded
birds:	feathers, lay eggs in hard shells. Warm-blooded
mammals:	hair, give birth to live young, feed them on milk. Warm-blooded

Invertebrate groups

- Go into a local area of rough grass and find a range of minibeasts. Sort the collection of minibeasts in a variety of ways suggested by the children. Teach the children that common land invertebrates (minibeasts) can be divided into:

The three main groups of common land invertebrates

worms:	including earthworms
molluscs:	including snails and slugs
arthropods:	all minibeasts with jointed legs.

Worms

Worms have bristles on their bodies (not to be confused with mammalian hair). Look in detail at the way in which they move.

Molluscs

Slugs and snails have a muscular foot that is fascinating to view from underneath, for example through the wall of a glass container.

Keep some snails and slugs in a vivarium. With luck they will lay eggs.

Jointed legs

Arthropods come in a bewildering range of forms. There are over 300 000 known types of beetle alone. Arthropods have an external skeleton that must be discarded as they grow.

Arthropods

- Collect minibeasts and classify them according to the number and arrangement of legs. Teach the children what the word arthropod means (*arthro* = joint, *pod* = leg) and that there are four main groups of arthropods:

Insects have six legs but spiders have eight.

insects:	six legs
arachnids:	eight legs
centipedes and millipedes:	one or two pairs of legs per segment
woodlice:	seven pairs of legs

Teaching strategy: lesson plans for Key Stage 2b

This suggestion for classroom organization focuses on the use of tree twigs in spring with a class of Year 5 or Year 6 pupils. However, many of the ideas could be simplified for use with other age groups.

Lesson plan 1

Theme:	CLASSIFYING TREES
Learning objective:	The children will learn to group and classify tree twigs in a variety of ways.
Lesson introduction:	*Look at the five or six types of twig on the table.* (These should be taken by the teacher from local trees using a pair of secateurs.) *Talk about the appearance of each one.* Show the children that some of the leaves are simple and that others are compound. Draw simple and compound leaves on the board.

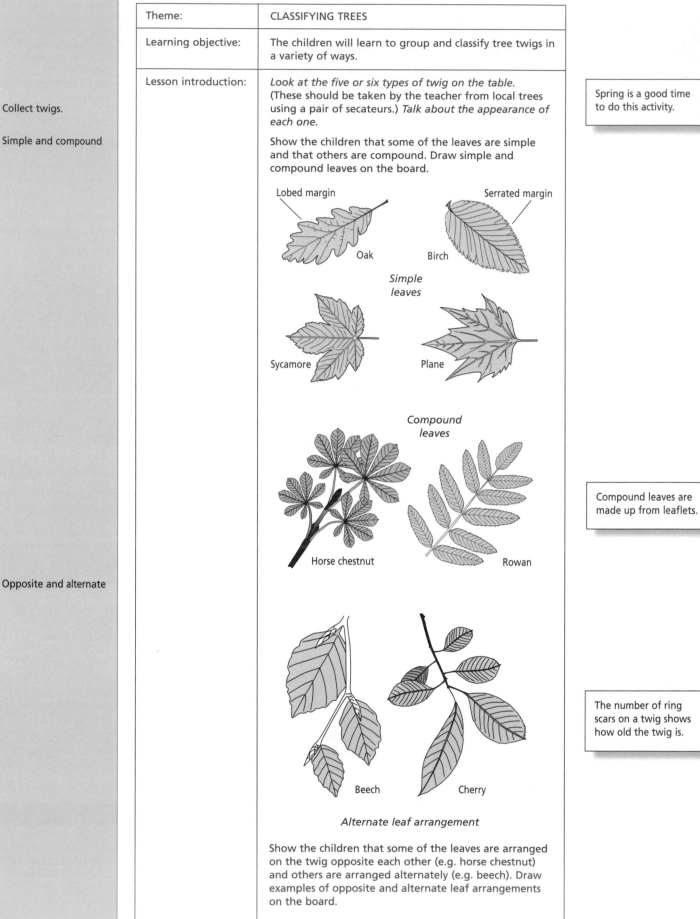

Collect twigs.

Simple and compound

Opposite and alternate

Spring is a good time to do this activity.

Compound leaves are made up from leaflets.

The number of ring scars on a twig shows how old the twig is.

Lobed margin — Oak

Serrated margin — Birch

Simple leaves

Sycamore

Plane

Compound leaves

Horse chestnut

Rowan

Beech

Cherry

Alternate leaf arrangement

Show the children that some of the leaves are arranged on the twig opposite each other (e.g. horse chestnut) and others are arranged alternately (e.g. beech). Draw examples of opposite and alternate leaf arrangements on the board.

	CLASSIFYING TREES *(continued)*
Lesson development:	*Draw two groups of twigs: twigs with leaves arranged opposite each other and twigs with leaves arranged alternately. Draw two groups of leaves: compound leaves and simple leaves.*
Recording:	*In what other ways can you group the twigs and leaves?*
Extension:	*Complete a Carroll diagram. This one has been partly filled in:*
Assessment:	*Criterion:* Has the child grouped the twigs and leaves in several ways? *Mode:* Look at the children's drawings.

Grouping

Carroll diagram

Extension Carroll diagram:

	SIMPLE LEAVES	COMPOUND LEAVES
ALTERNATE BUDS	lime oak	rowan
OPPOSITE BUDS	sycamore maple	ash horse chestnut

> If the children find the Carroll diagram too difficult they can complete just the top line of this example.

Lesson plan 2

Theme:	USING A KEY
Learning objective:	The children will learn to use a tree identification key to name twigs and leaves.
Lesson introduction:	Show the children the key from a good, easy-to-use book such as *The Clue Book of Trees.* Alternatively duplicate the limited key below remembering to refer only to the trees named if using it.

Identification book

A simple key

Bud scales

Lobed simple leaves

1. Wide flat leaves — Go to 2
   Needles — Go to 8*

2. Opposite — Go to 3
   Alternate — Go to 6

3. Compound — Go to 4
   Simple — Go to 5

4. Black bud scales and smooth silvery bark — Ash
   Sticky buds and brown bark — Horse chestnut

5. Five points with smooth underside — Sycamore
   Five points, small leaf, downy underneath — Field maple

6. Simple — Go to 7
   Compound — Go to 9*

7. Leaf very downy underneath — Whitebeam
   Small leaf with lots of lobes — Hawthorn
   Leaf large and lobed — Oak
   Leaf long and thin — Willow
   Leaf heart shaped — Lime
   Leaf small with saw-tooth edges — Birch

   * *These and subsequent questions are not shown.*

> *The Clue Book* (Allen, G. and Denslow, J., Oxford University Press) is a classic series with some of the easiest-to-follow keys. Look for the six titles that have been reissued in revised editions (1997). Teachers who are uncertain about identification will find books like this very useful.

> The insects and other arthropods you bring in with the twigs are bound to create interest, too.

Memory test

Map

Using a key

	USING A KEY *(continued)*
Lesson development:	Go out into the neighbourhood or school grounds and identify trees from memory.
Recording:	*Draw a map of the neighbourhood or school grounds, positioning and naming the trees.*
Extension:	Give the children six twigs as a basis for making up their own keys.
Assessment:	*Criterion:* Can the children use a key to identify leaves?

Mode: Give the children pictures of three leaves. In each case, can they name the tree using a key? |

Ask the children to write 'A guide to our playground' including a map showing trees.

Lesson plan 3

Binary or dichotomous tree database

Save the file.

Using keys created by other groups

Theme:	COMPUTER KEY
Learning objective:	The children will learn to use a computer to devise a binary key.
Lesson introduction:	Remind the children about making a key to identify tree leaves and twigs. Show the children how *Branch and Sort,* or any other binary (dichotomous) tree database, can be used to classify items.
Lesson development:	In groups, children take it in turns to design and save their own binary key on the computer. Once this has been done, each group then opens the file saved by another group and uses its binary key. This will take some days if only one computer is used.
Recording:	The computer file.
Extension:	The children can make other types of branching key.
Assessment:	*Criterion:* Is it possible to use a group's binary key to identify tree twigs?

Mode: Demonstration of the use of the key. |

For information about binary (dichotomous) keys, see page 24.

To save time, allow each group to classify a maximum of five or six twigs.

Living things in the environment

Habitats	**Ecology**

Ecology
Plants and animals interact with their environments to create habitats. Ecology is the study of these interactions.

The world can be divided into a number of large regions called biomes. Each biome is characterized by a particular climate and is usually named after the dominant plant type to be found in it:

tundra biome	very cold	lichens, mosses, small shrubs
coniferous forest biome	cold	coniferous trees
temperate forest biome	varied but cool	deciduous trees
grassland biome	dry	grasses
savannah	dry	grasses and some trees
desert	very dry	thorn shrubs and cacti
tropical rainforest	hot and wet	tall tropical hardwoods

The coastal fringes of South America have all these biomes within very short distances of each other as a result of rapid changes in altitude.

Parts of northern Britain are in the tundra biome.

Most of Britain is in the temperate forest biome.

Ecological succession
Whenever an area of land is cleared, for instance by a forest fire or digging, a succession of different plants will grow there, culminating in climax vegetation (the final type of vegetation). This stage results in a climax community, which is very stable. The biomes listed above represent the climax communities for different climatic zones.

Willowherb, bramble and birch are amongst the first colonizers.

Microhabitats
The place where an animal or plant lives is its habitat. Some habitats are very small and are called microhabitats. A rotting tree trunk is a microhabitat for a range of plants, fungi and animals. It is part of the much bigger forest habitat.

A habitat has to supply all the needs of the animals and plants that live in it. The rotting tree provides ready-made chemicals for bacteria and fungi to break down. These in turn, along with the rotting wood, provide food and shelter for larger animals such as woodlice and wood chewing insects. Other animals, such as woodpeckers, might visit the habitat from time to time to eat insects and grubs that live on the decaying wood.

Bring a rotting log into the classroom. It will contain a huge range of organisms and excite considerable interest.

Sidebar labels: Habitats · Biomes · South America · Climax vegetation · Supplying the needs of its animals and plants

Animal and plant
communities

Food web

Carbon and nitrogen
cycles

The animals and plants that share a habitat are locked together in an
interdependent community. Within a pond there is a community of
plants, micro-organisms and animals. They form a food web which is
dependent on the energy of the sun.

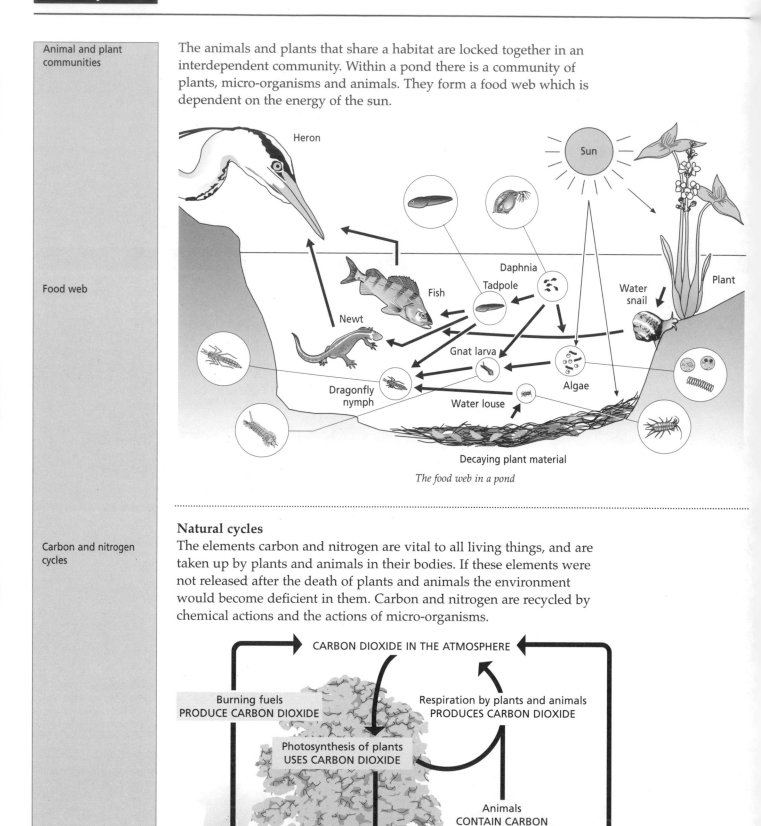

The food web in a pond

Natural cycles

The elements carbon and nitrogen are vital to all living things, and are
taken up by plants and animals in their bodies. If these elements were
not released after the death of plants and animals the environment
would become deficient in them. Carbon and nitrogen are recycled by
chemical actions and the actions of micro-organisms.

The carbon cycle

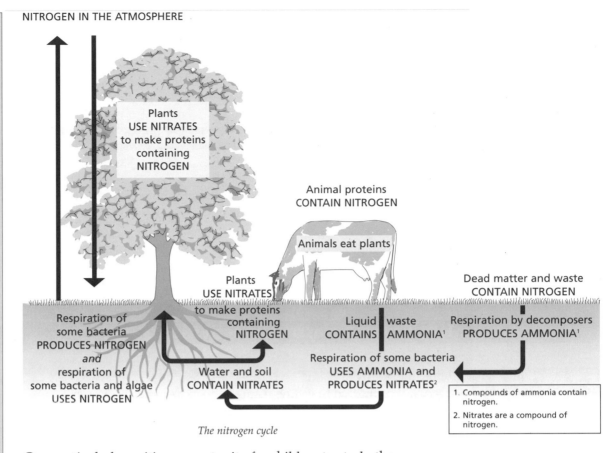

NITROGEN IN THE ATMOSPHERE

Plants
USE NITRATES
to make proteins
containing
NITROGEN

Animal proteins
CONTAIN NITROGEN

Animals eat plants

Plants
USE NITRATES
to make proteins
containing
NITROGEN

Dead matter and waste
CONTAIN NITROGEN

Respiration of
some bacteria
PRODUCES NITROGEN
and
respiration of
some bacteria and algae
USES NITROGEN

Liquid waste
CONTAINS AMMONIA[1]

Respiration by decomposers
PRODUCES AMMONIA[1]

Water and soil
CONTAIN NITRATES

Respiration of some bacteria
USES AMMONIA and
PRODUCES NITRATES[2]

1. Compounds of ammonia contain
   nitrogen.
2. Nitrates are a compound of
   nitrogen.

The nitrogen cycle

New habitats

One particularly exciting opportunity for children to study the
relationship of living things with their environment is when a new
habitat is opened up. This might happen if a temporary classroom on a
previously grassy site is removed. The territory that emerges is virgin
land which is subsequently colonized by waves of plants and animals.
In much of lowland Britain the natural climax vegetation is oak forest,
which is part of the deciduous forest biome.

As it silts up, a pond or
stream will show a
range of colonization.

Common misconceptions

Shelter and nest

Home or habitat?
Children may regard the place where an animal sleeps or breeds as its
home. So they will say that birds live in nests and that bears live in
caves. Strictly speaking those are places where the animals shelter or
hide their offspring. Their homes are the habitats they live in, such as
an area of suburban gardens or a coniferous forest.

This misunderstanding
is largely semantic.

List of resources

**Resources for studying
living things in the
environment**

- magnifying glass on stand
- microscope with × 20 maximum magnification
- minispectors
- disposable plastic gloves
- trowel
- sieve
- wooden pegs to push into soil

- 10 m lengths of string knotted every 50 cm
- 20 m lengths of nylon string marked every metre
- metre sticks
- trundle wheel
- long tape

Summary of the programmes of study

Key Stage 1 Sc2: 5a–b

Children should be taught about the following:
- the types of animals and plants in the environment
- differences between environments that affect the plants and animals living there

Key Stage 2 Sc2: 5a–d
- adaptation of animals and plants
- feeding relationships

Key Stage 1 classroom activities

Urban or rural, any area has many types of plants.

Looking locally
- Ask the children to list the plants and animals they notice on a walk. Talk about the places where the animals and plants are found and ask the children why they are found there.

Their observations might be that the worms are in the soil or the moss is growing on a wall. They might offer explanations, such as that the birds are in the trees to keep safe from cats.

Different plants are found in different places.

- Go to a variety of places such as: a flowerbed, the soil at the base of a wall or around trees in the playground, a small area of grass. Ask the children what plants are growing there. Discuss which plants were put there by gardeners and which arrived naturally. Discuss how the latter group got there. Take samples, draw them and press them.

> Try to obtain a range of seeds of plants such as dandelion, goosegrass (cleaver) and poppy. Tell the children about how the seeds are spread.

Plants are able to exploit different habitats depending on their mode of growth. Daisies can survive being cut because they grow low and sprout very close to the surface of the soil. Docks can grow in places where there is little moisture because their long tap root reaches down to the damper layers of the soil.

Simple quadrats

- Use quoits to focus the children's attention on a small area. Put the quoits on grassy areas and look at the plants framed by the hoop. Do not attempt a sophisticated survey; simply record if a plant is, or is not, present in the hoop.

> Compare the plants found in the quoit in the middle of a grassy field with those found under a hedge.

Quadrats (normally one square metre) are used to sample areas of ground but hoops and quoits can be used instead.

Minibeasts

Different animals are found in different places.

- Ask the children to look for minibeasts in a variety of places. Compile a table to show where the children found the biggest number:

WHERE?	HOW MANY?
under the hedge	12
in the flowerbed	6

Types of minibeasts

- Alternatively you can compile a list showing the number of minibeasts and where they were found:

WHERE?	HOW MANY?	NOTES
under the hedge	12	spiders and woodlice
in the flowerbed	8	worms

- In either case graph the results.

The needs of minibeasts

Minibeasts need to find a place (a habitat) where there is food, moisture, shelter from predation and a place to breed.

Shelter

Minibeasts shelter under stones and other objects during daylight because these are places that do not dry out and are safe from predators like birds. They tend to forage at night to get food. Woodlice need a moist place to keep their gills working; slugs need shelter during the day since they make a good meal for thrushes and other birds.

> Lay out old carpet two weeks before your hunt. This makes a good shelter for minibeasts that enjoy cool and shade, and gives them protection from birds.

Key Stage 2a classroom activities

There is a variety of habitats near most schools.

Environmental vocabulary

- Ask the children to write an estate agent's description of three or four places, e.g. 'damp area that rarely gets the sun – would suit someone who likes it wet and cold'.

- Teach the children to use the words 'habitat' and 'environment' correctly when discussing the places they identify in their estate agent's descriptions. Thus they could talk about a treetop habitat which is 'breezy and has a good view'.

> The children could put together their habitat adverts and make them into a page of a newspaper featuring habitats local to the school.

Habitat

Environment

Physical and biotic factors

A 'habitat' is a place in which a particular organism can survive. A worm can survive in the habitat of the soil. 'Environment', on the other hand, is the sum of all the conditions in a habitat that affect the organism. These include physical factors, such as temperature and rainfall, and biotic factors, such as predation by animals. For instance, the water snail lives in a freshwater environment that gets very warm by day (physical factor) and carries the threat of sticklebacks eating its eggs (biotic factor).

Animals and plants are suited to different habitats.

Adaptation

- Ask the children to note the plants and animals found in each habitat. Discuss why certain living things seem to prefer certain areas. Talk about the adaptation of worms and centipedes for a life in the soil. Look for the features of bees that help them survive.

Adaptation examples

Adaptation describes the characteristics of an organism that help it to survive in its environment. For example, a swallow's beak is adapted to catching flies, a fir tree has a shape that is adapted to shedding heavy snowfall, grass grows from a point just above the soil so that it can resist close cutting or grazing.

> Rabbit adaptations include: colour (for camouflage), ears (for acute hearing), incisors (for gnawing), and claws (for digging).

Food chains

Food chains start with green plants.

- Trace back some of the children's food to its source in the food chain: cows eat grass; cornflakes are the seeds of a green plant. Challenge the children to find a food that does not start with a green plant. (Even mushrooms need dead plant material to grow on.)

Energy from the sun

The energy for plant growth comes from the sun. Plants use the sun's energy to convert water and carbon dioxide into food. Plants build their bodies from water and carbon dioxide and animals use this to make their own bodies.

The only exceptions

The only food chains that do not start with energy from the sun are those around the deep ocean vents, where bacteria feed on sulphur-rich water coming from within the Earth. Most scientists now also recognize communities of incredibly slow-growing bacteria that live deep within the rocks of the Earth's crust. These form another food chain separate from the sun's energy.

> Even mushrooms and other fungi indirectly use the energy of the sun since they live on the decaying bodies of dead plants and animals that once relied on the sun for energy.

Key Stage 2b classroom activities

Sampling

Living things in a habitat can be systematically recorded.

- Show the children how to use hoops (see page 68) and line transects to sample vegetation. Line transects simply record which plant (or bare soil) is closest to a knot or mark made every 50 cm along a five-metre string.

Many habitats

- Select a small area for the class to work in, such as under a tree, in the open, near a wall, across a trampled path, near the goalmouth of a football field or between paving slabs. Split the class into groups. Each group selects two habitats within this area. Ask the groups to record the plants and animals found in their small sample. Ask them to write an illustrated comparison of the two habitats and suggest why different plants and animals are found in each.

- Use the results to draw a graph showing the changes in type or height of vegetation within the area, for example as you go away from a tree, wall or hedge.

Sampling

It is impossible to notice and count every plant or animal in an area. Ecologists use the technique of sampling one small area and suggesting that it is representative of the wider habitat.

Valid sample

The way in which the sample area is chosen is important to the degree of validity that the sample has. For instance, if you are looking at a field and choose to sample only areas where there are bright blue flowers it is unlikely that these will be representative of the field as a whole.

> A line transect is particularly useful when looking at the differences that occur between one part of a habitat and another.

> Introduce some simple ways of making a random sample selection. For instance, throw a ball and sample the area where the ball lands.

Ecosystem

What is an 'ecosystem'?

- Study a pond. Ponds are very small and self-contained ecosystems. Use books and videos to help the children understand the roles of the different animals within the pond ecosystem.

Pond ecosystem

- Teach the children about the plants and animals that can be found in two contrasting ecosystems. These ecosystems might be: polar, rainforest, desert, sea.

> As an extension the children could compare any two of these areas and say why, for instance, a polar bear is unable to survive in a desert.

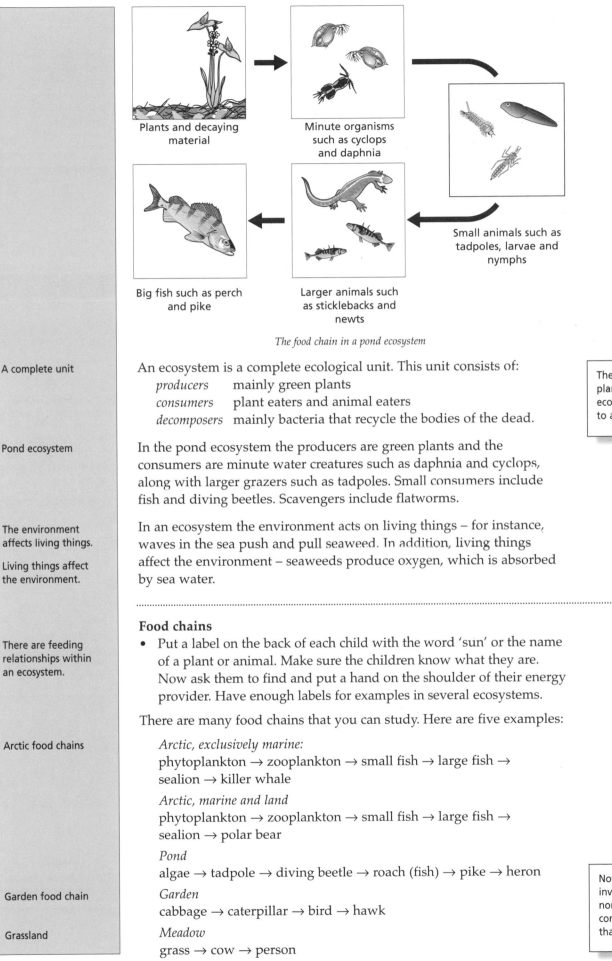

The food chain in a pond ecosystem

Plants and decaying material

Minute organisms such as cyclops and daphnia

Small animals such as tadpoles, larvae and nymphs

Big fish such as perch and pike

Larger animals such as sticklebacks and newts

A complete unit

An ecosystem is a complete ecological unit. This unit consists of:

producers	mainly green plants
consumers	plant eaters and animal eaters
decomposers	mainly bacteria that recycle the bodies of the dead.

> The animals and plants that live in an ecosystem are referred to as a community.

Pond ecosystem

In the pond ecosystem the producers are green plants and the consumers are minute water creatures such as daphnia and cyclops, along with larger grazers such as tadpoles. Small consumers include fish and diving beetles. Scavengers include flatworms.

The environment affects living things.

Living things affect the environment.

In an ecosystem the environment acts on living things – for instance, waves in the sea push and pull seaweed. In addition, living things affect the environment – seaweeds produce oxygen, which is absorbed by sea water.

Food chains

There are feeding relationships within an ecosystem.

- Put a label on the back of each child with the word 'sun' or the name of a plant or animal. Make sure the children know what they are. Now ask them to find and put a hand on the shoulder of their energy provider. Have enough labels for examples in several ecosystems.

There are many food chains that you can study. Here are five examples:

Arctic food chains

Arctic, exclusively marine:
phytoplankton → zooplankton → small fish → large fish → sealion → killer whale

Arctic, marine and land
phytoplankton → zooplankton → small fish → large fish → sealion → polar bear

Pond
algae → tadpole → diving beetle → roach (fish) → pike → heron

Garden food chain

Garden
cabbage → caterpillar → bird → hawk

Grassland

Meadow
grass → cow → person

> Notice that food chains involving water are normally longer and contain more levels than land food chains.

Artificial habitats

Vivariums for small
animals

- Show the children how to make an artificial home for small animals. A home like this is known as a vivarium. Start with a large plastic box or old aquarium. Children should explain how their vivarium will be made and managed. They could put cacti in a gritty compost with rocks, or woodlice in damp soil with potato skins.

It is unlikely that you will be able to create inside a vivarium a fully integrated ecosystem with all materials recycled and no input other than sunlight.

The carbon cycle

Carbon is just one of the elements that is recycled within the environment. Micro-organisms play a vital role in releasing the element from the bodies of dead plants and animals.

> Vivariums containing people have been tried, with limited success, in the USA, where groups in sealed containers have tried to simulate a two-year-long space flight.

Teaching strategy: Key Stage 2a lesson plans

Lesson plan 1

Theme:	HABITATS
Learning objective:	The children will learn that there is a variety of living things and a variety of habitats.
Lesson introduction:	Go for a walk around the school playground. Take notes on the animals and plants the children see and exactly where each is seen. Draw attention to the place (habitat) and conditions (environment) in which the animal or plant lives.
Lesson development:	In the classroom talk about the different places where the children noticed living things. Their observations might include: weeds in the gap between a wall and tarmac moss on a wall ants in the soil under paving slabs trees in the playground worms in the soil in a rose bed. Tell the children that the word for the place where an animal lives and gets food and shelter is 'habitat'. Ask them: *What is the habitat ... of the ants?* (the soil under the paving slabs) *... of the weeds?* (the gap between a wall and tarmac) *... of the worms?* (the soil in the rose bed). Now ask the children to describe the environment of each habitat: *What is it like ... under the paving slabs?* (dry and hot in summer) *... in the soil of the rose bed?* (dark and damp) *... on the wall?* (mostly in the shade, and damp).
Recording:	*Fill in this simple table:* 	NAME OF THE LIVING THING	HABITAT IT LIVES IN	WHAT THE HABITAT IS LIKE	 |---|---|---| 				 Less able children can be given a shorter table with a simplified version of the first two columns: 	NAME OF LIVING THING	PLACE IT LIVES	 |---|---| 			 All children can illustrate their work with careful pencil drawings of some of the living things they noticed.

Variety of habitats

Environment of each habitat

What lives in each habitat?

Describe the environment

Simple table

> The objective should be something that the children will know or be able to do at the end of the lesson. It should be fairly easy to assess.

> Emphasize that 'habitat' is a place and 'environment' describes conditions.

> You can differentiate here by simplifying the recording procedure.

	HABITATS *(continued)*

An estate agent's description

Extension:	Early finishers can write an estate agent's description of the habitats they have seen and talked about.
Assessment:	*Criterion:* Do the children know that plants and animals live in a range of habitats? *Mode:* Examine their tables for evidence of knowledge.

Lesson plan 2

Adaptation

Theme:	ANIMAL ADAPTATION
Learning objective:	The children will learn how two animals are adapted to their different environments.

A list of the local animals

Lesson introduction:	Ask the children to make a quick list of some of the different animals that live in the school grounds (at this stage avoid plants). Select two animals, preferably as different from each other as possible, for closer consideration. For example, you might decide to compare sparrows and worms.

Suited to their environment

Lesson development:	Talk about how the two animals are adapted to their environment. If possible, bring in some examples to look at in detail (worms are easy, and the school might own some stuffed birds). Ask *What is the worm's environment like?* (See Lesson 1.) *How are worms suited to their environment?* (They are long and thin so they can burrow through the soil. They are slimy. They have hairs to grip the soil. They don't need eyes. They eat rotting leaves and so don't need to move fast.) *What is the sparrow's environment like? How are sparrows suited to their environment?* (They have wings so they can fly to safety. They have feathers to keep them warm. They have sharp eyes so they can spot their food. They have beaks to get at their food. They have legs to move around on the ground.)

Draw the animals

Recording:	*Draw a picture of each animal. Say where it lives and the conditions it lives in. Write about how each one is adapted to its environment.*

Comparisons

Extension:	Early finishers write a comparison of the two animals.
Assessment:	*Criterion:* Does the child know how two animals are adapted to their environment? *Mode:* Examine their written account.

Lesson plan 3

Theme:	FOOD CHAINS

Food chains start with green plants.

Learning objective:	The children will learn that every food chain starts with a green plant.
Lesson introduction:	Ask the children where their food comes from.

Where does our food come from?

Lesson development:	Ask the children to trace back their food to its ultimate source. Make a diagram showing the food chain behind the materials we eat. For example: the sun → grass → cow the sun → plants → small fish → cod Ask the children if there are any foodstuffs that are not connected to a green plant at some point in the chain.

Children generally find animals more interesting than plants.

Local museums can sometimes provide stuffed animals.

Comparisons can be made in the form of a table.

Start from a meal and work out the food chains that produced it.

		FOOD CHAINS (continued)
Drawing food chains	Recording:	*Draw a small picture of the sun in the centre of a sheet of paper. Draw a short arrow to a plant, then to an animal or animals, then to a person.*
Long chains	Extension:	*What is the longest food chain that starts with a plant and ends with a person?*
	Assessment:	*Criterion:* Does the child know that each food chain starts with a green plant?
		Mode: A few days after the lesson ask the children to write down three food chains that end with something they eat. Take in the children's books and check their answers.

Delay the assessment for several days to check longer-term recall.

Micro-organisms

Key ideas

Diversity

Types of micro-organisms

Micro-organisms include viruses, bacteria, fungi and single-celled plants and animals.

Bacteria were probably the first living things on the planet and have been evolving for over three billion years. They are amongst the most evolved and specialized living things. Some experts suggest that we have classified less than one per cent of bacteria species.

> Most micro-organisms are microscopic. An amoeba is about the size of a pinhead.

Effects of micro-organisms

Very few micro-organisms are dangerous to people, but as some of them cause disease we have to take care that children working with them are not exposed to unnecessary danger.

Micro-organisms are vital to us in many ways:

Sewage

- They break down sewage effluent by anaerobic (without oxygen) respiration. In the process they give off methane gas, which can be used to provide heat.

Compost

- Bacteria and fungi break down dead plants to form compost.

> See habitats on page 65.

- In the wider environment bacteria and fungi play a vital role in the nitrogen and carbon cycles.

- Bacteria are used to make butter and cheese, producing lactic acid, which curdles milk.

> Although words like 'bacteria' are commonly used, check that the children share your understanding of what they mean.

Beer and wine

- Yeasts are used to raise bread and turn sugar into alcohol in wine and beer making.

- Bacteria can turn alcohol into vinegar.

Antibiotics

- Fungi are an important source of antibiotics, used to kill bacterial infection. Green mould produced the first antibiotic, penicillin.

Silage

- Bacteria that work anaerobically help farmers preserve grass for animal fodder in the form of silage. The bacteria produce lactic acid, which preserves the grass and stops other micro-organisms making the grass decay.

> **Safety:** When carrying out work with micro-organisms, take care to keep the samples in sealed containers.

- Many of the processes of genetic engineering are carried out using bacteria.

Gut bacteria	• Human beings have an intimate relationship with bacteria. Large numbers of bacteria live in the human gut and play an important role in keeping us healthy.

Common misconceptions

Too small to see Beneficial microbes	**The role of micro-organisms** Most children will have never seen a micro-organism because of their minute size. The role that micro-organisms play in decay is not likely to be easily understood, and many children will believe that decay happens through something spontaneous occurring within the decaying object. This was a common view before the work of Louis Pasteur. Micro-organisms have had such a bad press that it is unlikely children will easily accept the notion that many are harmless and, indeed, that some are vital to our existence.

List of resources

Resources for studying micro-organisms	• magnifying glass on stand • microscope with × 20 maximum magnification • clear plastic boxes of different shapes and sizes • disposable plastic gloves • jam jars • petri dishes • roll of small plastic bags • roll of sticky labels • screw-topped plastic containers • yeast • sugar

> Condensation can spoil the view into small containers. Using larger containers, such as aquaria, avoids this problem.

Summary of the programmes of study

Key Stage 2 Sc2: 5e	Children should be taught about the following: • micro-organisms exist and many may be beneficial whilst others may be harmful

Key Stage 2b classroom activities

	Size and diversity • Teach the children about the variety of micro-organisms. Tell them about the size and diversity of these organisms. Micro-organisms are extremely small and can have good and bad consequences for people. Micro-organisms include:
Viruses	*viruses*, e.g. tobacco mosaic virus, flu virus, HIV
Bacteria	*bacteria*, e.g typhoid virus, *E. coli,* pneumonia
Fungi	*fungi*, e.g. yeast
Protozoa	*single-celled organisms*, e.g. amoeba, *Trypanosoma.*

> Introduce micro-organisms by looking first at the effects they cause, such as plant damage, illness or fermentation. Something is causing these effects, but whatever it is, it is not easily visible.

Immunization

Viruses

- Discuss the need for immunization. Ask the children to find out from their parents what diseases they have been immunized against. Talk about why older people may be immunized against flu.

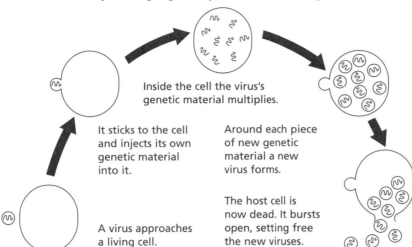

Inside the cell the virus's genetic material multiplies.

It sticks to the cell and injects its own genetic material into it.

Around each piece of new genetic material a new virus forms.

The host cell is now dead. It bursts open, setting free the new viruses.

A virus approaches a living cell.

How a virus reproduces

> Viruses cannot reproduce by themselves. They have to invade a living cell and use that cell to reproduce.

We can only protect ourselves from viruses by warning the body's immune system through immunization. This involves injecting dead viruses into our bodies. When our bodies detect a virus, our immune system goes into action. It produces antibodies that are designed to fix on to specific viruses and destroy them. Antibodies made in response to dead viruses stay in our bodies and will attack any future invasion by a live virus of the same type.

Washing hands

Bacteria

- Teach the children about the need to wash their hands before eating. Tell them that bacteria can get on their hands after they have used the lavatory and then transfer to their mouths.

Breeding bacteria

- Discuss the need to keep food fresh. Tell the children that bacteria cannot breed rapidly if the temperature is low. If the temperature is high, bacteria can double in number every 20 minutes. Imagine you start with one bacterium in some meat that is then kept warm. Calculate how many bacteria there will be after 20 minutes (two), and after six hours (over a quarter of a million). Discuss safe ways to handle frozen food and prepared meals.

> There is a general lack of understanding about food poisoning and how to avoid it.

Structures of bacteria

Bacteria vary greatly in structure and appearance. They occur as spheres, rods or spirals. They often clump together or form chains. Most bacteria are harmless but some have evolved to grow inside the human body and can produce illness.

Experiments with yeast

Yeast

- Buy fresh yeast. In a class demonstration use six clean clear glass or plastic containers. Number them one to six. Add yeast and water to all of them, then one special ingredient to each:

Container 1 – sugar	Container 4 – salt
Container 2 – raisins	Container 5 – saccharine tablet
Container 3 – flour	Container 6 – nothing

Ask the children to predict what they think will happen to each jar. Observe the jars over the next few hours. Draw the results and tabulate what is seen.

Yeast in baking and brewing

Yeast comes in a great many varieties. Wine makers, bakers and beer makers use a wide range of different strains of yeast. Yeast occurs naturally; it forms the bloom on grapes, for instance.

Yeast respires without oxygen.

In normal respiration carried out by plants and animals, oxygen is needed to break down sugar into carbon dioxide and water. In anaerobic respiration, as carried out by yeast, sugar is broken down without oxygen into carbon dioxide and alcohol.

Respiration with air

aerobic respiration:
glucose + oxygen = carbon dioxide + water + energy

Respiration without air

anaerobic respiration:
glucose = carbon dioxide + alcohol + energy

The yeast lives and multiplies in the fruit juice, feeding on sugar. Its anaerobic respiration produces carbon dioxide and alcohol.

The airlock, which contains water, allows carbon dioxide to escape from the demijohn and prevents other micro-organisms from entering. These could, for example, turn the alcohol into vinegar.

Anaerobic respiration in home wine making

Add sugar, water and yeast to a narrow-necked bottle. Pull the neck of a balloon over the top of the bottle and watch what happens. Ask the children to explain what they see.

Anaerobic respiration is inefficient. There is a great deal of energy locked up in alcohol, as anyone on a diet will know!

Make bread

Fresh yeast or fast-acting?

- Find a simple recipe for bread. Demonstrate making bread to the whole class first, then allow small groups to make some over the next few weeks. Use fresh yeast if you can, but fast-acting yeasts sold in packets are very effective. Weigh bread dough before and after baking. Why is it lighter afterwards?

Gas bubbles

Leaving dough in a warm place allows time for the yeast to multiply and respire. The yeast produces bubbles of carbon dioxide, which are trapped in the strands of gluten within the dough. When the dough is put in the oven the heat causes these small bubbles to expand and make the dough light and full of holes.

To speed up the process, make nan breads. These are made flat, allowed to rise for 30 minutes, then grilled.

Soil micro-organisms

Vary the conditions.

- Plan a series of investigations with the children to see what materials decay in pans of soil. Look at the pans every week or so. Vary the conditions of the soil. See if the same material decays more or less quickly in dry, damp or compacted soil.

A material that is surprisingly resistant to decay is orange peel, which can take many weeks to break down.

Micro-organisms break down waste in soil.	• Establish temporary compost heaps outside the classroom. Investigate the best ways of producing good compost.

- Establish temporary compost heaps outside the classroom. Investigate the best ways of producing good compost.

- Put a thermometer in a large bag of grass cuttings in the classroom. Make a record of the changes in temperature inside the bag. Remove the bag once the temperature starts to decline.

> Use a datalogger, if you have one, to make a line graph of the changes in temperature.

In a single spoonful of soil there may be many millions of bacteria. They, and fungi, break down any dead organic material that enters the soil. They do this by secreting digestive enzymes on to the dead material and digesting it through the process of aerobic respiration.

Materials such as plastics, which are not easily broken down by bacteria and fungi, will not rot quickly.

For materials to decay in soils:

Oxygen
- oxygen must be present to allow aerobic respiration of bacteria (anaerobic respiration results in lactic acid, which stops decay – see page 75 for the use of this in silage making);

Temperature
- the temperature must be fairly high in order for bacteria to work efficiently (in very cold conditions decay is extremely slow – frozen mammoth meat has been found in good condition in Siberia thousands of years after the animal's death);

Water
- there must be water to help fungi to germinate and bacteria to multiply.

Food decay

Micro-organisms cause the rotting of food.

- Teach the children about the way that materials decay once they are dead. Observe the decay of items such as carrots and bread.

When living things die, bacteria and fungal spores from the air will already be present on them. When an organism is alive it has many defences that stop micro-organisms consuming it. Wood, for instance, has to resist infection if a tree is to survive for hundreds of years. Other airborne micro-organisms will land on the dead organism and feed on its tissue. Many micro-organisms secrete liquids which speed up the breakdown of tissues.

Airborne microbes

> Wooden chopping-boards seem to have natural, in-built ways of killing the bacteria that land on them.

Food preservation

You can prevent micro-organisms working.

- Cut rings of carrot or apple and ask the children to devise several ways of preserving the food. These might include:

      coating it with sugar
      coating it with salt
      keeping it cold
      drying it.

Yoghurt

- Preserve milk by making yoghurt using clean equipment, warm milk and some natural yoghurt as a starter. After the starter has been added to the milk, the mixture needs to be kept warm for about 24 hours.

Stopping microbes

There are many chemicals that will stop microbes from working. These include vinegar, sugar and salt. For decay to take place, there needs to be oxygen, warmth and water.

> Although proper yoghurt-making equipment is fairly foolproof to use, a wide-necked thermos flask should keep the milk and yoghurt warm for long enough for the culture to breed.

Killing microbes	Food can be preserved by:

Food can be preserved by:

heating it in a container to kill all organisms and keeping air and other microbes out using a lid

keeping it cold to slow the rotting process

drying it to remove water and so prevent the germination of microbes

adding salt, sugar or vinegar.

Lactic acid

Yoghurt is preserved when the bacteria used in its production make sufficient lactic acid to preserve the food.

Teaching strategy: Key Stage 2b teacher demonstrations

Lesson plan 1

Theme:	YEAST AND BREAD
Organization:	Half the class works with the teacher and half works independently.
Learning objective:	The children will be able to create and fill in a table of results showing how yeast works with a variety of foods and under a range of conditions.
Lesson introduction:	The children working independently are given a selection of breads. Instructions have been written on the board: *Carefully draw cross-sections of at least three kinds of bread.* *Label the drawings.* *Look at the crust area under the microscope and draw what you can see.* *Write comparisons between two of the bread types.* The children working with the teacher are shown fresh yeast (this can be obtained free from many supermarkets). Smell it, touch it, eat a little of it (keep the portion for eating separate and clean). Talk about what it is and what it is used for.
Lesson development:	Discuss what yeast needs in order to grow. *How could we test this?* Suggest different conditions yeast could be kept in. *What will it feed on?* Set up experiments in a series of labelled jars or test tubes.
Recording:	Ask the children to design a table to record the results of their tests.
Extension:	Each half of the class now does the other half's activity.
Assessment:	*Criterion:* Can the children design and fill in a table of results? *Mode:* Is the table of results filled in correctly?

Side labels:
How does yeast work?
Cross-sections of bread
Handling yeast
Growing yeast
Classroom organization

Margin notes:
Bubbles are formed by the respiring yeast and expand dramatically in the oven.

Yeasts feed on sugar or starch.

Lesson plan 2

Theme:	DECAY
Organization:	Half the class works independently and the other half works with the teacher.
Learning objectives:	The children working independently will learn to make accurate drawings and records of decaying objects. The children with the teacher will be able to predict the results of an experiment.
Lesson introduction:	In groups, the children working independently make drawings and write about what they notice is happening in three decay tanks set up the previous week. The tanks contain cake, bread, apple, carrot and other vegetable remains. The children working with the teacher talk about compost and the things gardeners put on their compost heaps. *What eventually happens to bodies buried in the soil?*
Lesson development:	Show the children three seed trays of soil. *What conditions could we place each of these in?* The children might suggest: dry and warm, dry and cold, damp and warm. Place the same six items (e.g. pieces of apple, plastic crisp wrapper, carrot, metal paperclip, orange peel, bread) in each soil pan. Mark each item with a lolly stick label. Leave the experiment for one week.
Recording:	Use a standard template for this. For instance: *Title* *Diagram* *Equipment list* *What we wanted to find out* *What we did* *What we think will happen and why* *What happened* *What we have learnt*
Extension:	Play a video with time-lapse photography showing some of the ways in which objects decay.
Assessment:	*Criterion:* Do the children explain what they think will happen and why? *Mode:* Write-up of an experiment.

Keep the samples sealed in the tanks.

One teaspoon of soil can contain millions of bacteria and fungal spores.

Recording templates are discussed on page 12.

Lesson plan 3

Theme:	AVOIDING POISONING
Organization:	Half the class works independently and the other half works with the teacher.
Learning objectives:	The children working independently will learn that there are common-sense precautions that can be taken to avoid food poisoning. The children working with the teacher will be able to draw conclusions from experimental work.

	Theme:	AVOIDING POISONING *(continued)*
Using healthcare information	**Lesson introduction:**	Tell all the children about common-sense ways to avoid food poisoning (you can obtain information from organizations such as your local health centre or community healthcare trust). The children working independently then design a leaflet either for younger children or for parents.
		The children working with the teacher should be shown the range of different ways of preserving food from spoiling by microbes. Take a piece of apple and discuss what could be done to stop it going bad. The children's ideas might include: drying it on the radiator or in the sun sealing it in a bag sprinkling sugar on it sprinkling salt on it putting it in vinegar putting it in the fridge.
Changing the conditions	**Lesson development:**	Set up six investigations based on the children's suggestions. Remember to leave one piece of apple out on a saucer as a control.
Drawing the results	**Recording:**	*Fold a piece of paper into six. In each section made by the folds, draw and write about what happens to the apple under the six different conditions.*
	Extension:	Each half of the class now does the other half's activity. This time, to add a further variable, use a carrot in the preserving investigations.
Describing what was noticed	**Assessment:**	*Criterion:* Can the children say which ways of preserving the apple or carrot work? *Mode:* Oral response or short test item.

Food poisoning is on the increase as people become less knowledgeable about handling food.

Setting up six demonstration conditions is more feasible than allowing each group to do their own.

Grouping materials

Where does it come from?

Fired clay

Elements

Compounds

The source of materials

Ultimately, all the materials we use come from animals or plants, are dissolved in the sea or are dug from the ground. In some cases we use these natural materials as they are, and in others we alter them to make new, manufactured materials. Brick and pottery, for instance, are manufactured materials that have been chemically altered. Before human beings created them, brick and pottery did not exist on the planet.

Materials comprising one type of atom are called elements. Oxygen, hydrogen, sodium and chlorine are examples of elements. When elements combine, the resulting material is called a compound. Water is a compound of oxygen and hydrogen. Salt is a compound of sodium and chlorine.

Common materials can be loosely classified according to the properties listed in this table:

> All the materials we use are from one of three sources.

	METAL	PLASTIC	TEXTILE	WOOD	ROCK
EXAMPLES	iron aluminium gold	polythene polystyrene PVC	cotton wool nylon	pine beech oak	granite sandstone marble
MAIN PROPERTIES	makes a ringing sound when struck; cold to touch	easy to mould into complicated shapes; warm to touch	easy to cut and make into sheets; very warm to touch	easy to saw and cut into shape; warm to touch	hard and cold to touch
HARDNESS	often very hard	usually quite soft	soft	hard	very hard
CONDUCTS ELECTRICITY?	all do	no	no	no	no
CONDUCTS HEAT?	yes, all do very well	most are poor conductors	most are poor conductors	most are poor conductors	most are fairly good conductors of heat
WHERE DOES IT COME FROM?	mixed with rock in the ground (ores)	made from oil	animals, plants and chemicals	trees	the ground

Hard and soft materials

Hard: diamond

Soft: talc
Metals

The hardest natural material is diamond, which is a form of carbon. Drills are coated with diamond to make them very hard. The softest mineral found in rocks is talc, which is made into talcum powder. Hard and strong metals include steel and iron, used for bridges and girders. Soft metals include lead and aluminium, which are easy to shape.

Toothpaste is made from hard, ground-up rock.

Magnetic properties

Only iron, steel, nickel and cobalt are magnetic. Steel is used for compass needles. You can magnetize a steel needle by stroking it with a magnet.

Conductors and insulators

Heat conductors

Good conductors of heat are substances with free electrons in their structure. In metals, these electrons can carry electrical current as well as heat energy. Metals are good conductors of both heat and electricity. Metal pan handles feel hot because they conduct heat to our hands. Wooden and plastic pan handles feel cooler because they do not conduct heat. Metal is used in radiators to transfer the heat from hot water into the air.

Heat insulators

Poor conductors of heat, such as fur and wool, are used to stop heat escaping from our bodies. In a similar way, fibreglass is used to insulate the roofs of houses to keep in the heat. Polystyrene is used to stop the heat of the sun warming a picnic in a cool box.

Insulators slow the movement of heat from a hot place to a cold place.

Poor conductors of heat = good thermal insulators.

Good conductors of heat = poor thermal insulators.

Electrical conductors

Electrical insulators

All metals conduct electricity because they have free electrons. Plastic and wood do not conduct electricity because they do not have free electrons; all electrons in these materials are tightly bound into the chemical structure. Plastics are electrical insulators. In our homes, electricity is conducted in wires made from metal whilst plastic is used to coat those wires and make the casing of plugs, insulating the electrical flow from contact with other conductors, such as people!

Gold is the best electrical conductor; gold-plated connections are used in top-of-the-range hi-fi systems.

Rocks and minerals

Rocks

Granite

Rocks are mixtures of minerals. A mineral is a chemical compound that has a consistent chemical formula. Coal, oil, quartz and iron ore are minerals. Granite is a rock that is principally a mixture of three minerals: quartz, feldspar and mica.

There are three categories of rocks:

Igneous rocks

Igneous rocks (e.g. granite and basalt) are made from solidified lava emitted as molten rock from volcanoes or from deep underground. They are hard, and grains do not rub off them. Their structure is often composed of crystals.

When igneous rocks have cooled slowly their crystals are large. Granite is a good example of this.

Sedimentary rocks

Sedimentary rocks (e.g. sandstone, chalk, limestone and shale) are made from grains of mud, sand or pebbles that have settled in water. They are usually soft and grains will rub off them. They sometimes contain fossils.

Metamorphic rocks

Metamorphic rocks (e.g. marble – made from heating limestone, and slate – made from heated and squashed mudstone) are igneous or sedimentary rocks transformed by heat or pressure. They are often banded.

Manufactured rocks

Soil

Concrete and bricks are manufactured rocks.

Soil comprises ground-up rock and plant remains. When you mix soil with water and let it settle, the biggest rock particles settle first and the clay settles last.

Cement is made by heating up limestone and mixing it with clay.

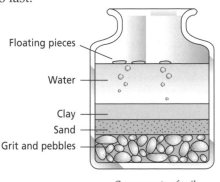

Components of soil

Floating pieces
Water
Clay
Sand
Grit and pebbles

Properties

States of matter

The differences between solid, liquid and gas are in ease of flow, maintenance of shape, and volume. Here are examples of each state:

SOLID	LIQUID	GAS
water ice	oil	carbon dioxide
wax	vinegar	oxygen
iron	liquid water	wax vapour
wood	melted wax	water vapour

Solids

Liquids

Gases

Solids: keep their shape
do not flow easily
can be cut.

Liquids: take the shape of a container
flow easily
cannot be cut.

Gases: fill any space they are in
flow very easily.

Water: volume as liquid and volume as ice

In terms of volume, most materials expand when heated. This means that generally a substance in its liquid state has a slightly larger volume than in its solid state. An important exception to this is water. Water in the form of ice has a significantly greater volume than liquid water. The expansion of water on freezing explains why, in water, ice floats.

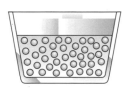

Liquid water

In their liquid state, water molecules are packed more closely together than they are in their solid state, ice.

The solid is lighter for its size than the liquid, which is why ice floats in water.

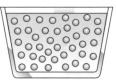

Solid ice

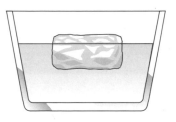

This odd behaviour is referred to as the anomalous expansion of water.

Why ice floats in water

Common misconceptions

Flow

Grains

Clouds

Condensed droplets

Polystyrene

Powders as liquid

Children's confusion of powders with liquids has been well documented. Powders have many of the properties of liquids in that they flow, take up the shape of the container they are in, and have a surface that is approximately level. Let the children look at coarse powders such as salt under the microscope. They will see that individual grains are in fact solid.

Condensed liquid drops

Clouds and fog are also often misunderstood by children, who are told (correctly) that clouds are the result of water vapour rising into the atmosphere after it has evaporated off the oceans and land. Because clouds and fog stay up in the air, many children believe that they are water vapour itself. However, clouds and fog are actually condensed water vapour. They are formed out of tiny droplets of water that are too small to fall to the ground. Look at a kettle. You can see the changes that happen to water vapour leaving the spout.

> Probe children's understanding of evaporation and condensation before teaching the water cycle.

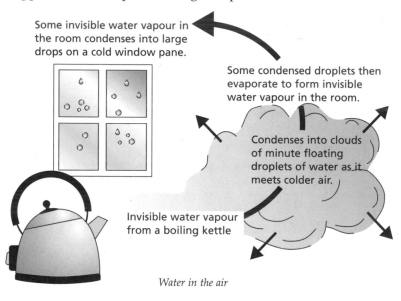

Some invisible water vapour in the room condenses into large drops on a cold window pane.

Some condensed droplets then evaporate to form invisible water vapour in the room.

Condenses into clouds of minute floating droplets of water as it meets colder air.

Invisible water vapour from a boiling kettle

Water in the air

Is it really warm?

When you touch a material that is an excellent heat insulator, like polystyrene, it is easy to believe, as many children do, that it is warm. In fact it is the same temperature as other objects in the same environment. It *feels* warm because it prevents heat being conducted away from your warm hand. To test this idea, put a thermometer in some polystyrene. You will see that the polystyrene is the same temperature as the surrounding air.

> Many adults find this difficult to accept.

List of resources

Resources for studying the classification of materials

- balls of wool
- cloth samples
- filter paper

- greaseproof paper
- metal samples
- steel wool
- tissue paper
- wallpaper samples
- powders
- microscope with × 20 maximum magnification
- lenses
- rock samples
- soil samples
- magnets
- electrical circuit equipment

> Most classrooms have an interesting range of different types of paper.

Summary of the programmes of study

Key Stage 1 Sc3: 1a–e

Children should be taught about the following:
- using senses to explore and recognize the similarities and differences between materials
- sorting materials into groups
- recognizing and naming common types of materials and knowing that some are found naturally
- many materials have a variety of uses
- materials are chosen for specific uses

Key Stage 2 Sc3: 1a–e

- comparing everyday materials on the basis of their properties
- some materials are better thermal insulators than others
- some materials are better electrical conductors than others
- describing and grouping rocks and soils on the basis of characteristics
- recognizing the differences between solids, liquids and gases

Key Stage 1 classroom activities

Objects have a variety of properties depending on material and shape.

Objects are made from materials.

The properties of objects
- Look at a number of different objects. Ask the children to draw them or write about their:

| colour | hardness | size |
| texture | strength | |

Objects are made from materials. The same material can be made into quite different objects. For instance, steel can be used for piano wire, girders, knives or car panels.

> Young children understand about objects much more readily than they do materials.

What is it made from?
- Select a range of different objects and discuss with the children what they are made from. Some, of course, will be made from a number of materials. Give able pupils examples of objects made from several materials to study, and give less able pupils objects made from one or two materials.

Every object is made from a material or materials. This book is made from paper. Scissors are made from metal. Windows are made from glass. Cars are made from a huge range of materials.

Feeling comparisons

- Use a feely bag to focus on the texture of a material. Place some interesting textures in the bag, such as a washing scourer, a powder puff, a metal block, a sponge, a rough rock and a polished pebble.

Surface texture

It is difficult to divorce the properties of the material from the properties of the object. Surface texture is often an attribute of the material. Feeling cold to the touch is characteristic of metals and stone.

Paper

Different papers have different properties.

- Paper is an excellent material on which to carry out a range of tests and investigations. It is cheap, and there are many varieties in the average classroom.

Paper tests

> Will water soak into the paper quickly?
> Is it easy to write on?
> Is it attractive to use to wrap a present?
> Can you make a rubbing of a coin through it?

Paper qualities

Absorbent paper, such as in a paper towel, has coarse fibres. Shiny papers for magazines are filled with clay to give them a smooth surface. Gift wrap papers are coated with metal to make them shine. Writing paper has a surface that does not absorb excessive amounts of ink. Watercolour paper has an absorbent surface.

> You can see the paper fibres if you press sticky tape on to newspaper then rip it off. The fibres stick to the tape, making them easy to see.

Properties of materials

Why is it made out of that?

- Ask the children to write down a list of objects made from the same material. Talk about why the material has been used to make those objects. Here are some examples:

wood	strong and light	chairs
		tables
		pencils
metal	very strong	door hinges
		door handles

Some silly questions

- Ask some amusing questions about materials, such as 'Why aren't shoes made out of card?' 'Why aren't umbrellas made from bricks?' 'Why don't we use jelly to make chairs?'

Properties

The properties of a material include being waterproof, transparent, warm to the touch, absorbent or elastic.

Wool

Wool relies for its warmth on the way the fibres crinkle and trap warmth. The fibres are springy and soft.

Plastic

Plastic makes good bags because it is strong, light and cheap.

Paper

Paper is used to write on because it absorbs ink well and is light and cheap.

> Bags can be made from plastic, paper or cloth. Evaluate each material.

Wood

Wood is used for structures because it is very strong, can be cut easily into interesting shapes and can be joined easily.

Metal

Metals such as copper can conduct electrical current. They are easily beaten into shape or can be cast into new shapes.

Natural or manufactured?

- Collect a variety of natural and manufactured objects. Ask the children to put them into two sets: manufactured and natural.

- Make a list of materials and where they come from under the headings of 'plants', 'animals' and 'other'.

- Make a list of materials the children know about that have been dug from the ground.

- List materials that are made by people.

Materials that are found naturally include sheep's wool and wood. But you would not expect to find a jumper or a table occurring naturally.

To help you with your preparation, construct a Carroll diagram to clarify the distinction between natural and manufactured, and object and material. Children of this age often find these concepts difficult.

	NATURAL MATERIAL	MANUFACTURED MATERIAL
NATURAL OBJECT	pebble twig pine cone feather	none occur
MANUFACTURED OBJECT	wooden table woolly jumper	nylon sock plastic pen

> At this point the important distinction between a material and an object must be completely clear in the teacher's mind.

Recycling

- Show the children how to mix paper pulp with dry grass, thin rags, thread and scraps of coloured tissue.

  To make recycled paper, use three sheets of white paper tissue:
  1. Shred it
  2. Mix it with water.
  3. Spread it out on clean scrap paper.
  4. Roll it out.
  5. Leave it to dry.
  6. Write on it.

> Do not try to recycle newspaper – the ink gets everywhere and is very difficult to remove.

Paper is the classic example of a material that can be recycled. In recycling, scrap paper is shredded and mixed with water to make a pulp. It is then spread out and rolled into flat sheets before being dried.

Key Stage 2a classroom activities

Elasticity

- Collect different types of clothing elastic. Test which would be the best type to use for an elasticated waistband for a pair of tracksuit bottoms. The children might try to see which sort cuts into them most, which is strongest, and which goes out of shape quickly.

Some objects are manufactured, others are found naturally.
Where do materials come from?

Objects and materials

Some materials can be recycled.

Materials can be compared on the basis of their elasticity.

Stockings	• Hang a stocking from a clamp or from a stick between two chairs. Add a small mass to the toe. Measure the length of the stocking. Add more mass and measure the distance the stocking stretches. Using worn-out clothes compare the stretch of different types of sock, leggings and stockings.

Use different coloured tights or stockings to make it easier to distinguish between them.

Nylon and rubber

All materials change shape when they are pulled or pushed. Elastic materials can be bent a great distance and will return to their original shape once the force has been removed. The nylon in tights and the rubber of elastic bands are good examples of elastic materials.

Springs

Springs will stretch in proportion to the force that is pulling them. However, once they are 'overstretched' they cannot return to their original shape.

Strength

Materials can be compared on the basis of their strength.

• Ask the children to plan a test comparing the strength of different supermarket plastic bags. Hang the bags from a pole set between two tables and ask the children to see how many full tins each will carry before breaking.

Protect floors and feet when testing the strength of materials.

• Compare the strength of different types of paper.

Strength of paper

If you compare the strength of paper samples you will notice that the wider they are the stronger they are. This means that very narrow strips are best for safe strength tests. Use thin tissue as ordinary paper is far too strong.

Construct a weight carrier from a plastic plant pot. Make three holes in the rim with a paper punch and thread strings through the holes. Hang the carrier from the item you are testing.

Equal amounts of material make the test fair.

The amount of force that an object can resist before breaking is its strength. To compare materials fairly you have to use equal amounts of each material.

Electrical conductors and magnetic materials

Some materials conduct electricity.

• Set up a simple circuit and test a variety of materials to see if they allow electricity to pass through them.

For more on conductors, see page 84.

Bulb

Battery

Test material is attached to the circuit here.

A simple circuit for testing the electrical conductivity of materials

Be aware that some metal objects, such as wire coathangers, are coated with varnish or other materials that are non-conductive and will prevent the flow of electricity.

All metals and a few non-metals, such as carbon, silicon and germanium, conduct electricity. This is because they have free electrons in their structure that can carry electrical charge. Other materials, such as plastics, wood and paper, will not conduct electricity.

Some materials are attracted to magnets.

• Ask the children to test a variety of materials to see which are magnetic.

Only iron, steel, cobalt and nickel are attracted to magnets.

Heat conductor

- Let the children handle a warm hot water bottle through different materials. Note the effects, and compare wool with foil.

- Let the children hold a plastic bag of ice cubes using gloves made of different materials. Which type of glove allows most heat to be drawn out of the hand?

Heat energy from the hot part of a material moves to the cold parts.

This is a table showing the relative heat conductivity of different materials, assuming that the reading for glass is 1:

copper	350	brick	0.5
steel	70	water	0.5
concrete	5	wool	0.05
glass	1	air	0.02

You can see that wool conducts heat very slowly whereas concrete conducts heat quite quickly. This explains why wool is used for carpeting, to prevent heat from bare feet being conducted away into the floor.

Cold is merely the absence of heat. So it is quite incorrect to say that coats keep the cold out. It is more accurate to say that they keep the heat in.

Wallpapers

- Let the children test a variety of wallpapers. Look at their resistance to stains, their ease of cleaning and their resistance to fire.

Warning: Vinyl wallpapers produce toxic fumes if burnt.

Many wallcoverings consist of vinyl plastic coated on paper. This plastic is hard-wearing and easy to wipe clean. It is waterproof and stain resistant. Formica is a similar but more rigid material, being paper coated in a tough, thick layer of plastic.

Some materials are good conductors of heat.

Measures of conductivity

Wool is warmer to touch than concrete.

You can conduct heat, but not cold.

Wallpaper tests

Alternatively use a radiator – but take care to test it first as it may be too hot.

Investigate which is the best wallpaper for a kitchen.

Key Stage 2b classroom activities

States of matter

- Ask the children to list the properties of solids, liquids and gases, and to give examples of each state.

All matter is made from particles (usually atoms or molecules). In solids these particles are bound together very firmly. In liquids the particles are free to move within a fixed volume. In a gas the particles are not bound at all.

Solids, liquids and gases have different properties.

For more on states of matter, see page 85.

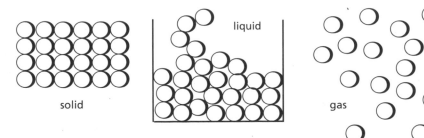

solid · liquid · gas

Viscosity

- Set up experiments with the children to see which of a range of liquids flows most easily. Put drops of water, syrup, shampoo and washing up liquid on a clean tray. Look at how warmer liquids flow in comparison with cold liquids.

All liquids can flow. Some flow more easily than others. The ease of flow is referred to as viscosity. The more viscous a liquid is the 'stiffer' it is.

Since this requires a range of equipment it may be better done as a demonstration or as part of a circus of activities.

Density

- Let the children handle a range of solids and talk about how heavy each feels. Comparing the heaviness of a piece of lead with that of a similar-sized piece of aluminium is a good way to experience the density of different materials.

A material's density is its mass per cubic centimetre of its volume. Density gives an indication of how heavy a certain quantity of material is for its size. Below is a list of densities. It shows the mass of one cubic centimetre of each material.

The children may not easily understand the concept of density but they will feel that some materials are heavy for their size.

gold	19.3 grams	aluminium	2.7 grams
mercury	13.6 grams	water	1.0 gram
lead	11.4 grams	cork	0.2 grams

Gases are real

- Balance two inflated balloons on a beam balance. Prick one, and note the way the scale goes down on the side of the balloon that is still inflated.

- Let the children experiment with pumps, syringes and inflated balls to feel the way that air is easily squashed, yet quickly returns to its original shape.

If you attach a piece of sticky tape to the balloon and prick it through that, the balloon will deflate slowly.

Bottled butane gas is sold by weight. An empty gas cylinder weighs less than a full one.

Gases are easily compressed and feel squashy when they are compressed. Pumps, syringes, tyres and balls show how gases can act as springs when compressed.

Wood

- Ask the children to compare different types of wood:
  Which would make the best chopping board?
  Which would make the best flooring for a factory?
  Which would make the best raft?
  Which would make the most beautiful table top?

Balsa wood rafts have been made that can cross the Pacific Ocean.

- Look at manufactured wood-based materials such as plywood, hardboard, MDF and blockboard. Ask the children to find out how they are made and write an illustrated report.

Wood comes from various tree species such as pine, oak, ash and mahogany. It can be made into manufactured materials such as hardboard and plywood, which are composites of wood and glue.

Plywood is made from thin sheets of wood. These are glued together so that the grain of one sheet is at right angles to the grain of the next, giving it great strength.

Each type of wood has its own distinctive set of properties. Oak, for instance, is dense, hard and closely grained. Balsa, on the other hand, is soft, light and open grained.

Some materials occur as powders that have particular properties.

Powders

- Show the children a range of powders. Tell them how to carry out some basic tests on the powders and allow them to devise some tests of their own. Ask them to tabulate their findings using headings like:

Texture	Does it dissolve?
Smell	What happens when you add vinegar?

Put the information on to a database, or a branching database, then let the children use this information to identify a powder from the group they have tested.

Many everyday materials occur as white powders: flour, bicarbonate of soda, sugar, salt, washing powder, cream of tartar and citric acid.

Rocks and soils can be grouped.

Rock properties

- Show the children a range of different rocks and tell them how some were formed. Ask them what sorts of things they want to find out about rocks. Let them list the questions they want to try to answer.

Secondary sources will be needed to find the answers to many of the children's questions about rocks.

- Let the children examine a range of rocks, note their features, then make careful drawings and paintings of them. Important features to look out for include:

> Grain size
> Can you rub off grains?
> Can you scratch it easily?
> Does the rock make a mark if you rub it on a paving stone?
> Colour
> Patterns such as bedding
> Fossils

See page 84 for information on rock types.

Teaching strategy: Key Stage 2b materials trail

Around the school

- Devise a short trail around the school for the children to follow. An example is shown on pages 94–95. Start with easy questions then introduce questions that require an inference to be made.

- Once the children have finished working on your trail, ask them to devise trails of their own. Older children could take infants for a walk around their trail.

Ensure that the walk is safe and that unsupervised children do not leave the school grounds.

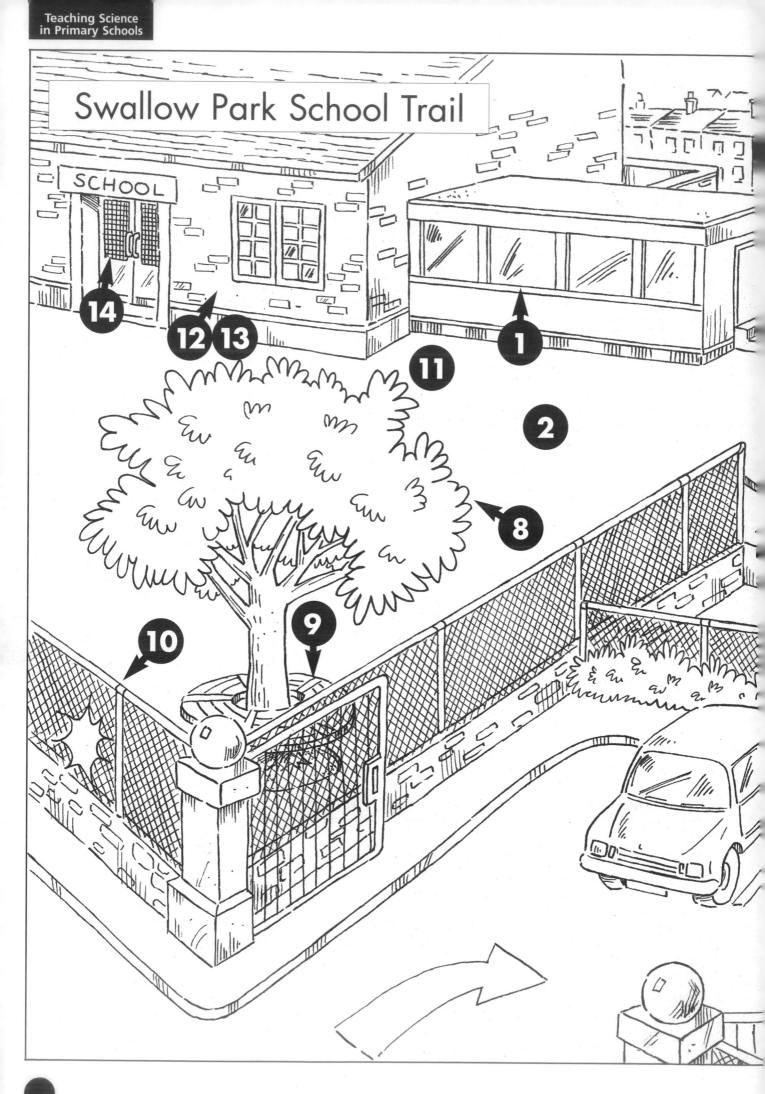

Swallow Park School Trail

Look at the picture. Answer the questions.

1. What material is this window pane made from?

2. What material is the playground made from?

3. What do you notice about the metal in this fence?

4. What material is the handrail made from? Does it feel warm or cold to the touch?

5. Is the roof of the shed waterproof?

6. The school might make a climbing frame here for the nursery. What materials should it use?

7. Stand at the fence and look into the car park. Look at one of the cars. List all the materials that the car is made from.

8. What material can we get from this living thing?

9. What material is the bench made from?

10. What would you replace this fence with? What materials would you use? Explain your choice.

11. Look at the outside of this temporary classroom. In what ways is it different from the main school building?

12. What material is this wall made from?

13. Is the wall made from a natural or a manufactured material?

14. Look at the glass in the doors. How is it different from the glass in the windows?

Changing materials

Key ideas

Solution
Suspension
A temperature line
Water cycle

Dissolving

Some solids dissolve and form a solution in water. A solution is transparent and the solids do not settle to the bottom. Salt, sugar, coffee powder and soap powder are all soluble in water.

Some materials do not dissolve in water. They might mix with the water but the mixture is cloudy and the solids settle to the bottom. Flour, custard powder, paint powder, sand and soil are insoluble in water. The mixture they form is called a suspension.

Temperature

Temperature is measured in degrees Celsius (°C). There is no upper limit to how hot something can be.

Home ovens go up to 250°C

Frying oil is at about 170°C

Water boils at 100°C

Body temperature is about 37°C

Most home freezers are -18°C

Absolute zero is -273°C or 0 K. This is the lowest possible temperature.

Reversible changes

Some changes can be reversed. Melting, evaporating, freezing and condensing are normally reversible.

In the water cycle, water evaporates from the sea, lakes, plants and animals. This water vapour is invisible. Water vapour condenses to form clouds. Clouds are tiny drops of liquid water. The water drops get heavier and fall from the cloud as rain. Your breath makes clouds on a cold winter's day.

Carbon dioxide goes straight from a solid state (dry ice) to gas.

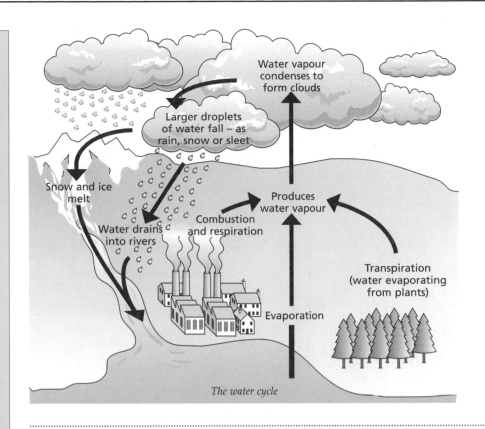

The water cycle

Permanent change

When food is cooked it changes. These changes are not reversible. For instance, dough changes into bread, raw egg changes into fried, scrambled or boiled egg, cake mix changes into cake.

When materials burn the fuel combines with oxygen. Wood, wax, oil and gas are fuels. All are hydrocarbons because they are compounds of hydrogen and carbon. For example, CH_4 is the chemical composition of methane or natural gas. This means that it is four parts hydrogen and one part carbon.

> Many children do not think that wax burns.

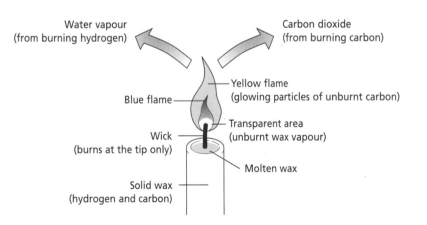

Processes at work when a candle burns

As a candle burns many interesting changes take place. When you light a new candle, the heat of the match sets the wick burning. Then the flame dies down before leaping up as the heat of the burning wick starts to vaporize the wax, and the wax vapour starts to burn. From then on the heat of the burning wax vapour continues to vaporize more wax. Wax is the fuel.

> Night lights burn for a long time because the wick is thin.

Products of burning	The products of the complete combustion of a hydrocarbon are water and carbon dioxide. However, burning often leaves behind unburnt materials, such as ash when wood and coal are burnt. Wood ash cannot be turned back into wood – burning is usually irreversible. However, when hydrogen is burnt it combines with oxygen to produce water. Water can be turned back into hydrogen and oxygen using electricity, so the burning of hydrogen is reversible.

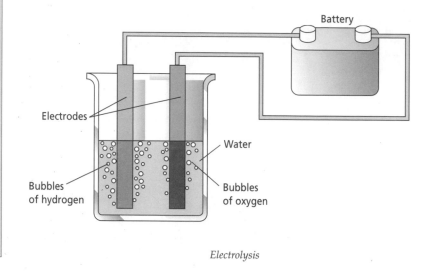

Electrolysis

> Heat does not split water into oxygen and hydrogen. Water is split using electricity.

Common misconceptions

What's burning?

String burns poorly.

Wax vapour will light.

Candles

When a candle burns it appears at first sight that the wick is burning. When asked what the wax is for, many children say that it is to hold the wick up. When asked what happens to the wax, they say it runs down the candle. To show children that it is the candle wax vapour that burns, give them a small piece of candle wick (ordinary string). They will see that it burns very poorly. Demonstrate that a spent match, when soaked in wax, burns freely. Now blow out the candle and carefully draw a lighted match towards the wax vapour streaming from the hot wick. See the vapour ignite.

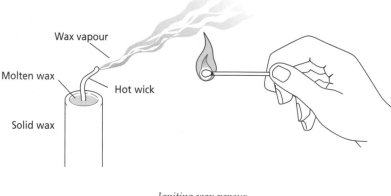

Igniting wax vapour

> The wicks of 'magic' birthday-cake candles contain small fragments of phosphorus. These cause the wick to spark slightly, even when just smouldering, which is enough to re-ignite the hot wax vapour.

Many children find it hard to believe that one material can be found in different states. The idea that wax will turn into a liquid and then into a gas seems highly unlikely to them.

Dissolving

Solute disappears.

When a solid dissolves it literally disappears from sight. However, some children will believe that the solid is no longer present. Many are surprised when salt reappears after brine has been left to evaporate.

Condensation

Invisible vapour

When water condenses on the outside of a cold drinks can it is not surprising that many children believe that water has oozed out of the can itself. Water vapour is invisible in the air and its appearance as condensation on cold surfaces is remarkable.

Even adults find the concept of condensation difficult to understand. Condensation on walls and windows in damp flats is often due to the water vapour produced by sleeping bodies. Exchanging the damp air for dry air from outside is the only cheap cure for damp walls.

> Simulate this effect using a chilled coloured drink inside a clear plastic bottle. The children will see that the condensation, unlike the contents of the bottle, is clear.

Evaporation

Disappearing water

The disappearance of water via evaporation leads to the misconception that water no longer exists. The idea that it has merely changed state is difficult for some children to grasp. Water does not need to boil to evaporate, although this is implied in some books. Material such as bread will dry out and go stale even in a fridge.

> Water vapour condenses on the ice box in a fridge, then freezes.

Is it really cool?

A fan doesn't blow cool air – it only helps your sweat to evaporate more rapidly, and this makes the air from the fan feel cool. Confirm this by holding a dry thermometer in the stream of air from a fan.

List of resources

Resources for studying changes in materials

- ice
- butter
- lard
- chocolate
- wax
- candles
- matches
- candle holders
- sugar
- salt
- flour
- sand
- custard powder
- instant coffee
- washing powder
- sieves
- filter papers
- filter funnels

> Having a good selection of candles, including night lights, household candles and 'magic' birthday-cake candles, is extremely useful.

Summary of the programmes of study

Key Stage 1 Sc3: 2a–b

Children should be taught about the following:
- objects made from some materials can be changed in shape by processes including squashing, bending, twisting and stretching
- some everyday materials change when they are heated and cooled

Key Stage 2 Sc3: 2a–f

- mixing materials can cause them to change
- heating and cooling materials can cause them to change, and temperature is a measure of how hot or cold they are

- some changes can be reversed and some cannot
- dissolving, melting, boiling, condensing, freezing and evaporating are changes that can be reversed
- the water cycle
- the changes that occur when most materials are burnt are not reversible

Key Stage 1 classroom activities

Clay can be made into different shapes.

Clay
- Talk about processes such as pushing and pulling that can be used to make clay change shape. Use a variety of tools to squash and mark clay.

In terms of its properties clay is plastic; it will change shape but not return to its original shape. Compare this property with elasticity. Clay minerals occur in flat sheets with very weak bonds to adjacent sheets above and below them.

The term 'plastic' simply means that a material can hold a new shape.

Clay changes when it dries out.

- Ask the children to make models using clay. Weigh the models before and after they have dried. Look at the change in appearance of the clay after it has dried. Discuss what has caused this change. Vary the factors that affect drying, for example by placing a model in a plastic bag and comparing the way it dries with a model left in the open air.

Clay minerals

Water in clay

Clay gets lighter both in colour and in weight as it dries. Weight loss is a temporary change; clay minerals can be rehydrated by the addition of water. A permanent change can be brought about by firing the clay. Clay minerals have places in their molecular structure to which water molecules can bond. This is why a clay soil holds moisture for longer than a light, sandy soil.

Stretchy

Fabric
- Let the children handle and change the shape of stretchy materials including tights, knitted fabrics and lycra cloth. Compare these materials with woven cloth, which is far less stretchy. Start with samples of the same size and see how far each stretches. Show the results on a bar chart or simply use unifix bricks to show how far each material has stretched.

Knitted fabrics made out of an elastic material such as lycra or nylon tend to be much stretchier than cotton.

Bread changes

Heat changes
- Demonstrate that bread changes with heating. Get the children to compare the stages it goes through, from fresh bread, through light toast to burnt toast. Use pencil crayons to match the colour changes. Discuss the changes in texture as well as colour.

Bring in an electric toaster from home. Supervised children can safely carry out much of the work themselves.

Making toast involves chemically changing bread. If you continue with the process until the toast is burnt you are left with carbon. In addition water is evaporated, resulting in crisp, dry bread.

Warming food safely

- Place chocolate, lard, cheese and bread in separate foil dishes and set these up in some hot water. Ask the children to predict what will happen to the food in the dishes. Draw their attention to the changes that occur as it heats up.

Lard facts

Lard is an interesting material. It is partly crystalline at room temperature, and this makes it appear translucent as a solid. Lard makes a clear liquid.

> Light can pass through translucent materials, but not well enough for clear images to be visible.

Heating graph

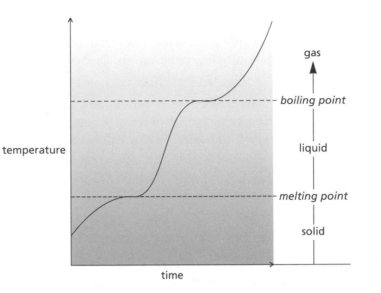

Changes in temperature and state as a substance is heated

> Heat energy is needed for solids to change into liquids, and for liquids to change into gases. A solid will stay at its melting point until all of it has melted.

Changes to ice

Making plans

- Give the children ice challenges. Who can make equal-sized ice cubes last longest? Who can make them melt quickest? Let the children plan what they will do before you give them the cubes. They could draw their plans, tell you about them or write them down. Discuss why the cubes melt quickly in warm water and why they melt slowly if wrapped in layers of newspaper.

Heat energy is absorbed.

Ice absorbs heat from its surroundings. This causes things nearby or touching it to cool down. Most of the heat energy absorbed by the ice is used to break the bonds that make it a crystalline solid.

Key Stage 2a classroom activities

Dissolving

Some materials dissolve in water.

- Demonstrate that sugar dissolves in water and compare this with mixing flour and water. Children will need to be shown what a solution and a suspension look like before they begin their own practical work. Leave dry spoons in the powders, which can be on the front table, and have one wet spoon per group for stirring.

> See the detailed lesson plans on pages 105–106.

Solute, solvent, solution, dissolve, suspension

For information about solutions and suspensions, and definitions of related terms such as solute, solvent and dissolve, see pages 96 and 107. Materials that dissolve in water break down into individual molecules, ions or atoms, which form a loose bond with the water molecules.

> See *Science for Primary Teachers*, page 23.

Use a variety of sugars.

- Give the children three or four types of sugar: icing, granulated, cube, brown sugar, coffee crystals. Ask the children which of the sugars will dissolve most quickly. Discuss how they will make a fair test. Talk about how to measure the time each sugar sample takes to dissolve.

> Discuss what would be sensible quantities of sugar and water to use in this activity.

Sugar dissolves more quickly in warm water and if you stir it. Different types of sugar dissolve at different rates. However, don't assume that because icing sugar is fine it will dissolve faster than granulated sugar – it doesn't.

Some sugars dissolve more quickly than others.

Evaporation

- Listen to the children's ideas about where the water goes when washing dries, puddles evaporate or sweat dries from their skin. Let the children wet three or four paper hand towels. Discuss places where the towels will dry quickly and slowly.

- Look at a variety of containers, some wide and shallow and others tall and thin, filled with equal quantities of water. Listen to the children's ideas about which container's water will evaporate the quickest.

Water will evaporate quickly if:
    the air is warm
    the air is moving
    the air has low humidity
    the water has a big surface area.

Water does not need to boil to evaporate. Even cool water will evaporate rapidly if the air around it is dry. Leave some water in the fridge – it will evaporate quite quickly.

Water can evaporate at different rates.

Drying towels

Evaporation rates

Factors affecting evaporation

Things dry out in the fridge.

> Humid air contains a great deal of water vapour, so water will not easily evaporate into it.

Condensation

- Take several cans from the fridge. Let the children examine the condensation on the cans and talk about where it comes from. Breathe on mirrors and other shiny surfaces (metal and glass are best). Talk about where the children see condensation in everyday life. What do they do to get rid of it?

If air that is already humid (has plenty of water vapour in it) is cooled, water will condense out of it either on to a cold surface or as droplets of water. A cool shower room will often have clouds of steam and condensation on the walls for this reason.

Water will condense out of the air on to a cold surface.

Humid air is the culprit.

> Some children will think that condensation is the liquid inside the can seeping out.

Water drops

- Give the children dropper pipettes and ask them to place single drops of water on a variety of materials. Look carefully at what happens when the drops are placed. Look at a drop of water on a feather or on a cabbage leaf. Compare that with a drop of water on cotton or paper.

Some materials absorb water.

Water drop repelled by surface   *Water drop attracted by surface*

> Feathers repel water wonderfully. On a flight feather, water drops roll around like quicksilver.

Water repelled Water attracted	Waterproof surfaces repel water. A drop formed on a waterproof surface is very round, as the water tries to get as far from the repelling surface as possible. Other materials, such as paper towels or cotton, will attract the drop and make it very flat.

Rehydrating

- Weigh quantities of dried peas and beans, and find out their volume. Soak them. Weigh them again and calculate their volume now. Observe the differences between the dry and the soaked food.

Beans in particular dry out naturally. This is to prevent them from germinating until the conditions are right. Very dry food will not rot easily (see page 80).

> If you soak peas in water for more than 12 hours they begin to smell unpleasant.

Some foods change dramatically when mixed with water.

Key Stage 2b classroom activities

Thermometers measure temperature.

Sunny day

Expansion of alcohol

Amount of heat energy

Heat

- Measure the temperature of places and things, such as water from the taps, in and around the classroom. Use a variety of thermometers; do they all read the same temperature in the same place? On a sunny day, make a series of readings, both outside and inside the classroom. Draw a bar chart or a line graph of the results.

Most school thermometers use the expansion of liquid alcohol to measure temperature. If you have mercury thermometers take extra care when using them or give them to the local secondary school. Temperature is a measure of how hot something is; it is not a measure of its heat energy. For instance, a large object like a radiator may be at a temperature of only about 60°C but it contains more heat energy than a drop of water at 95°C.

Flame tests

Burning is not normally reversible.

Flames

- Take tiny scraps of fabric and test them to see which are flameproof. Note that many clothes are not flameproof.

Burning is the process through which a fuel combines with oxygen in a flame. Burning reactions are not normally reversible. However, the burning of hydrogen to produce water is reversible by electrolysis (see page 98).

> Perform burning tests only in a well-ventilated room.

Burning candle

Wax is a fuel.

Fuels

- Look at a candle burning. Note the colour of the flame. Draw the candle flame using pastel crayons on black paper. Challenge the children to make as long a list of observations about the candle flame as they can. Discuss what the children think is burning when the candle is alight. Demonstrate that it is the wax that is burning (see page 97).

Wax is a hydrocarbon. That means that it is chemically a compound of hydrogen and carbon. Hydrocarbons can consist of long chains of carbon molecules:

$$H-\underset{\underset{H}{|}}{\overset{\overset{H}{|}}{C}}-\underset{\underset{H}{|}}{\overset{\overset{H}{|}}{C}}-\underset{\underset{H}{|}}{\overset{\overset{H}{|}}{C}}-\underset{\underset{H}{|}}{\overset{\overset{H}{|}}{C}}-\underset{\underset{H}{|}}{\overset{\overset{H}{|}}{C}}-\underset{\underset{H}{|}}{\overset{\overset{H}{|}}{C}}-\underset{\underset{H}{|}}{\overset{\overset{H}{|}}{C}}-\underset{\underset{H}{|}}{\overset{\overset{H}{|}}{C}}-\underset{\underset{H}{|}}{\overset{\overset{H}{|}}{C}}-\underset{\underset{H}{|}}{\overset{\overset{H}{|}}{C}}-\underset{\underset{H}{|}}{\overset{\overset{H}{|}}{C}}-H$$

Hydrocarbons burn with a blue flame when there is complete combustion. A yellow flame is caused by glowing particles of unburnt carbon.

hydrogen + oxygen = water
carbon + oxygen = carbon dioxide

Reaction with water

- Make a mould from plasticine by pressing an object into it. Mix some plaster of Paris with water and pour the creamy liquid into the mould. Leave it to set. Make casts of seashells and fossils, leaves and twigs, keys and coins.

Step 1: Make a plasticine tray with shallow walls. Press the leaf carefully into the base of the tray to make a mould, then remove it.

Step 2: Mix plaster of Paris with water until the consistency of the mixture is like double cream. Pour it into the mould

Step 3: Leave the plaster to set for one hour then carefully tip the cast out of the mould.

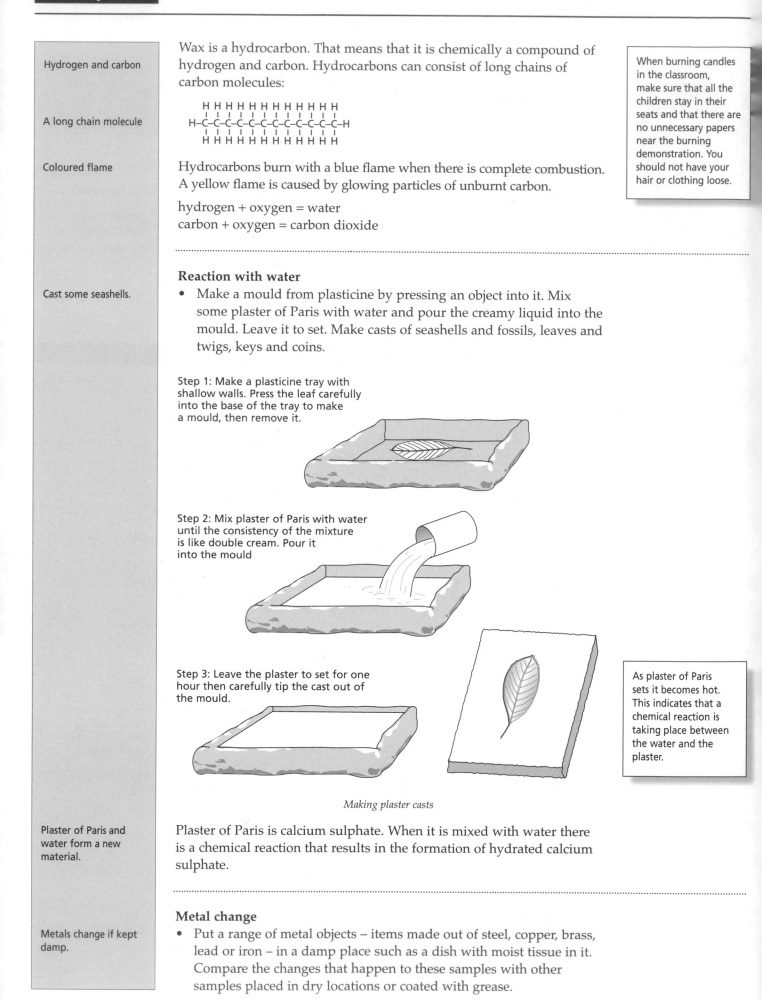

Making plaster casts

Plaster of Paris is calcium sulphate. When it is mixed with water there is a chemical reaction that results in the formation of hydrated calcium sulphate.

Metal change

- Put a range of metal objects – items made out of steel, copper, brass, lead or iron – in a damp place such as a dish with moist tissue in it. Compare the changes that happen to these samples with other samples placed in dry locations or coated with grease.

Side notes (left margin):

Hydrogen and carbon

A long chain molecule

Coloured flame

Cast some seashells.

Plaster of Paris and water form a new material.

Metals change if kept damp.

Side notes (right margin):

When burning candles in the classroom, make sure that all the children stay in their seats and that there are no unnecessary papers near the burning demonstration. You should not have your hair or clothing loose.

As plaster of Paris sets it becomes hot. This indicates that a chemical reaction is taking place between the water and the plaster.

| Copper turns green. | Metals such as iron and steel will oxidize, forming rust if left in a damp atmosphere. Copper forms verdigris, which is copper carbonate produced by a reaction with slightly acidic water. Rusting can be avoided by keeping the metal dry or preventing air from reaching it. | Find out what effect salt water or vinegar has on the metals. |

Teaching strategy: structuring the classroom for Key Stage 2b

| Structure the lesson. | **Introduction** |
| | When experimenting with materials you need a highly structured classroom organization. If your organization is weak, you will have a frustrating and unstructured lesson. In these examples, we will assume there are 32 children in the class and suggest how they can be organized in a way that maximizes learning and minimizes confusion. |

Lesson 1

Theme:	WHAT DISSOLVES?	
Objective:	The children will learn about materials that dissolve in water.	
Introduction:	Explain to the children what they are going to do. Demonstrate that some materials dissolve in water whilst others do not. Show sugar mixed with water and flour mixed with water. Many will think that because flour has mixed with water it has dissolved. Explain that this is not the case.	Soap powder gives a hazy solution.
Central equipment:	Set out on one long table six or seven different types of powder, each in a separate bowl or dish, labelled. Each bowl has one (dry) spoon.	
Group equipment:	Give each group: • 1 jug of water • 1 spoon for stirring • 1 clear calibrated container • 1 bowl for dirty water	
Organization:	Arrange the children into groups of four. In each group everyone has a job: • the *gofer* goes out to get the powder • the *gaffer* records the results • the *stirrer* stirs • the *pourer* pours water Choose one group to demonstrate the routine: • the gofer goes to the powder with the small clear container, puts into it one small spoonful of powder, and returns • the pourer pours in 50 ml of water • the stirrer stirs • all look • the gaffer records what they see • the pourer empties the container into the bowl	This minimizes movement around the classroom.
Recording:	Show the children how to record using a simple table.	Children can design their own table or copy one from the board.
Summary:	Once equipment is tidied away discuss the children's results. Ask them to write about what they did. Make sure each group designs a table in which to record its results.	

Left margin notes:
Everyone has a job.

Demonstrate the routine.

Tidy away.

Lesson 2

Theme:	HOW QUICKLY DOES SUGAR DISSOLVE?
Objective:	Investigate the factors that make sugar dissolve quickly in water.
Central equipment:	• 3 bowls of different types of sugar • 1 dry spoon in each bowl • 2 containers of hot water from the tap (or simply go straight to the tap)
Group equipment:	Give each group: • 1 thermometer • 1 jug of cold water • 1 spoon for stirring • 1 clear container marked up to 50 ml • 1 timer for each group (or use the classroom clock)
Organization:	Arrange the children into groups of four. In each group, everyone has a job: • the *gofer* gets the sugar and warm water • the *gaffer* records the results • the *stirrer* stirs • the *pourer* pours water The routine is similar to that used in Lesson 1. However, in this activity there will be fewer child movements around the classroom, so the gofers can wash out their containers in the sink between each test. Choose one group to demonstrate the routine.

Introduction:	Before you start the practical work, discuss what the children want to find out. Questions will probably include:
	    Will sugar dissolve more quickly if we stir it?
	    Will sugar dissolve more quickly if we use warm water?
	    Which type of sugar dissolves the quickest?
	
	Discuss what will be kept the same in the investigations and what will be altered. Each group should design a table to record their results. Unless you have a lot of time, do not ask for a written plan – this will take the children too long to produce and in any case the table should neatly summarize what they are going to do.

Recording:	Use the tables designed by the children to record the data. In each instance the dependent variable will be the time taken for the sugar to dissolve. Graph the results. On a bar chart, show the time taken for different types of sugar to dissolve. On a line graph, show the time taken for sugar to dissolve at different temperatures or with different numbers of stirs per minute.

Set up the groups.

Allow the children to decide what they want to find out.

This could be set in the context of the manufacture of soft drinks.

Not all groups will need to use a thermometer.

Use the planning template suggested on page 12.

Graphing results is a good opportunity for differentiation.

Mixtures of materials

Key ideas

Sieves of different sizes
Sieving soil gives several grades of material.
Solutions pass through filters.
Suspensions can be filtered out.
Evaporation removes liquid.
Distillation recovers liquid.

Sieving
Solid particles of different sizes can be separated using sieves of different sizes. Wholemeal flour can be sieved to trap coarse bran, letting finer particles fall through the mesh. Soil can be sieved using different mesh sizes:

> Pebbles are caught in a coarse sieve.
> Gravel, sand and clay particles are caught in progressively finer sieves.

Filtering
A solution is a mixture of a dissolved solid and a liquid in which the solid can no longer be seen. A solution is clear; the solute will not settle out and cannot be filtered out of the solution.

> The *solute* is a solid, such as salt.
> The *solvent* is a liquid, such as water.

A suspension is a mixture of solid and liquid, but the mixture is cloudy and the solid can be filtered out. If left for a time the solid will settle out of a suspension.

Separating solutions
There are several techniques that can separate mixtures in solution:

The liquid is boiled away and the solid remains. This is how salt is obtained from sea water.

The liquid is heated, evaporated and then cooled and condensed, leaving behind the solid. This is how drinking water is obtained from sea water.

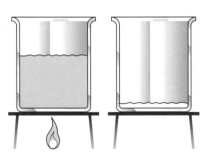

Evaporation

Distillation

Fractional distillation recovers two liquids.

Two liquids of different boiling points are heated together. The liquid with the lower boiling point evaporates first, and is then condensed and cooled, leaving the other liquid behind. This is how alcohol is separated from water in distilleries.

Fractional distillation

Chromatology moves pigments through a medium.

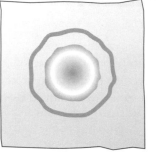

Different dissolved solids are absorbed into a substance like paper at different rates. Make a solution of the colour in the sugar coating of a sweet, and put several drops on a filter paper. Chromatography will separate the dissolved solids that make up the colour.

Chromatography

Saturation

Full up

Hotter water

When no more solid will dissolve in a liquid the solution is saturated. In 100 ml of water you can dissolve about six teaspoons of salt. You cannot dissolve more salt by warming the water. In 100 ml of cold water you can dissolve about 200 g of sugar. If the water is hotter, much more sugar will dissolve. Over 400 g of sugar can be dissolved in 100 ml of water at 90°C.

Common misconceptions

Saturation

When learning about the concept of saturation analogies can be helpful, but they do have their limits.

An analogy

Particles

A useful way of visualizing dissolving and saturation is to think of a room with tables set aside for storing parcels. The room is the liquid and the tables are the places within the liquid's structure where solid atoms, ions or molecules can be put. When all the tables are full then no more parcels can be stored – just as when a liquid is saturated no more solid can be stored.

> Analogies are very useful when discussing abstract concepts.

A limited comparison

The problem with this analogy is that no more tables are created as the room/liquid becomes hot – and when sugar is dissolved in warm water rather than cold this is effectively what happens. The analogy relies on an understanding of particle theory and must be approached with care at primary level.

List of resources

Resources for studying mixtures of materials

- sieves
- flour
- wholemeal flour
- soil
- sugar
- salt
- sand
- instant coffee
- filter paper
- filter funnel
- measuring jugs
- teaspoons
- dropper pipette
- thermometers
- food dyes
- magnet
- felt-tip pens

Wholemeal flour is an interesting material that contains husks and wheatgerm.

Summary of the programmes of study

Key Stage 2 Sc3: 3a–e

Children should be taught about the following:
- solids of different sizes can be separated by sieving
- some solids dissolve
- insoluble solids can be separated from liquids by filtering
- dissolved solids can be recovered by evaporating the liquid from the solution
- there is a limit to the mass of a solid that can be dissolved in a given amount of water

Key Stage 2a classroom activities

Dry powders

Sieving
- Sieve mixtures, such as wholemeal flour and dry soil, through different size meshes. Look at the different materials you trap and let through with each grade of mesh.

The solids you are sieving have to be extremely dry or the grains will clump together, preventing them from passing through the sieve.

You can obtain kitchen sieves of different grades from hardware shops.

Filtering

Coffee filter papers are easily available.

- Let the children dissolve salt and mix sand with water. Let them try to filter each mixture. Use standard filter papers – or coffee filter papers if laboratory ones are not available.

Separate molecules pass through filters.

Sieves and filters are not able to catch individual, separate molecules, ions or atoms. Liquids pass through sieves because their molecules are not closely attached to each other. Undissolved solids cannot pass through filters because they never break down into molecular size.

Filtering water

Removing bacteria

- Discuss the ways in which drinking water is treated before it is potable. Add soil to dirty water and get the children to filter it with sand and gravel. The top part of a drinks bottle makes a good funnel that can be filled with a variety of gravel, sand, perlite and rock. Visit a water treatment works to see how filtration is done on an industrial scale. You might have a water bottling plant nearby that could supply information.

Investigate which combination of materials makes the clearest water.

Water treatment

Water treatment involves cleaning and disinfecting water. The first step is to filter out particles and some of the bacteria, initially through sand and gravel.

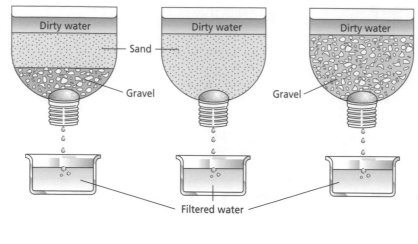

Bottle-neck water filters

Wash day

Testing washing powders

Fat and oil

Attracted to water

- Test different methods of soaking and washing dirty cotton/nylon with and without detergent. Test a variety of washing powders and assess which is most efficient.

Fat and oil are difficult to remove from clothes using only water since both repel water. Soaps and detergents are chemicals made from long chains of hydrocarbon molecules with a group of atoms of carbon, oxygen and sodium at one end. This group of atoms is highly attracted to water whilst the hydrocarbon molecules are highly attracted to fat.

Washing separates the 'mixture' of dirt and clothing.

This is a piece of cloth with a fatty stain being washed in detergent in water. The hydrocarbon end of detergent molecule chains are attracted to the fat.

The clusters of carbon, oxygen and sodium atoms at the other end of the detergent chains are attracted to the water, and this attraction starts to pull at the chains, plus the fat they are clinging to. This action lifts the fat out of the cloth.

As the fat is pulled free, the hydrocarbon ends of the detergent chains continue to be attracted to it until its surface is completely covered. The fat is now suspended in the water.

Detergent action

When fatty stains are washed out of clothes, the hydrocarbon plus fat is pulled off the clothing material by the attraction of the other end of the detergent chain to the water.

Reflecting light

Detergents also contain whitening agents, which reflect ultraviolet light as visible light, literally making the wash appear 'whiter than white'.

Key Stage 2b classroom activities

Saturation

Reaching saturation

- Find out how much salt will dissolve in 50 ml of water at 20°C and at 40°C. Do the same for sugar. Draw a line graph to show the increase at higher temperatures in the amount of sugar that dissolves.

Saturated sponges

When a sponge is saturated it can no longer absorb any more water. The same principle probably applies to someone's brain when it is too full of knowledge – such as during a teacher training course!

Salt's solubility does not change with temperature.

In liquids there are particular sites where dissolved solids can be accommodated. In the case of salt, where the sodium ions and chlorine ions form ionic bonds with the water, there is no increase in the amount of solid that will dissolve as the water gets warmer. Sugar, on the other hand, does not form ionic bonds with water, and the amount of sugar that can be dissolved increases dramatically with temperature.

Saturation points

Salt forms a saturated solution at this level:
   30 g per 100 ml of water.

Sugar forms a saturated solution at these levels:
   200 g per 100 ml water in cold water
   400 g per 100 ml water in hot water.

> If you want to move the lesson along, give one group the task of finding the saturation point of sugar at 20°C, another the job of finding the saturation point of water with sugar at 30°C, and so on. The results can be pooled at the end and conclusions drawn.

Crystal culture

Evaporating the liquid

- Dissolve salt in water. Leave the solution in different places until the water has evaporated. Examine the salt crystals under a microscope.

Liquids can change state to gas at low as well as high temperatures. The water in saucer of salt solution will evaporate at any temperature. As the solution dries out, the salt recrystalizes. If this happens slowly, at a low temperature, the salt crystals form as beautiful cubes. If it happens quickly, as a result of heating the water, the salt crystals look like fine powder.

Microscopic examination

Growing large crystals

Make a saturated solution.

- Show the children how to grow large crystals using a saturated solution of alum. Buy alum from a chemist's shop. Make a saturated solution by dissolving as much alum as possible in warm water and letting the solution cool. As cooling occurs alum solids will come out of solution because warm water can dissolve more alum than cold. Allow the water to evaporate slowly at a constant temperature. If the solution warms up excessively and then cools down, your prize crystals will be redissolved.

> Compare what happens to the size of the crystals that result when the water is evaporated rapidly and slowly.

Beautiful crystals

Grow alum and copper sulphate crystals either separately or together in one mixture.

Warning: Copper sulphate is a poison.

> Grow a crystal garden using one of the commercially available kits.

Mixtures

Separating complex mixtures

- Ask the children to separate mixtures in which one element is soluble, one can float, one is insoluble and one is magnetic. For instance, make up a mixture of salt, wax chips, sand and iron filings. Ask the children to devise mixtures for others to separate.

Get the children to record this work as a series of cartoon drawings.

How to separate a complex mixture.

To separate a mixture of salt, wax chips, sand and iron filings:

1. First attract the iron filings to a magnet wrapped in paper.
2. Next mix the salt, wax and sand with water.
3. Skim off the floating wax.
4. Filter the mixture to trap the sand.
5. Leave the remaining salt solution to dry out – the salt will be left behind.

Chromatography

Wash the colour through a filter paper.

- Place a dot of food colour, water-soluble ink from a felt-tip pen or a sugar-coated coloured sweet in the centre of a circle of filter paper. Place four or five drops of water on to the item using a dropper pipette. Watch the colours spread out as the water washes the different components of the pigment into the paper.

Brown Smarties are best!

Pigments

Colours are made from a mixture of pigments. The molecules that make up pigments are of different sizes. Large, heavy molecules will not move far in a filter paper. Small, light ones will travel further.

Have you noticed how the outer edge of many stains is brown?

Black felt-tips have many pigments

Black or dark colours comprise a range of different pigments since they have to absorb all the colours of the spectrum to appear dark. These colours are the most interesting on which to perform chromatography. Yellow dyes are composed of yellow pigments only, and don't give such interesting results.

Survey the inks from several black felt-tip pens. Each will have a distinctive pigment mix.

Do they do it at Key Stage 3?

Chromatography is part of the Key Stage 3 programme of study. Check with your local secondary school if they do work on chromatography – not all do. Use this opportunity to discuss other issues of progression between Key Stages 2 and 3.

Teaching strategy: Key Stage 2a reports for a purpose

Introduction

Audience

When children are writing reports of scientific investigations, the teacher needs to bear in mind the intended audience for the reports. Sometimes it is possible to have a real audience. For instance, reports can be written for:

Many organizations welcome letters from children.

> the local bakery on the quality of their bread
> the local supermarket on the quality of their washing powder
> the police on the effects of simulated collisions using toy cars
> the local garden centre on the quality of different composts

However, in this short section we look at writing a report for an imaginary, highly specialized audience.

Rock salt

Purification

Salt is a mineral.

First impressions

Report for the prospector

Lesson plan

Theme:	WHAT'S THAT STUFF?
Materials:	You will need some rock salt – the caretaker may have some. Mix in a little sand to give the filter more to catch.
Learning objective:	The children will learn how to purify rock salt.
Lesson introduction:	*We have been sent some material by a prospector digging for minerals. She found this material in the county of Cheshire and wondered what it was made of. She sent a map showing where it was found. (Show the children a map of Britain with a place in Cheshire marked.)* *Look at the sample of the mystery substance on each table. What do you think it is? What tests could you do on it? What do you need to get a closer look at the stuff? Make drawings and keep notes about what you do.*
Lesson development:	*Can you purify the material? (Use the techniques described above for the Key Stage 2b activity Mixtures.)*
Recording:	*Write up a report for the prospector.*
Extension:	*Read about how rock salt is extracted from the ground and make notes and diagrams. Read about the uses for salt.*
Assessment:	*Criterion:* Does the report give a clear idea of what the substance is and how it can be purified? *Mode:* Report to the prospector.

Cheshire was the site of an inland sea about 350 million years ago.

Hot water is pumped into the ground, dissolving the salt, which is brought to the surface in solution.

Magnetism

Key ideas

Forces that work at a distance

Magnetism and gravity are the two forces studied by primary children that work at a distance. When looked at in detail these forces seem mysterious and puzzling, yet they are also so much part of our world that they are usually taken for granted. As distance increases, the strength of both forces decreases.

Effect of distance

Magnetic forces

Magnetism is a force. Iron and steel are the only common materials that are attracted to magnets. Nickel and cobalt, which are less common, are also attracted to magnets. The Earth itself acts like a huge bar magnet. The Earth's geographic North Pole is actually a magnetic south pole. This is logical, if confusing. The north pole of a compass is called 'north' because it points towards the Earth's geographic North Pole. However, like poles repel, so what attracts the north pole of a compass must, magnetically speaking, be a south pole.

Nickel and cobalt are also magnetic.

Magnetic south pole at geographic North Pole

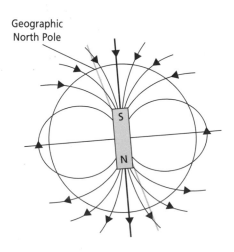

Section through the Earth's magnetic field

The Earth's magnetic field flips over every hundred thousand years or so. No one really knows what effect this has on living things.

Lodestone

The ancient Greeks used pieces of natural magnetite, called lodestone, to attract pieces of iron. In the twelfth century the Chinese discovered that, if hung from a thread, a lodestone always aligned itself north to south. In the sixteenth century English sailors learnt how to transfer the magnetism of a lodestone to a piece of steel.

Steel compass

Poles and dipoles

Magnetic force is concentrated at the ends or poles of a magnet. If you break a bar magnet in half the two pieces will each have a north and a south pole. Right down to a group of molecules or a single molecule, pieces of magnetic material have polarity. Single molecules of magnetic material are called dipoles.

In their unmagnetized state, the dipoles of iron are arranged randomly. When magnetized they align themselves. No substance has yet been found with a north pole and no south pole.

Magnetism is concentrated at the poles.

If there is a north pole there has to be a south pole, too.

The poles of a polo magnet are on the two flat faces.

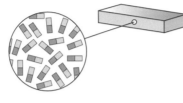

Dipoles are grouped in domains. In unmagnetized magnetic material, the domains are arranged randomly.

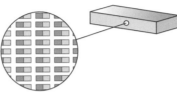

In magnetized material, the domains are aligned.

When any piece of magnetized material is broken, each fragment is a new magnet.

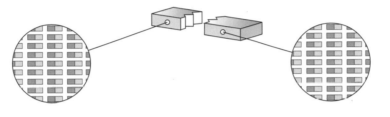

Magnetic material and dipoles

Electricity and magnetism

The connection between magnetism and electricity was first investigated by Oersted in 1819. He found that when an electric current flowed through a wire it affected the needle of a nearby compass. In 1825 an English scientist discovered that an iron core wrapped in wire became magnetized when the wire carried electricity but lost its magnetism when the electricity was turned off. This was electromagnetism, and it formed the basis of inventions like the telephone, electric motor, dynamo and electric bell.

Electromagnet

Most magnets are created by placing steel in a strong magnetic field produced by electricity.

Common misconceptions

Poles

Many children believe that circular (polo) magnets do not have a north and south pole. They also imagine that all bar magnets have their poles at their ends whereas many have poles on their faces.

Children often think that if you snap a bar magnet at the line separating the blue and the red parts you will have one north pole and one south pole. This concept is difficult to disprove without extreme prejudice to your stock of magnets!

Circular magnet poles

Just snap that magnet, will you?

Children currently find ideas about lines of force more accessible than they did some years ago. They are used to the idea that in science fiction spaceships have force shields around them.

Bigger isn't always better.

Magic
The wonderful way in which magnets work across empty space leads some young children to believe this is magic – literally.

Size doesn't count
Children believe that the bigger the magnet the stronger it is.
A more important factor is way in which it was made. In general, the type of material and the strength of the field that created the magnet is more important than the magnet's size.

List of resources

Resources for studying magnetism

- ceramic bar magnets
- polo magnets
- large nails
- electromagnet (commercially produced)
- lengths of wire
- selection of other magnets
- small plotting compasses

Iron filings should be kept in the teacher's drawer since, if spilled directly on to them, they are difficult to remove from the magnets. If you intend to attract iron filings, always wrap the magnet in paper first to facilitate removal of the filings.

Ceramic magnets keep their magnetism for much longer than standard steel magnets. However, they are contained in a hard plastic cover. You might prefer 'alinco' magnets, which are far stronger. Polo magnets are the same shape as the mint with the hole and have poles on each face.

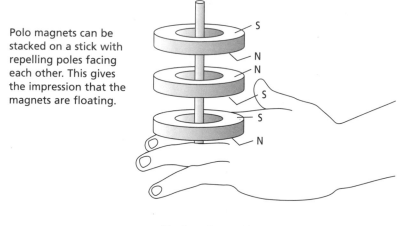

Polo magnets can be stacked on a stick with repelling poles facing each other. This gives the impression that the magnets are floating.

Floating polo magnets

Summary of the programmes of study

Key Stage 1 Sc3: 1b

Key Stage 2 Sc4: 2a

Children should be taught about the following:
- sorting materials on the basis of whether they are magnetic or non-magnetic
- there are forces of attraction and repulsion between magnets, and forces of attraction between magnets and magnetic materials.

Key Stage 1 classroom activities

Attraction

What objects will a magnet attract?

- Test objects around the classroom using a single bar magnet. Be aware that the distinction between objects and materials is difficult for children of this age.

Pennies and two-pence pieces made since the late 1980s use an alloy that contains a substantial amount of iron, making the coins magnetic. Earlier coins are not magnetic.

Magnets attract iron and steel.

The only materials that are attracted by magnets are iron, steel, nickel and cobalt.

Many samples apparently made out of zinc and tin will in fact be plated. They will have steel underneath!

Poles

Magnets have two poles.

- Place magnets on a table. Feel the attraction and repulsion of the magnetic poles.

Opposite poles attract, like poles repel.

- Float a bar magnet on a dish. Bring other magnetic poles near the floating magnet.

In magnetic materials, every molecule acts like a tiny magnet. These molecules are called dipoles.

Keep the dish away from the metal framework of the table – for obvious reasons!

The pull is at the poles.

- Test the strength of a magnet's pull at its poles and compare this with the pull at the middle. Use small paper clips as a measure of attraction.

The lines of magnetic force are concentrated at the poles of a magnet.

It is often impossible to make a paperclip hang from the centre of a magnet.

Key Stage 2a classroom activities

Strength

Magnets vary in strength.

- Collect three different magnets and ask the children to devise an investigation to test which magnet is the strongest.

Look after your magnets.

How magnets are made.

Magnets lose their magnetism over time. If they are treated roughly, stored incorrectly or heated they become less magnetic. Not all magnets are the same. Expensive, heavy magnets are likely to be stronger than cheap, small ones. Most magnets are made by passing an electric current through a wire wrapped round a piece of iron or steel. If a strong current is used then the resulting magnet will be strong as well.

Use a weak magnet to investigate how a compass needle can be affected by other magnets.

Distance

- Test a variety of materials to see which ones magnetism will work through.

Working through space

Magnetic attraction can work through space (a vacuum) and through all materials except cast iron – unless, of course, the magnet is touching it. Cast iron both carries magnetic force and shields objects from it.

Variety of magnets
- Examine rubber fridge seals, and bar, polo and horseshoe magnets.

Rubber magnets are made by mixing tiny pieces of iron, which are single dipoles (see above), into molten rubber. The molten rubber is then placed in a strong magnetic field that aligns the dipoles permanently.

Rubber magnets

> Children may be confused by these since they are clearly not metal.

Compasses
- Put a bar magnet in a dish and float it in water. Observe how the floating magnet aligns itself with the Earth's magnetism.

Earth's magnetic field

> This develops the Key Stage 1 activity.

The cork will prevent pricked fingers.

- Push the point of a needle a little way into a cork. Gently stroke the needle with a magnet. Float it on water on a tiny piece of polystyrene. It should align north-south.

Since like poles repel, there must be a south magnetic pole at the geographic North Pole. If not, the north pole of the floating magnet would not point to the north.

Making compass needles

By stroking a steel needle with an existing magnet you create a new, permanent magnet. Doing the same with an iron nail creates only a temporary magnet. This is because the domains of steel stay aligned once magnetized but the domains of iron return to their original position after the magnetic force has been removed.

> Naturally occurring lodestone was once used like this to magnetize the needles for ships' compasses.

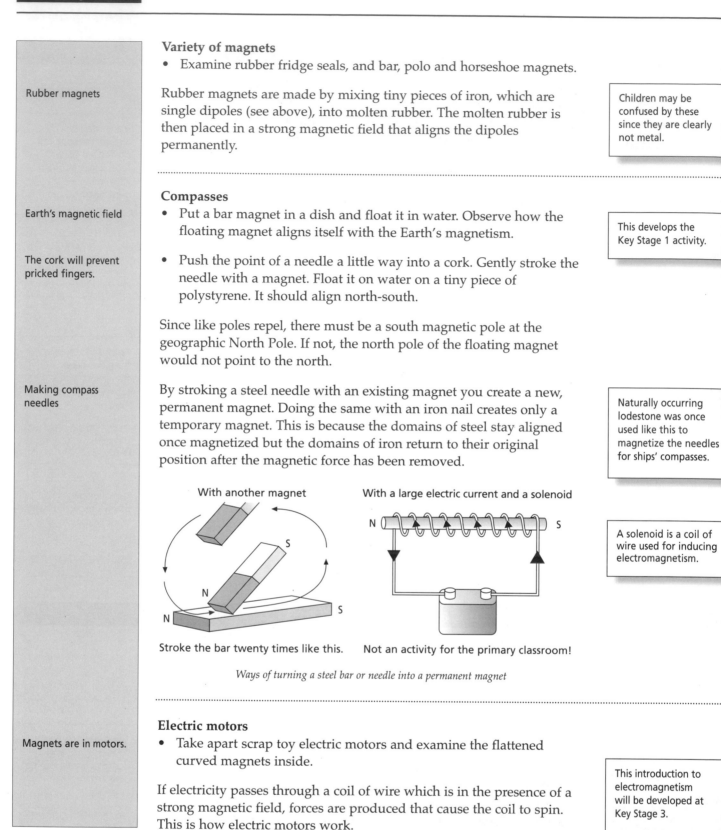

With another magnet

Stroke the bar twenty times like this.

With a large electric current and a solenoid

Not an activity for the primary classroom!

> A solenoid is a coil of wire used for inducing electromagnetism.

Ways of turning a steel bar or needle into a permanent magnet

Electric motors

Magnets are in motors.

- Take apart scrap toy electric motors and examine the flattened curved magnets inside.

If electricity passes through a coil of wire which is in the presence of a strong magnetic field, forces are produced that cause the coil to spin. This is how electric motors work.

> This introduction to electromagnetism will be developed at Key Stage 3.

Teaching strategy: circus of activities for Key Stage 2a

Introduction
Work on magnetism can form part of a circus of activities. After an initial introduction from the teacher the children, working in groups, move between the different activities.

Differentiation

Attraction

Coin attraction

Metal attraction

Activities five and six are a little more demanding so you will need to start more able children there. Amend the recording for the less able children. In activity six, for instance, ask the less able children just to write down the number of paperclips attracted to magnet 'A', and in activity five simply to draw what happens.

The materials that follow show how work at Key Stage 2a can be organized using a series of workcards arranged on different tables.

Workcard 1

What things will the magnet attract?

Write a list with these headings:

IS ATTRACTED TO A MAGNET   IS NOT ATTRACTED TO A MAGNET

> Workcards should be very easy to read.

Equipment
- 1 basket (or more) of small items – about 10 in total
- enough bar magnets for the children to have one each

Workcard 2

Look at the coins.

Which are attracted to a magnet?

Write down the dates of the coins attracted to the magnet.

Equipment
- 10 coins of 1p and 2p denominations
- 2 bar magnets
- 1 or 2 hand lenses

Workcard 3

Which of these metal objects are attracted to the magnet?

Write a list with these headings:

ATTRACTED   NOT ATTRACTED

> Avoid any samples made out of steel plated with another metal as this will confuse.

Equipment
- a set of metal samples
- 1 magnet

**Magnetic attraction
and repulsion**

Workcard 4

> **Bring the ends of the magnets close
> together.**
>
> What do you notice?
>
> Draw a coloured picture showing the
> magnets attracted.
>
> Draw another picture with the magnets
> pushing apart.

The red ends of
magnets are usually
north poles and the
blue ends south poles.

Equipment
- 2 pairs of red-blue magnets
- red and blue coloured pencils

Floating magnet

Workcard 5

> *Please do not touch the dish or the bowl –
> the magnet may sink.*
>
> **Look at the magnet in the dish that is
> floating in the bowl. Slowly bring another
> magnet towards the outside of the bowl.**
>
> Write three sentences about what you
> notice.

A block of polystyrene
makes a buoyant raft
for the magnet but it
can get stuck to the
edge of the bowl by
surface tension.

Equipment
- a magnet in a dish that is floating in a bowl containing a few
  centimetres of water
- 1 additional bar magnet

Strength of magnet

Workcard 6

> **How many clips are attracted to the ends
> of each magnet?**
>
> How many are attracted to the middle of
> each magnet?
>
> Write the numbers in this table:
>
> | | AT THE ENDS | IN THE MIDDLE |
> |---|---|---|
> | MAGNET 'A' | | |
> | MAGNET 'B' | | |

Equipment
- 1 magnet labelled 'A'
- 1 magnet labelled 'B'
- 20 paperclips

Electricity

Key ideas

Galvani

Early history

Luigi Galvani was a teacher of anatomy in Italy who accidentally discovered, in 1791, that he could make a dissected frog's leg twitch by touching it with two different metals.

Volta

His fellow countryman Alessandro Volta used this observation to make the first battery. This consisted of a stack of copper and zinc discs separated by salt-water-soaked cloth.

> These scientists have given their names to units of measurement (volts, farads) or processes (galvanisation).

Faraday

In 1831, Michael Faraday found that when a magnet was moved near a coil of wire an electric current flowed in the wire. This discovery was the basis for many later inventions, such as generators and dynamos.

Circuit

A complete electrical circuit is needed to make bulbs, motors or buzzers work. Electricity goes all the way round a circuit. Conventionally electricity is shown to flow from a positive electrode to a negative one. However, since electrons are negatively charged they in fact flow from a negative electrode to a positive one.

Conventionally, flow is shown as positive to negative.

> This key idea about electricity is often misunderstood.

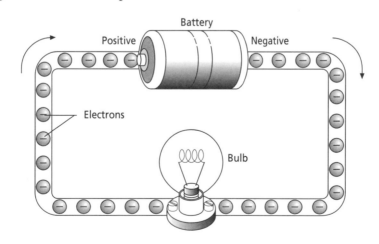

Electron flow in a circuit

Current

Electron flow

Current is carried by electrons that flow around a circuit. It is measured in amps using an ammeter. The current is the same throughout a circuit.

In the circuit shown below, each ammeter is indicating the same flow of electricity.

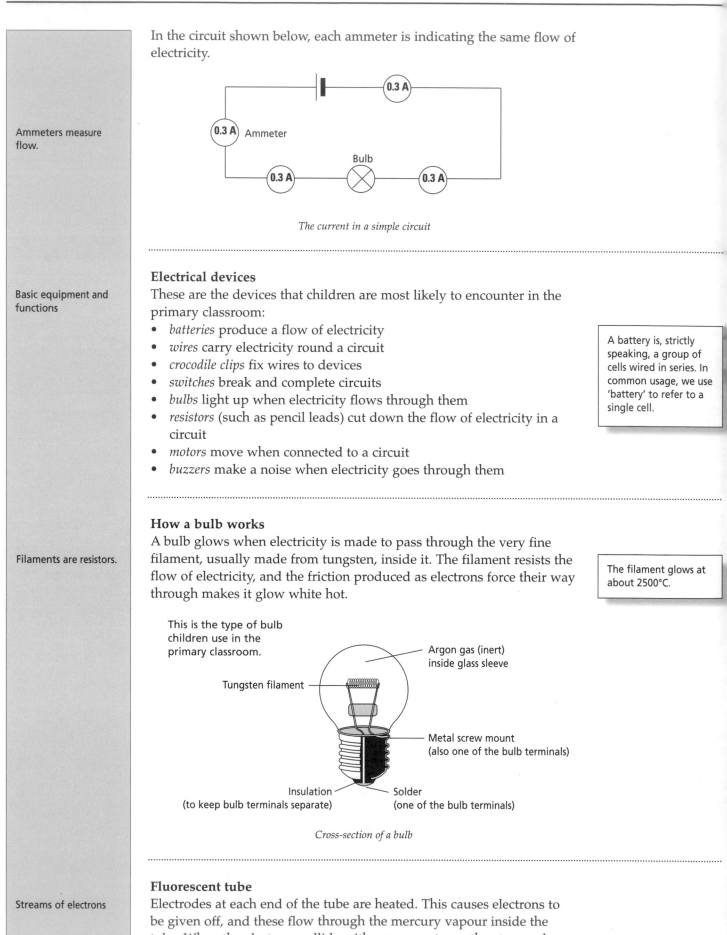

The current in a simple circuit

Ammeters measure flow.

Electrical devices

These are the devices that children are most likely to encounter in the primary classroom:

- *batteries* produce a flow of electricity
- *wires* carry electricity round a circuit
- *crocodile clips* fix wires to devices
- *switches* break and complete circuits
- *bulbs* light up when electricity flows through them
- *resistors* (such as pencil leads) cut down the flow of electricity in a circuit
- *motors* move when connected to a circuit
- *buzzers* make a noise when electricity goes through them

Basic equipment and functions

> A battery is, strictly speaking, a group of cells wired in series. In common usage, we use 'battery' to refer to a single cell.

How a bulb works

A bulb glows when electricity is made to pass through the very fine filament, usually made from tungsten, inside it. The filament resists the flow of electricity, and the friction produced as electrons force their way through makes it glow white hot.

Filaments are resistors.

> The filament glows at about 2500°C.

Cross-section of a bulb

Fluorescent tube

Electrodes at each end of the tube are heated. This causes electrons to be given off, and these flow through the mercury vapour inside the tube. When the electrons collide with mercury atoms, the atoms release ultraviolet radiation. When the radiation hits the phosphor coating inside the tube, the phosphor glows.

Streams of electrons

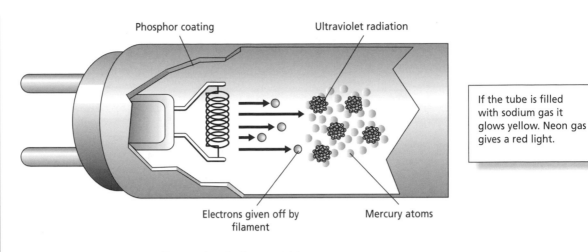

Phosphor coating   Ultraviolet radiation

Electrons given off by
filament   Mercury atoms

If the tube is filled
with sodium gas it
glows yellow. Neon gas
gives a red light.

Cross-section of a fluorescent tube

Electrical switches

When switches are open ('off') they make a gap in a circuit. When switches are closed ('on') they complete a circuit.

A *tilt switch* turns electricity on and off when the device itself is tilted.

A *reed switch* is operated by a magnet, which causes two strips of steel to attract.

Collect scrap switches
from a variety of
sources.

Resistance

The unit of measurement for resistance is the ohm (Ω). High resistance cuts down the flow of electricity. The resistance of an electrical component can be calculated if you know the voltage drop across it (in volts) and the current flowing through it (in amps). This is the relationship:

$$\text{resistance } (\Omega) = \frac{\text{voltage drop (V)}}{\text{current (A)}}$$

You can use a wire made of nickel and chrome (heating wire) to test the resistance effect of longer and shorter lengths of wire.

A voltmeter measures
voltage by sampling
it in parallel. The
meter is connected to
a circuit at two points,
such as either side
of a component. It
compares the *energy*
of the current flowing
at these points.

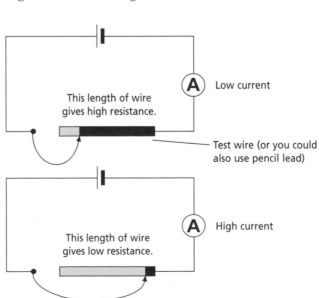

This length of wire
gives high resistance.

A Low current

Test wire (or you could
also use pencil lead)

This length of wire
gives low resistance.

A High current

The best resistor to
use in the primary
classroom is a length
of pencil lead.

The resistance of a wire increases with its length

Tilt switch

Reed switch

Ohms

Resistance wire

Vary the current.	To vary the electrical current you need to increase the number of batteries (cells) or change the resistance of the circuit.

To make a bulb glow more brightly you need:
> more batteries
> new batteries
> fewer resistors in the circuit, such as other bulbs.

To make a bulb glow more dimly you need:
> fewer batteries
> old batteries
> more resistors in the circuit, such as bulbs or a piece of pencil lead.

Brighter glow

Dimmer glow

Circuit diagrams

Common components

Series circuit diagram

Parallel circuit diagram

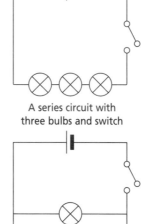

Bell

Buzzer

Bulb

Motor

One cell

Three cells

Switch

Variable resistor

A series circuit with three bulbs and switch

A parallel circuit with three bulbs and switch

> In the parallel circuit the electricity has two possible routes at each branch.

Some commonly used circuit symbols and examples of their use

Series and parallel

The difference between series and parallel circuits is important. In a series circuit you calculate the total resistance by adding together the resistance of all the resistors in the circuit. This is because there is only one route through the circuit for the electricity to take.

Add the resistance.

Imagine a one-way system that consists of one street full of cars to which you add a series of road works. The more sets of roadworks you add, the slower the traffic flows. The roadworks are like resistors in a series circuit.

Resistors are like roadworks.

More than one route

In a parallel circuit the traffic in the one-way system has one or even more alternative routes to follow. When you add sets of roadworks you are not having such a big effect on traffic congestion overall. In other words there will be less resistance in the circuit.

> Electricity will always flow along the line offering least resistance.

Amount of flow	The current that can flow in a series circuit with two bulbs is much less than the current that can flow in a parallel circuit with the same two bulbs.

Voltage and current

An analogy

Think about a battery as a pump that pushes water up to a pool at the start of a series of waterfalls. The height the water reaches is like electrical voltage; this is the energy available to it. The amount of water flowing is the current.

> To explore these ideas fully you will need to use a voltmeter and an ammeter.

The waterfalls are users of energy, like bulbs in a circuit. They convert it into other forms, such as noise and movement. The bigger a waterfall, the more energy it is able to convert. When the water returns to the pump, it has no energy (0 volts) left. The pump recharges it to complete the circuit again.

Waterfalls and pumps

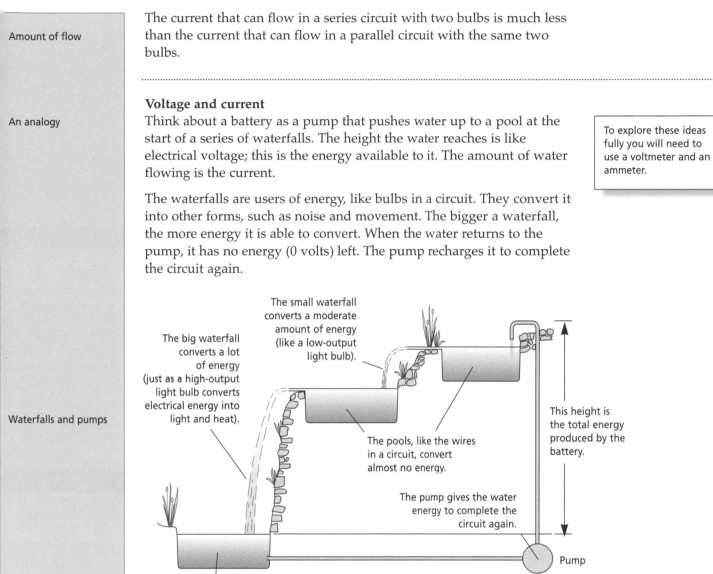

The small waterfall converts a moderate amount of energy (like a low-output light bulb).

The big waterfall converts a lot of energy (just as a high-output light bulb converts electrical energy into light and heat).

The pools, like the wires in a circuit, convert almost no energy.

This height is the total energy produced by the battery.

The pump gives the water energy to complete the circuit again.

The water in the bottom pool has no energy left.

Pump

Common misconceptions

Current

Children think that current gets used up.

There is a substantial literature concerning common misconceptions about electricity. When children are asked to describe what happens when current meets a bulb, most think, incorrectly, that the current flowing out of the bulb is going to be less than the current flowing into it. It is difficult to correct this idea without the use of an ammeter to show that the flow of electricity is in fact the same throughout the circuit.

> None of the current is in fact used up.

Pigs at the trough

Which bulb is brightest?

Another common misconception is that in a series circuit the bulb closest to the source of the electrical flow is brightest. This is thought of on the same principle as pigs at a trough, in which the one nearest the food supply gets the most. This is not the case with electricity. Again, it is difficult to put forward the scientifically correct idea without the use of voltmeters and ammeters. However, if you put several bulbs of

Swap the bulbs.	different ratings into a series circuit then swap their positions, it becomes clear that it is the type of bulb and not its position that determines brightness. Bulbs with higher resistance are brighter. One can think of electricity struggling mightily to get through a bulb with high resistance, causing the bulb filament to glow brightly, whilst getting easily through the filament of a low-resistance bulb and causing less upheaval in the process.
Voltage is not the flow but the energy of the flow.	Many trainee teachers confuse voltage with electrical flow. Voltage is the energy of the electrical flow. The analogy of waterfalls described above provides a useful mind picture of how to think about voltage.

List of resources

Resources for studying electricity	• 2 plastic bulb holders • 2 size D or size C single cell holders • 2 size D or size C 1.5 V cells (dry cells, not rechargeable ones) • 6 wires with crocodile clips attached to each end • 2 bulbs (2.5 V – standardize on these) • 1 buzzer • 1 motor • 2 or 3 switches (manufactured, not home-made) • 1 piece of soft wood or fibreboard approximately 10 cm square

> Equipment has to be compatible: batteries and bulbs should be standard sizes and voltages.

Summary of the programmes of study

Key Stage 1 Sc4: 1a–c	Children should be taught about the following: • everyday appliances use electricity • simple circuits use wires, batteries, buzzers and bulbs • electrical circuits will not work if there is a break in the circuit
Key Stage 2 Sc4: 1a–d	• a complete circuit is needed to make electrical devices work • switches can be used to control electrical devices • current can be varied in a circuit • circuit diagrams represent circuits

Key Stage 1 classroom activities

	Safety • Tell children never to play with any mains device or attempt to plug in or unplug one.
Mains electricity is dangerous.	If someone touches a live mains wire, electricity will flow through their body and possibly kill them. The small batteries we use in school produce an electrical flow of such low power that we cannot usually feel it at all.
Many appliances use electricity.	**What uses electricity?** • Group devices according to what they do when they are plugged in. • Sort devices into those that are battery operated and those that are mains operated.

Electricity has the following effects:
    heat
    magnetism
    light
    movement
    sound.

Heat

Heat is produced when a current runs through a wire that resists the flow of electricity. The element of an electric fire resists electricity and this produces heat.

See filament bulbs on page 122.

Magnetism

A magnetic field is produced around any wire through which electricity runs. This field can be magnified by wrapping the wire round an iron nail. The magnetic effect of electricity is used to make motors turn and bells ring and creates temporary magnets such as those used on security doors.

See fluorescent tubes on page 122.

Light

Electricity is converted into light in a number of devices including bulbs, tubes, television screens and LED warning lights.

Circuit

- Give the children a bulb, a battery and some foil and see if they can make the bulb light.

This experience strips away all the unnecessary clutter and helps the children focus on the bulb and the battery.

Bulb and battery holders

- Show the children the devices used to make a circuit and ask them to construct their own simple circuit using two wires, one bulb and its holder, and one cell and its holder.

A bulb has two terminals. One is the screw mount and the other is the blob of solder at the base.

Connecting the bulb

Using foil with a bulb and a battery, both of these arrangements make the bulb glow:

Buzzers

Buzzer wires are quite delicate.

- Show the children that they need to take care with buzzer wires – they are very fragile. You may want to attach a small block connector to the wires to stop them being pulled off.

Buzzers work using electromagnetism.	Buzzers will only work with the current flowing in one direction. If when connected it fails to operate, simply swap the terminals round. Buzzers use the magnetic effect of electrical current to make a membrane vibrate very rapidly.

Switch
- Make a circuit with a switch in it. Ask the children to tell you how they think the switch works.

A break in a circuit can be caused by an accident, such as a wire becoming loose or disconnected. However, a switch makes a break in a circuit by design. Switches can range from a simple piece of foil to more complex, manufactured switches.

Break in the circuit

Foil switch

> If a circuit fails to work, check the connections between the wires and the components.

Key Stage 2a classroom activities

Some materials conduct
- Test a variety of materials for their ability to conduct electricity. Remember that many metal objects are coated with another material, such as plastic or paint, which does not conduct electricity. Wire coat hangers, for instance, are varnished.

Free electrons

Only materials with free electrons are capable of conducting electricity. All metals conduct electricity because in their atoms the electrons are loosely bound.

Non-metal conductors

Non-metal elements that are conductors include carbon and germanium. These are resistors; they conduct electricity very poorly.

Poor conductors

Special mixtures, such as nickel and chrome (nichrome), do not conduct very well. They are used to make heating elements in fires.

> The electrons in plastic and wood are firmly bound into the molecular structure.

> Germanium is a metalloid.

Brighter bulbs
- Ask the children to note the brightness of the bulb in a simple circuit with one cell, then two cells, then three cells, in series.

Cells in series

> Note what happens if you connect two cells the wrong way round.

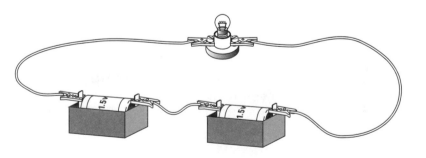

A battery

Two or more cells in series make a battery. You calculate the voltage of the current in a circuit by adding together the voltages of the cells in series.

Match the bulb and battery.

If the combined voltage of the cells is greater than the rating of a bulb, the filament of the bulb is likely to overheat and burn out, causing the bulb to 'blow'.

Key Stage 2b classroom activities

2B or not 2B?

Resistors
- Select pencil leads of different hardness. Use a simple circuit to test which has most resistance to electricity.

Longer resistors

The greater the length of a resistor the more it resists electrical flow. A long piece of pencil lead in a circuit with a bulb will make the bulb glow more dimly than a short piece of pencil lead in the same circuit. This is the principle of the variable resistor.

Volume controls

Variable resistors are used to change the volume of a radio, increase the speed of a motor or dim a light bulb. They do this by restricting the flow of electricity through these devices. The restricting effect of a resistor affects the whole circuit.

> Special resistance wire is used to make the heating elements of toasters, hair dryers and fires.

Series circuit

Identical bulbs in series

- Put two identical bulbs in a series circuit and ask the children to explain what they think is happening to the bulbs. (Only when you use identical bulbs from the same packet can you be sure that they will glow equally brightly in a series circuit.)

Dissimilar bulbs in series

- Now put two dissimilar bulbs in a series circuit. One will glow more than the other. Ask the children why. Swap the position of the bulbs. Note that the one that glowed brightest before is still the brightest. This shows that brightness is to do with the bulb and not its position in the circuit.

> Give children plenty of experience of experimenting with series circuits using a range of components. Avoid being drawn into over-complex explanations.

Regard the bulb as a resistor.

A bulb filament is a piece of very thin tungsten metal. It is a resistor, and electricity struggles to get through it. The struggle causes the filament to get hot. In the activity *Resistors* we noted that longer resistors produce greater resistance. If you put two identical bulbs in series you have twice the length of tungsten resistor of one bulb. If you put three identical bulbs in series you have three times the length of tungsten resistor.

Poor explanation

To suggest that the bulbs in these circuits are sharing the current is a misleading explanation since it encourages the misconception that the current is the same no matter how many bulbs are connected. The more bulbs in a series circuit, the smaller the current that is allowed to flow.

In this series circuit with two bulbs, both bulbs are resisting the flow of electricity.

In this series circuit with one bulb there is less resistance.

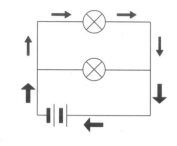

In this parallel circuit, more electricity is flowing in the wires that supply both bulbs than in the wires that supply a single bulb.

Symbols

Electrical symbols

- Teach the children the standard symbols for a bulb, cell, battery, switch, buzzer, bell, motor and variable resistor. Show the children that circuit diagrams using symbols are a simple way of recording the circuits they have made.

These symbols are shown on page 124.

Circuit diagram example

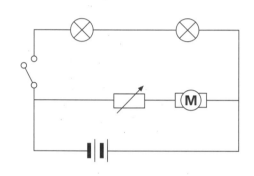

This is a circuit with two lamps and a 3 V battery. A motor is wired in parallel to the bulbs. The switch controls the bulbs and a variable resistor controls the motor.

There are ways of visualizing the flow of electricity for children.

Active analogy

- Current flow can be represented by the children jogging round a desk. Encourage them to go faster (this is the job of the battery). If there is nothing to slow the children they can move quite quickly.

- Put a chair close to the table to make a restricted passage that the children have to squeeze through.

The restriction is a resistance and works like a bulb in a circuit. It slows the flow of children like a bulb restricts and resists the flow of current.

The number of children passing a point in ten seconds can be a measure of flow. An ammeter works on a similar principle.

There are a number of analogies for electrical flow. All have strengths and weaknesses. Use them sparingly, and remind the children that this sort of work is only to help them have a mind-picture of what happens.

Teaching strategy: Key Stage 2b working at their own pace

Repetition

Revisiting

Introduction

It may be difficult to extend work on electricity for children in Years 5 and 6 without repeating work already done in Key Stage 2a. Some schools teach electricity once in Key Stage 1 then just once more in upper Key Stage 2. Others believe that revisiting the subject helps children's understanding. There is scope for a slightly more theoretical approach in Key Stage 2b if the basic ideas have been firmly established in Key Stage 2a.

Try to avoid giving over-detailed explanations of phenomena.

The strategy suggested below allows children to work at their own pace through a structured plan for learning about electricity. It has been devised on the assumption that there is sufficient equipment for three groups of three children to work on electricity at any one time.

The teacher will need to produce a sheet for each group giving them details of the activities they should complete. Keep a tick-sheet record of which activities each group has completed. Tell the children to keep notes of their work on paper or in an exercise book.

> Use the children's notebooks as a record of what they have covered.

Equipment considerations

Electricity groupwork

Notes to the children

Revisiting an earlier idea

Conductors

Probably new work

Focusing on voltage

Explaining what they think is happening

Work through each of these activities as a group.

Draw a diagram of everything you do. Make very short notes of what you notice.

Write down any questions you have and come to ask me about them at the end of your work.

If you get stuck, come and ask me for help.

1. Light a bulb using one cell and a length of foil. How many ways can you get the bulb to light using this simple equipment?

2. Screw a bulb into a holder and wire it up to a cell in a holder.

3. Make a circuit by joining up a 2.5 V bulb and a 1.5 V cell using three wires. You will have two free ends of wire at one point. Touch the crocodile clips of these wires together to make the bulb light. You will need this circuit for the next activities.

4. Hold different materials between the two crocodile clips. Which materials conduct electricity? Which materials stop electricity flowing? Make a table of conductors and insulators.

5. Instead of touching the two crocodile clips together to turn the bulb off and on, make a simple switch. Use two scraps of foil, two drawing pins and a piece of board. Hold one scrap of foil in each crocodile clip. Fix the scraps to the board with pins so that they always touch when held down together.

6. Find a pencil split lengthways with the lead showing. Grip each end of the pencil lead with the two crocodile clips, then move the clips closer together. What happens to the brightness of the bulb when you do this?

7. Add another 1.5 V cell to your circuit. Attach the positive end of one cell to the negative end of the other. This makes a battery of 3 V. The cells are wired in series. Make a table showing what happens to the 2.5 V bulb before and after you increase the voltage of the battery.

8. Change the bulb in the circuit for others of different voltages. Change the number of cells in the battery. Make a table for listing the voltage of the bulb, the number of cells in the battery and how brightly the bulb glows. Each time you make a change, write down in the table the result it has.

9. Add a second bulb holder to your circuit. Wire it into the circuit in series. Put identical bulbs into each bulb holder. Record what you notice.

10. Now put different bulbs into each bulb holder. Record what you notice. Write down explanations for what you notice.

> Store wires by clipping their crocodile clips to the edge of a rectangular piece of hardboard or plywood. This will stop them getting in a tangle.

> Prepare the pencil leads well in advance, taking great care. Many teachers prefer to use propelling pencil leads glued to lolly sticks.

Electrical models and extension activities

Simple projects

Choose and do one of the following activities from the science activities book *Electricity* (Wayland):

1. Make a Morse code signaller (p.17).

2. Make a burglar alarm to go under the carpet (p.18).

3. Make an Iron Man with eyes that light up when metal objects touch its lips (p.14). Add your own switch to the idea.

4. Make a quiz with a bulb that lights up when you get a right answer (p.16).

5. Wire three bulbs so that they work like traffic lights (p.15).

Activities like this are presented in a number of books. In addition to Peacock, G. *Electricity* (Wayland, 1993), titles include: Richards, R. *An Early Start to Science* (Simon and Schuster, 1993), Richards, R. *An Early Start to Energy* (Simon and Schuster, 1993), and Baker, W. and Haslam, A. *Electricity* (Two Can, 1992). There is little point in you writing them out again.

Types of forces

Newtons

Gravity and magnetism operate at a distance.

Air resistance and friction only affect moving things.

Which forces?

This section does not deal in detail with floating forces or upthrust, which are discussed in the next chapter.

Forces are pulls and pushes. They are measured in newtons (N) and include:

gravity	the pull of the Earth, which is felt as weight
magnetism	the pull of a magnet on a magnetic material
air resistance	which slows objects moving through air
friction	which slows moving objects as they rub against each other
upthrust	the push up from water (or, to a lesser extent, air)
forces between molecules	that hold solids and liquids together
direct pushes	from a person, animal or machine
direct pulls	from a person, animal or machine

> Forces give excellent opportunities for investigations.

All objects pull.

Gravity diminishes with distance.

Gravity

All large objects have a pull of gravity. The gravity we experience and which affects our world is the pull of the Earth. Very sensitive instruments, which operate like plumb lines, can detect the pull of massive objects like mountains or ocean liners. The further away from an object you are the less is the force of its gravity.

> The greater the density of rock, the greater its gravitational pull.

Moon gravity

There must be gravity in space or planets and moons would not stay in orbit around each other. Similarly there must be gravity on the Earth's moon otherwise astronauts would not fall back to its surface after jumping.

Weight

Weight is the pull of gravity on a mass. Weight is measured in newtons and mass is measured in grams and kilograms. The bigger the mass the more that gravity pulls on it.

> Weight is a force.

Mass is always the same.

Weight changes

The mass of a house brick does not change. Regardless of where it is, it contains the same number of molecules and the same amount of matter. However, on another planet or the moon, the pull of gravity is different from the pull of the Earth's gravity. Here the brick would have a different weight. On the moon it would weigh one-sixth of its weight on Earth.

> The pull of the moon results in tides on Earth.

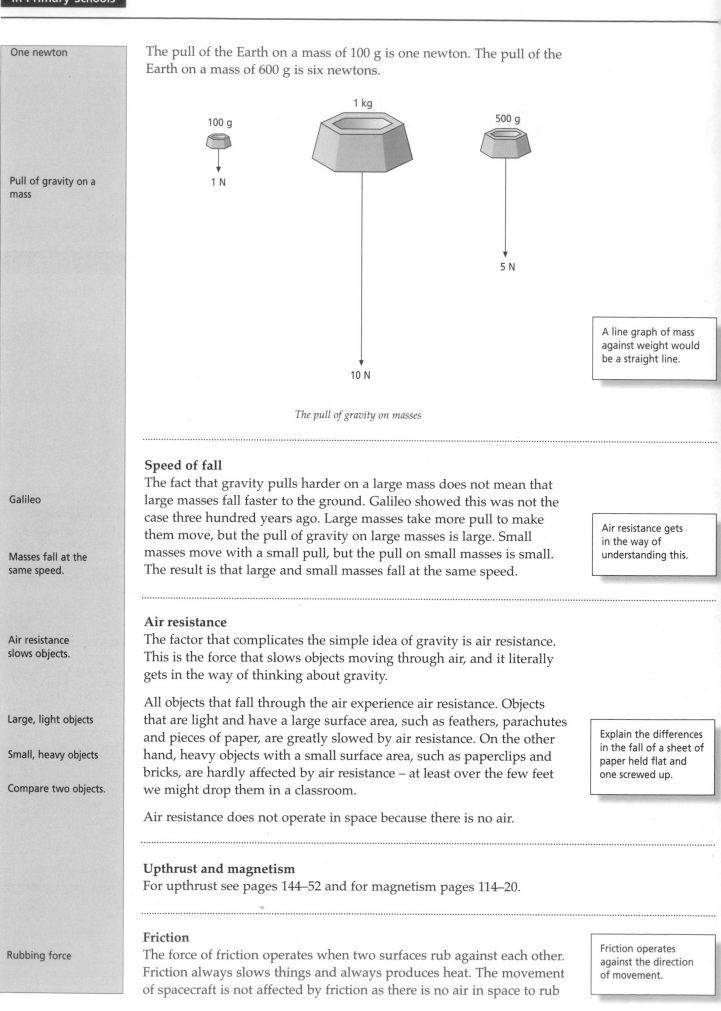

The pull of the Earth on a mass of 100 g is one newton. The pull of the Earth on a mass of 600 g is six newtons.

100 g	1 kg	500 g
1 N		5 N
	10 N	

The pull of gravity on masses

A line graph of mass against weight would be a straight line.

One newton

Pull of gravity on a mass

Speed of fall
The fact that gravity pulls harder on a large mass does not mean that large masses fall faster to the ground. Galileo showed this was not the case three hundred years ago. Large masses take more pull to make them move, but the pull of gravity on large masses is large. Small masses move with a small pull, but the pull on small masses is small. The result is that large and small masses fall at the same speed.

Galileo

Masses fall at the same speed.

Air resistance gets in the way of understanding this.

Air resistance
The factor that complicates the simple idea of gravity is air resistance. This is the force that slows objects moving through air, and it literally gets in the way of thinking about gravity.

All objects that fall through the air experience air resistance. Objects that are light and have a large surface area, such as feathers, parachutes and pieces of paper, are greatly slowed by air resistance. On the other hand, heavy objects with a small surface area, such as paperclips and bricks, are hardly affected by air resistance – at least over the few feet we might drop them in a classroom.

Air resistance does not operate in space because there is no air.

Air resistance slows objects.

Large, light objects

Small, heavy objects

Compare two objects.

Explain the differences in the fall of a sheet of paper held flat and one screwed up.

Upthrust and magnetism
For upthrust see pages 144–52 and for magnetism pages 114–20.

Friction
The force of friction operates when two surfaces rub against each other. Friction always slows things and always produces heat. The movement of spacecraft is not affected by friction as there is no air in space to rub

Rubbing force

Friction operates against the direction of movement.

against. That is why objects in space move at a constant speed and do not slow down.

Molecular forces

It is the forces between molecules that give solids their shape and make liquids retain a constant volume. These forces provide solids with their strength, which is why walls, floors and chairs can push back against heavy objects. Molecular forces also allow elastic bands to pull against the object that is stretching them.

There are no forces between gas molecules.

Direct push and pull

When a golfer hits a ball, or a bulldozer pushes some rock, or a tanker moves through the sea, or a person is pushed on a swing, there are direct pushes and pulls at work.

Once the push or pull stops, the object affected by the force starts to slow down. From the moment it leaves the racquet, a tennis ball is slowing down.

Direction of forces

Forces operate in specific directions. In diagrams, arrows are used to show the direction of the force. Long arrows indicate strong forces, short arrows indicate weak forces. Often more than one force is affecting an object at the same time. Here are some examples of this:

Parachutist at terminal velocity

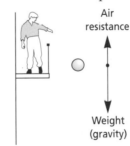

Ball just dropped from a balcony

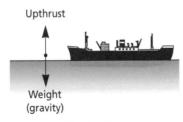

Floating ship

Ball (i) being kicked (ii) after being kicked

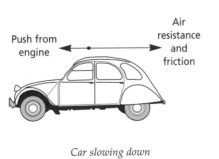

Car slowing down

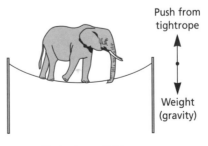

Elephant on a tightrope

Sidebar labels:
- Without friction, things carry on moving.
- Solid cohesion
- Elasticity
- Contact forces
- Force diagrams

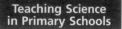

Forces can balance.	### Balanced forces

Forces balance when they cancel each other out. You know that forces are balanced when an object is:

- still
- moving at a constant speed in a straight line.

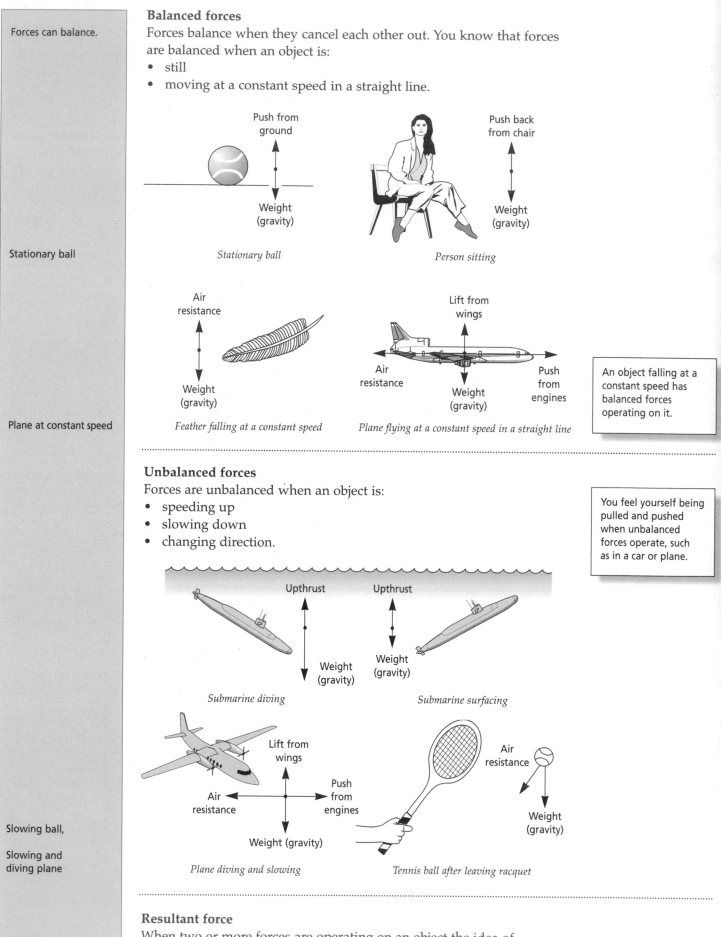

Stationary ball

Person sitting

Stationary ball	

Feather falling at a constant speed

Plane flying at a constant speed in a straight line

Plane at constant speed	An object falling at a constant speed has balanced forces operating on it.

Unbalanced forces

Forces are unbalanced when an object is:

- speeding up
- slowing down
- changing direction.

> You feel yourself being pulled and pushed when unbalanced forces operate, such as in a car or plane.

Submarine diving

Submarine surfacing

Slowing ball, Slowing and diving plane	*Plane diving and slowing* *Tennis ball after leaving racquet*

Resultant force

When two or more forces are operating on an object the idea of resultant force is very useful. Look at the size and the direction of the

Size of the forces	

force arrows in the diagrams above. If two arrows are opposed and one is longer than the other then there is a resultant force in the direction of the longer arrow.

Newton's laws

One law

Many of the ideas about forces are summarized in Newton's first law of motion:

> Objects stay still unless something makes them begin to move. Once they are moving, objects carry on going unless a force slows them down.

> Newton explained how the moon stays in orbit.

Common misconceptions

Direction of force

Model car slowing

Friction and air resistance

This area of science is more open to misunderstanding than any other. Children often associate direction of movement with direction of force. They think that if an object is moving in a particular direction then there must be a force pushing it in that direction. This is true only for as long as a force is being applied. For instance, when you push a model car there is a force in the direction of movement while your hand is in contact with the car. The moment you let go, the car is slowing down because of friction and, to some extent, air resistance.

> Forces do not always operate in the direction of movement.

Gravity

Moon gravity

Astronauts are affected by gravity.

When considering gravity many children think that there is no gravity on the moon or in space. They see pictures of astronauts bouncing around on the moon and floating in spacecraft and incorrectly conclude that there is no gravity beyond the Earth's atmosphere. Astronauts look as if they are unaffected by gravity, but they and their spacecraft are indeed orbiting around Earth under the influence of its gravity. For more about gravity, see page 133.

> Astronauts and their spacecraft orbit the Earth and so must be experiencing the effect of its gravity.

List of resources

Resources for studying types of forces

- spring balances calibrated in newtons
- toy cars
- ramps
- bricks
- tape measures
- scrap paper
- thin tissue for parachutes
- thin plastic for parachutes
- fish shapes cut from a variety of papers
- clean washing-up liquid bottle
- cotton thread
- paper clips
- sticky tape
- balloons

> Set up kits of equipment that can be used regularly, such as an air resistance kit, a floating kit, and a friction kit.

- stopwatches
- selection of very light objects
- selection of balls
- springs
- weight carriers
- hoops

Summary of the programmes of study

Key Stage 1 Sc4: 2a–d	Children should be taught about the following:
	• describing the movement of familiar things
	• pulls and pushes are examples of forces
	• forces can make things speed up, slow down or change direction
	• forces can change the shape of things
Key Stage 2 Sc4: 1c–h	• objects have weight because of the gravitational attraction between them and the Earth
	• friction as a force that slows moving objects
	• when springs and elastic bands are stretched they exert a force on whatever is stretching or compressing them
	• forces act in particular directions
	• forces can balance
	• unbalanced forces can make things speed up or slow down

Key Stage 1 classroom activities

Make it move

Flapping fish

- Play with paper fish. How many ways can you make flapping fish move? Have a flapping fish race.

Make it move.

- Look at a small toy figure. Think of ways to make the figure move. Include sliding down a ramp, floating in a boat, sliding down a rope, and travelling in a car.

- When the children are changing for PE talk about which clothes they pull and which they push.

Pushes and pulls make things move.

You pull something when you move it towards yourself. You push something away. An object that is stationary needs a push or pull to make it start moving. This paraphrase of part of Newton's first law of motion is easily understood by young children.

> When doing these activities ask the children what force is making the object move.

Large and small pushes

Small forces

- Investigate which objects in the classroom can be moved by blowing or pushing with a straw.

Large forces

- With teacher demonstration and supervision look at moving heavier objects. Can you push an empty chair on casters? Can you push the same chair with a child or a teacher sitting on it?

Newton's second law for infants

Large pushes result in large movements of small objects or small movements of large objects.

> Blowing or pushing with a straw is safe and avoids children hurting themselves by trying to push heavy objects.

Slowing down and speeding up

Hoops and balls

- Play with hoops and balls. Feel what happens when you make them start moving (apply a force). Feel what you have to do to stop them moving. A force is needed to make them change direction.

> Discuss what you have to do to make them change direction.

Speeding up and slowing down

Unbalanced forces are operating when an object speeds up and slows down. A push from a child will speed up a ball or hoop. Friction and air resistance will slow it down.

Ramps

How far does a car roll off a ramp?

- Let the children roll a car down a shallow ramp. How far does the car travel? How fast does it travel? Make the ramp steeper. What do the children notice now?

> This provides an excellent context for scientific investigation.

- Do the same with balls.

Acceleration

Gravity pulls cars and balls down ramps. If the ramp is steep, the ball or car accelerates (gets faster) all the way down the ramp.

Bubbles and feathers

- Blow bubbles in the playground. Make the bubbles go upwards. Make them go to one side. Make them hover in one place.

> Talk about the pushes and pulls on the bubbles. Do similar activities with feathers.

Very light objects are relatively unaffected by gravity.

Very light objects like bubbles and feathers are moved easily by small forces such as the push from moving air. They eventually fall to the ground because of the pull of gravity.

Change shape

Forces change the shape of objects.

- Ask the children to make three balls of clay and squash them using different masses or heavy books.

> When working with clay, talk about the forces – pulls and pushes – that change its shape.

Materials such as clay are plastic. It is easy to change their shape, and once in a new shape or position they stay in it.

Key Stage 2a classroom activities

Stationary objects

Forces are in balance when an object is still.

- Discuss the forces acting on stationary objects. Tell the children that the pull of gravity is always there. Ask someone to hold a book at arm's length for a few seconds to feel the pull of gravity.

- Look at a simple, stationary floating object. Tell the children about the push from the water and the pull of gravity.

This is another example of Newton's first law in action. The forces on an object, including a floating object, are balanced when it is still. On Earth the force of gravity is always present. Normally a still object is balanced by a push from the ground or upthrust from water or the air.

> Balanced forces are described on page 136.

Measuring forces

All forces can be measured in newtons.

- Pull objects with spring balances and note the amount of force needed to move them. For example, investigate the force needed to pull a bag, drag a shoe, open a door or lift a mass.

Forces are calculated by examining the stretch of a spring. Spring balances are really forcemeters. Strictly speaking they are not measuring mass but the pull of gravity on a mass, and should therefore measure in newtons. However, the pull of gravity is directly related to mass, so in fact spring balances do give an accurate indication of mass.

> Use a variety of spring balances. Ideally they should measure in both newtons and grams.

Stretchy forces

> Springs and other stretchy objects pull back against the things that are pulling them.

- Feel the pull back of an elastic band when you pull it. Feel the push back from a spring when you push it.

- Look at the amount that rubber bands, springs or stretchy cloth stretch when you attach weights to them.

> Put weights in the toes of coloured stockings. Do red stockings stretch more than black stockings?

The force of attraction between the molecules in objects like a spring or rubber band resists the forces that are pulling them apart. In this way the molecules can pull back against a force that is stretching them.

Key Stage 2b classroom activities

One newton

> Weight is measured in newtons.

- Use a spring balance to weigh masses. Fill in a table like this:

Mass	Pull of gravity
100 g	1 N
200 g	2 N
300 g	3 N

> All forces can be measured using a spring balance.

- Find the pull of gravity on objects. Fill in a table like this:

Object	Pull of gravity
bag	3.5 N
chair	20 N

> 100g = 1N

The pull of gravity on a mass of 100 grams is one newton (1 N). The pull of gravity and the mass are directly related.

Air resistance

> Air resistance affects the way paper falls.

- Drop one piece of paper edge-on and one piece flat. Which falls faster? Screw one piece into a ball and compare how it falls with a flat piece.

> Drop the pieces of paper from hip height. Dropping them from any higher makes their fall unpredictable.

- Make whatever changes you like to the other pieces of paper and compare how they fall with a flat piece.

If all the pieces of paper are the same weight then the pull of gravity will also be the same on them all, no matter what shape you form them into. A sheet of paper dropped flat will have a great deal more air resistance acting on it than an identical sheet dropped edge-on, folded or in a ball.

Light for their size

- Compare the speed of drop of four or five objects that are light for their size. In this investigation concentrate on the air resistance slowing the objects.

Balanced forces

Terminal velocity

- Give each child a piece of cotton wool. Who can make theirs fall the slowest?

- Look carefully at the way in which a very light feather falls. It neither speeds up nor slows down for most of its fall. This constant speed indicates that the forces acting on it are balanced.

Large, light objects fall slowly because the small pull of gravity on them is quickly balanced by air resistance. The speed at which the pull of gravity becomes balanced by air resistance is called terminal velocity. Relatively few children will understand the concept of terminal velocity, but you can challenge the most able with it and still give the rest of the children a very worthwhile practical experience.

Air resistance increases with surface area.

Parachutes

- Make parachutes of different surface areas. Calculate the areas. Time each parachute's fall. Graph the results. Draw force diagrams for each parachute.

> Thin plastic and tissue paper make the best parachutes.

- Time how long a parachute takes to fall when you add different masses to it. A large mass will lead to the parachute having a faster terminal velocity.

Parachutes work by increasing the air resistance of objects attached to them. With the same mass beneath, larger parachutes will fall at a slower speed than smaller parachutes.

More air resistance

Air resistance can slow a moving object rapidly.

- Screw up scrap paper into balls of different sizes. Throw them one at a time with the same force and measure how far they travel. Throw each one three times to obtain an average. Draw force diagrams for each ball.

> Make a simple catapult to fire the paper balls with consistent force.

A rope runway

- Let the children make a rope runway for small toys. Add cloaks to the toys and note the effect of air resistance on their travel. Ensure that the rope runway is located in a safe place in the classroom.

Balls of paper

A ball of paper with a large diameter will encounter more air resistance than a ball with a small diameter.

> Try this now with some of the scrap paper that teachers always seem to accumulate!

Force diagrams

The only forces acting on the balls are gravity and air resistance. Gravity is the same in each case, so it is air resistance that is making the difference.

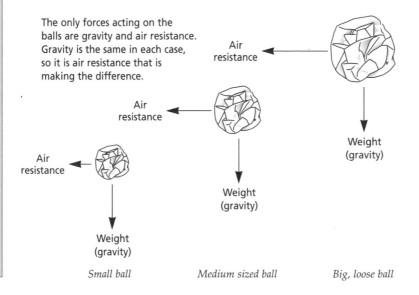

Small ball   *Medium sized ball*   *Big, loose ball*

Teaching strategy: Key Stage 2b workcards

Adapt the cards.

Introduction

Four workcards follow for Key Stage 2b. These can easily be adapted for use with Key Stage 2a. They can be used either as:

- a starting point for the whole class to work in groups of three on the same activity
- a circus of activities.

> With the whole class working together it is possible to compare results.

Simple equipment

No unusual or expensive equipment is needed, so equipping the class to do the activities is relatively easy. Activities of this kind involve a great deal of movement and it may be advantageous to have activities of a similar kind taking place simultaneously. However, you will need to clear plenty of space in the classroom or work in a room with more space.

Use a large space.

Make the focus clear.

COMPARING LIGHT OBJECTS
Very light objects fall slowly because of air resistance.

What you need
A selection of five very light objects such as:
- a feather
- a scrap of paper
- a scrap of tissue paper
- a small piece of polystyrene
- a scrap of plastic from a bag
- a piece of wool
- a piece of cotton wool

What to do
1. Choose five very light objects to test.
2. Predict which will fall fastest and which will fall slowest. Write a list of your predictions.
3. Test your predictions. Repeat the tests to check your results.

Recording
1. Write a report about what you did. Describe what happened. Explain why you think some things fell faster than others.
2. Tell your teacher about how you could improve your test.

> Objects that are heavy for their size are not affected much by air resistance.

Predicting

Testing

Reporting

Evaluating

> Less able or younger children can make comparisons about the different falls rather than timing them.

FALLING FASTER
Sheets of paper fall slowly when dropped flat. They can be made to fall faster by giving them less air resistance.

What you need
About ten sheets of A4 scrap paper

What to do
1. Hold two sheets of paper in front of you. Hold them at hip height. Drop both of them flat.

   Do this a few times. Do the sheets usually fall at the same speed?

2. Change the way you drop one of the sheets. You could crumple it up, fold it in two, or rip it in half first – or you could drop it on its edge.

   Remember to drop a flat sheet with it, as a comparison.

Recording
1. Write about what you did to change the sheets. What effect did this have in each case?
2. Explain your results.

> Dropping the paper flat maximizes the air resistance.

Altering one factor

Offer suggestions.

> All these procedures except one will reduce air resistance. The pieces of the ripped sheet will fall at about the same speed as the whole sheet.

Interpreting

Controlling variables

A ready-made table

Graphing

Looking for patterns

Minimal equipment

Designing a test

Simple table

Using evidence

CHANGING THE AREA OF PARACHUTES
One parachute is half the size of another. Does this mean its falls twice as fast?

What you need
- Squared paper
- Opened-out plastic bags
- Cotton
- Small weights (e.g. made of Blu-Tack)
- Timer

What to do
1. Make plastic parachutes of different areas, such as 100 cm², 200 cm², 300 cm² and 400 cm².
2. When you make the parachutes, think about what factors you will keep the same.
3. Time the drop of the parachutes you make.

Recording
1. Record your results in a chart like this:

AREA	LENGTH OF TIME			
	1ST DROP	2ND DROP	3RD DROP	AVERAGE
100 cm²				
200 cm²				
300 cm²				
400 cm²				

2. Draw a stick graph or a line graph of your results.
3. Describe any patterns you notice in your graph. Does a parachute that is half the size of another fall twice as fast?

> If you have insufficient timers or stopwatches, teach the children to count finger taps.

> This work ties in with investigating area in maths.

SCREWED-UP PAPER
The distance you can throw a very light object depends on the air resistance slowing it down.

What you need
- Scrap A4 paper
- Measuring tape or trundle wheel

What to do
1. Lightly screw up a piece of scrap paper. How far can you throw it?
2. Screw up another piece as tightly as possible. How far can you throw this one?

Design a test to find the information needed to fill in this table:

APPROXIMATE WIDTH OF BALL OF PAPER	DISTANCE THROWN		
	1ST THROW	2ND THROW	3RD THROW
10 cm			
8 cm			
6 cm			
4 cm			

Recording
1. Explain what you did and what you found out. Use graphs and drawings to help.
2. Explain why the tightly screwed-up piece travels so much further.

> Bullets are heavy and streamlined so that they travel quickly and far.

> Smaller surface area means less air resistance.

> Leaving the task open like this allows children scope for their own ideas.

Floating and sinking

Displacement pushes a liquid out of the way.	**Displacement** When an object is placed in water it displaces some of the water. This is true both for objects that float and those that sink.
Support from the liquid	**Buoyancy** When an object displaces water it is pushed up or supported by the water. This is true both for floaters and sinkers. This 'push up' is called buoyancy or upthrust. The amount of upthrust on an object is the same as the weight of the water displaced by the object. This is true both for floaters and sinkers.
Upthrust on floaters	An object that floats in water experiences an upthrust that is equal to its total weight. A floater is effectively weightless. The forces of gravity and upthrust are in balance (see the diagram of the forces acting on a floating ship on page 135).

Displacement

When an object is placed in water it displaces some of the water. This is true both for objects that float and those that sink.

Buoyancy

When an object displaces water it is pushed up or supported by the water. This is true both for floaters and sinkers. This 'push up' is called buoyancy or upthrust. The amount of upthrust on an object is the same as the weight of the water displaced by the object. This is true both for floaters and sinkers.

An object that floats in water experiences an upthrust that is equal to its total weight. A floater is effectively weightless. The forces of gravity and upthrust are in balance (see the diagram of the forces acting on a floating ship on page 135).

> When upthrust is equal to the weight of the object the forces are balanced.

An object that sinks in water loses some weight. The weight lost by a sinker is equal to the weight of the water that the sinker displaces (see the diagram of the forces acting on a diving submarine on page 136).

Density

Density is the mass of one cubic centimetre of a material or object.

  Density = mass divided by volume

The density of water is 1 gram per cubic centimetre (1 g/cm^3)

  Objects that float have a density less than 1 g/cm^3
  Objects that sink have a density more than 1 g/cm^3

> Instead of using this term, you can say that things are 'light for their size' or 'heavy for their size'.

Ships

Ships float, even if they are made of a dense material like steel, because they are hollow. The air inside them is very light. The total density of the hollow steel and air is less than 1g/cm^3. A ship displaces a weight of water equal to its own weight.

> Focus on the volume of water displaced by the ship.

Language

In primary science children should try to explain what they feel and see using appropriate language. Many will not be ready to cope with

Complex words	'density' but they may use phrases like 'the size stays the same but it gets heavier than the water'. This is far more valuable to their understanding than parroting Archimedes' principle.

Archimedes

Tell older children the story of Archimedes. He was asked by the king to come up with a way of finding out whether the royal jeweller was cheating him by adding base metal to his crowns; the king felt that the crowns were 'light for their size' but could prove no wrongdoing. Archimedes was supposedly in his bath when the thought struck him that he could find the volume of a crown by seeing how much water it displaced. All he needed to do then was divide the crown's weight by its volume. This would give him a precise figure (for its density). If he knew this figure for real gold he could test the crown to see if it was the same.

> Archimedes was in his bath when he had his insight into how to measure the volume of irregularly shaped objects.

Common misconceptions

Upthrust or lack of gravity?

Children may notice the reduction in the pull on a spring balance holding a stone or a ball as the object is immersed in water. They may incorrectly conclude that gravity does not act very effectively through water. To help them work this through you may need to emphasize the way in which water pushes up against things like balls and balloons when you hold them underwater (see page 146). Stress the connection between the water that is displaced and the push back from the water.

Volume or area?

Another common misconception surrounds the reason why boats and rafts float. Whilst scientists believe that it is the volume of water displaced by a boat that makes it float, some children and adults think it is the area of the bottom of the boat. There seems to be a connection in many minds between the reason why snow shoes stop you sinking in snow and the reason why boats do not sink.

Show that area does not play a significant part in making things float by getting some plasticine and spreading it out flat. Make sure it does not dome up or air may get trapped underneath when you try to float it. A flat sheet of plasticine will not float but a piece shaped like a boat, which displaces more water, will.

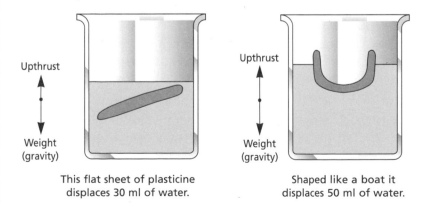

This flat sheet of plasticine displaces 30 ml of water.

Shaped like a boat it displaces 50 ml of water.

Upthrust and the volume of water displaced

List of resources

Resources for studying floating and sinking	

- variety of balls
- calibrated containers
- scales
- spring balances
- rocks

- plasticine
- toy boats
- containers to make boats
- aquaria
- elastic bands

Summary of the programmes of study

Key Stage 1 Sc4: 2b	
Key Stage 2 Sc4: 1f–h	

Children should be taught about the following:
- pulls and pushes are examples of forces
- forces act in particular directions
- forces can balance

Key Stage 1 classroom activities

Floating or sunk?

Some things float and some things sink.

Candles do not have air in them.

Has it sunk?

- Let the children see which of a range of objects float and which sink. Before they begin ask them to predict which they think will float. Use a see-through aquarium so that they can get a side view of the floating objects above and below the water line. Select several items to provoke discussion: candles (there is clearly no air in these), plastic practice balls (they are hollow and full of holes) and rubbers (they feel fairly heavy but some float).

- When considering if an object is floating or has sunk encourage the children to use only these two categories: floater and sinker. Some children try to use a third category for objects that are almost submerged but still floating. Try to steer them away from this unhelpful idea.

Floating objects can be submerged.

When an object is on the bottom of the container it has sunk. Otherwise objects are floating. Even objects that are completely submerged, yet not on the bottom, are floating. In air, helium balloons and hot-air balloons are described as floating even when they are hanging motionless in the air or are just a few metres off the ground.

> Try to use objects whose performance will be hard to predict. Polystyrene or iron objects are not going to make the children pause for a second.

Displacement and upthrust

Push a ball down into water.

- Supervise children pushing a large ball down into a half-full tank of water. The water level will rise. Push the ball further. Watch the water level continue to rise. The force with which the children have to push increases as more water is displaced.

Water pushes back.

It is the push back or upthrust from the water that makes objects float. When an object displaces more water it experiences more upthrust.

> Children will be able to feel the water pushing back. It is almost impossible to submerge an inflated beach ball.

Load some boats

Ready-made boats

- Give the children a range of objects to use as boats: margarine containers, the top halves of plastic bottles with their lids, plastic egg boxes, foil dishes. Let them load up the boats with marbles and see which one carries most.

Boats can carry weights because as they displace more water they get more upthrust from the water.

Displacement

These boats give the fun and experience of floating without the difficulty often found using plasticine boats.

Key Stage 2a classroom activities

Floating objects

Pull of gravity

• Let the children feel the weight of objects like a candle, a block of wood or a bottle of glue. Hang one object at a time from an elastic band and each time see how much the band is stretched. Ask the children what they think will happen when they dip the object into water. They will notice that the band goes completely slack. Ask them for their idea of why this happens.

The weight of floating objects is completely taken by upthrust.

When you dip wood or wax into water, upthrust pushes vertically upwards against it. This counters all the pull of gravity and removes all the pull on your hand. The push from the water completely relaxes the elastic band.

Talk about the direction of the forces on the wood or wax. Remind the children that gravity pulls down and upthrust from the water pushes up.

Rocks on bands

Rocks stretch rubber bands.

• Attach rocks, and other objects that sink, to elastic bands. See how much each one stretches the band. Ask the children what they think will happen to the stretch of the band when a rock is dipped into water. Ask them to explain their ideas.

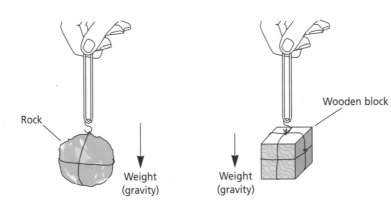

Stretch in air

The pull of gravity stretches the elastic band. In air, your hand gives a balancing pull in the opposite direction.

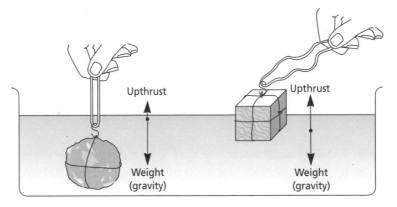

Stretch in water

When doing this work refer to upthrust from the water as a force which works upwards against gravity.

| Dip the rock into water. | • Let the children dip the rock into water, feel the reduction in pull and see the stretch on the band relax as the object is immersed. |

• Now lift the rock out of the water. Let the children feel and see the band stretch again.

Upthrust works in the opposite direction to gravity.

When you dip a rock into water upthrust pushes vertically upwards against it. This counters some of the pull of gravity and reduces the pull on your hand. This push from the water reduces the stretch of the elastic band.

More boats

Make boats.

• Make a boat by cutting the top ten centimetres off a clear plastic bottle, and use this top part as your boat. Put marbles in the boat to make it float upright. Float it in a calibrated container. Add more marbles and see what happens to the water level in the container. Also look at the water level on the side of the boat.

Water levels

Equal forces

To float, a boat must get a push back from water equal to its weight. When the boat is loaded with marbles it sinks lower, meaning that it is displacing more water.

> This activity extends a similar one introduced at Key Stage 1. Note here the possibilities for more numerical work and the use of measures of volume.

Key Stage 2b classroom activities

Measuring upthrust

Weighing in air and water

• Show the children how to use spring balances to measure the weight of objects in air. Do this with objects that float and with some that sink.

• Weigh the same objects immersed in water.

Recording table

• Ask the children to complete a table showing:
  weight in air
  weight in water
  difference in weight

> The weight of all floating objects will be zero on the spring balance.

Upthrust

Upthrust pushes up objects in water. Spring balances show how much upthrust water gives to an object. Objects that float experience upthrust equal to the force of gravity.

Which unit of measurement?

Units are a problem here. Ideally we should be measuring upthrust and the pull of gravity in newtons (N), which are the units of force. But this introduces decimals (e.g. 3.5 newtons instead of 350 grams) and a unit of measurement that is less familiar to children than grams. It is possible to compromise simply by talking about the reading on the spring balance. Provided you use either grams or newtons consistently there should be little confusion.

Grams measure mass only.

> Teach the children how to use a spring balance accurately. They will need to avoid parallax error, which is explained on page 50 in *Science for Primary Teachers*, the companion volume in this series.

The weight of displaced water

Finding displacement

• Fill a calibrated container to a convenient level, such as 100 cm³. Float a ball in the container. How much water does it displace when floating? How much does this amount of water weigh? What is the weight of the object?

> 1 cm³ = 1 ml. Both units measure volume.

An example

A ball has a mass of 70 grams. It floats in water, so it must have an upthrust that is equal to its weight (0.7 N or 70 grams). To experience this amount of upthrust it must have displaced 70 cm³ of water.

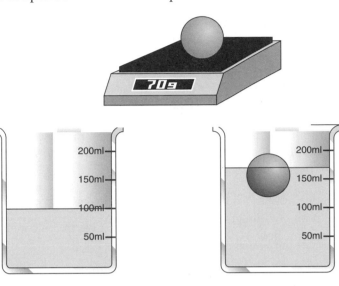

The weight of 100 ml of water is 100 g.

The weight of water displaced by the ball is equal to the ball's weight.

> The weight of water displaced by a floating object is equal to its weight.

Weight and upthrust

Boats float because they displace water.

The displacement of boats

* Take a plasticine ball and weigh it. Put it into a calibrated container of water and watch it sink. How much water does it displace? How much does this amount of water weigh? Now make the ball into the shape of a boat. Float it in a container of water. How much water does it displace? How much does this amount of water weigh?

> The weight of a boat is often expressed as its 'displacement' (of water).

A ball of plasticine does not displace sufficient water to make it float. Made into a boat, it displaces a much greater volume of water, and the upthrust from the water is enough to balance the pull of gravity on the plasticine.

This piece of plasticine weighs 90 g and has a volume of 40 cm³.

1 cm³ is the same volume as 1 ml. The weight of 100 ml of water is 100 g.

Why boats float

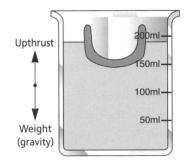

In a ball the plasticine displaces 40 cm³ of water, not enough to balance its weight.

Shaped as a boat it displaces 90 cm³ of water. This balances its weight.

Displacement volume, weight and upthrust

What is important is the volume of water that the boat displaces. The amount of air in the boat shape is not directly responsible for the boat floating.

Find the mass.

Salt and fresh water

- Challenge the children to find the difference in mass between the same volumes of salty water and fresh water.

Density of water

Fresh water (e.g. tap water) has a density of 1 g/cm³. Salt water has a greater density than fresh water. When objects are immersed in salt water they do not need to displace as much of it as they would fresh water to get the same push back.

> 1 cm³ of salt water has a greater mass than 1 cm³ of fresh water.

Swimming

You will notice how much higher you float in the sea than you do in a swimming pool. Swimmers in the Dead Sea, which has an extremely high salt content, float very high in the water.

Floating eggs

Objects in salt water

- Show the children that a bar of soap and an egg will float in salt water but not in fresh (tap) water. Wrap the soap in cling film to stop the water going cloudy. Hard boil the egg to avoid nasty accidents.

> Make the salty water as salty as possible to ensure the children see a difference in the way the objects behave in the two types of water.

Density of soap

An egg and a bar of soap both have a densities a little higher than the density of fresh water, so they do not get enough upthrust from the water to make them float. Conversely, salt water has a density a little higher than the egg and the soap, so both float in it.

For example, a bar of soap with a mass of 100 g and a volume of 95 cm³ will sink in fresh water because the soap has the greater density. The upthrust from the water is 0.95 N, less than the soap's weight of 1 N.

> Challenge the children to find or make things which float in salt water but sink in tap water.

Plimsoll line

Ships are painted with a Plimsoll line to stop them being overloaded in salt water and sinking when they reach fresh water.

Dropper pipettes are sometimes used for ear drops.

Cartesian diver

- Make a 'diver' by half filling a dropper pipette with water. Attach paper clips to the stem of the pipette. Place the diver in a beaker of water and add more clips or Blu-Tack until it is just floating.

> Do this in a wide-necked beaker. It makes it easy to remove and adjust the diver if it sinks, or floats too high.

- Now carefully remove the diver and its weights from the beaker and place it in a plastic bottle full of water. Put on the lid. Squeeze the bottle. Watch the diver fill with water and sink. Release the bottle and watch the water leave the dropper. It will now float to the top of the bottle.

Density of the diver

As you squeeze the bottle you increase the pressure inside it. This pushes water into the pipette, so that the density of the diver becomes greater than the density of the surrounding water. The diver no longer displaces its own weight in water, so it sinks. When you release the bottle the pressure inside it drops. The air in the diver expands, pushing some of the water out of the pipette. This reduces the density of the diver, and it floats.

> Submarines alter their density by adding water to their tanks to sink and expelling it when they want to float.

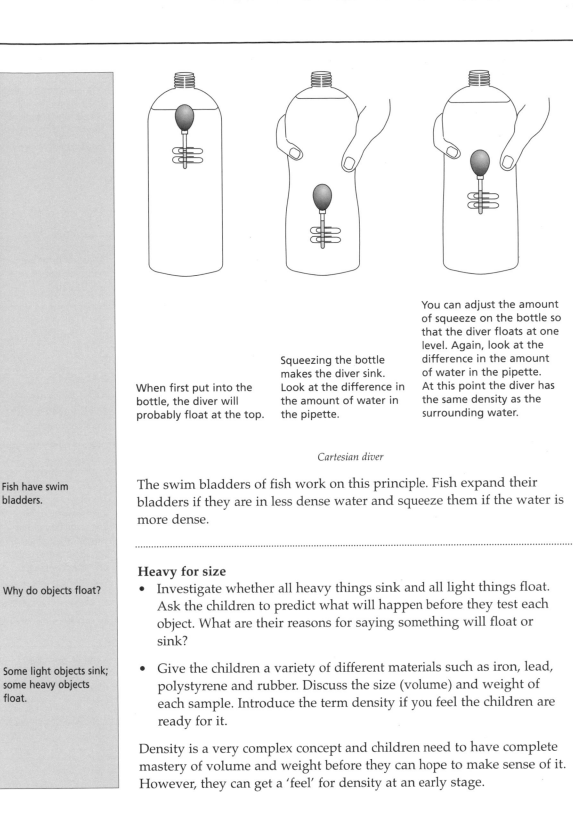

When first put into the bottle, the diver will probably float at the top.

Squeezing the bottle makes the diver sink. Look at the difference in the amount of water in the pipette.

You can adjust the amount of squeeze on the bottle so that the diver floats at one level. Again, look at the difference in the amount of water in the pipette. At this point the diver has the same density as the surrounding water.

Cartesian diver

Fish have swim bladders.

The swim bladders of fish work on this principle. Fish expand their bladders if they are in less dense water and squeeze them if the water is more dense.

Why do objects float?

Heavy for size

- Investigate whether all heavy things sink and all light things float. Ask the children to predict what will happen before they test each object. What are their reasons for saying something will float or sink?

Some light objects sink; some heavy objects float.

- Give the children a variety of different materials such as iron, lead, polystyrene and rubber. Discuss the size (volume) and weight of each sample. Introduce the term density if you feel the children are ready for it.

Density is a very complex concept and children need to have complete mastery of volume and weight before they can hope to make sense of it. However, they can get a 'feel' for density at an early stage.

> Objects that are denser than water sink. Objects less dense than water float. In other words, objects that are light for their size float and objects that are heavy for their size sink.

Teaching strategy: teacher demonstrations

Discussion and exposition

Introduction

Work on floating and sinking can be done as a series of teacher demonstrations followed by limited small-group activity. This approach acknowledges the fact that equipment is difficult to organize for these activities, which are potentially very messy, and that the quality of the discussion between pupils and teacher is the most important factor. There are also relatively few opportunities for open-ended investigations in floating and sinking.

The following sequence of teacher demonstrations covers several weeks and is relevant to the whole of Key Stage 2. Teachers will want to use their judgement about how far to take this work.

It is important to keep focusing on the main theme and not allow too many distractions.

Reduction of stretch	1	Show the children that the pull on a thin elastic band attached to a rock is reduced when you dip the rock into water. Show them that when you attach an object that floats to the elastic band then dip the object in water, the band goes entirely slack. Let all the children feel these effects. Ask them to draw pictures and write about what they notice.
Loading boats Simple table	2	Make a simple boat out of the top ten centimetres of a clear plastic bottle. Float it in a large calibrated container. Load it with marbles. See how the boat sinks lower and displaces more water as more marbles are added. Give small groups the opportunity to experiment with this equipment. Ask them to fill in a table like the one below, make notes and complete diagrams.

The stability of bottle boats increases as marbles are added.

Number of marbles	Level of water in jug
5	
10	
15	
20	

This is a good subject for a bar chart.

Weigh in air and water. Upthrust = weight Misconception	3	Show the children how to weigh objects in air and water. Demonstrate that floating objects apparently weigh nothing in water. This is because upthrust on the object is equal to the object's weight. Show the children the table below. Demonstrate how to fill it in.

Object	Weight in air	Weight in water	Difference in weights

The reduction in the weight of an object is the same as the weight of water the object displaces.

If time and equipment allow, the children should do weighing tasks in groups. Discuss why objects seem to weigh less in water. Take care to check what the children think is happening. Some may come to the wrong conclusion that gravity is affected by water. You may not want to tackle this misconception head-on. It will help you and the children to refer frequently to 'upthrust from the water'.

Displacement Weight of object	4	Float a fairly heavy object such as a cricket ball or a sealed glue container in a calibrated vessel. Notice how much water it displaces. Weigh the object on an accurate kitchen scale in grams. (As already discussed, it is not proper to weigh force in grams, but it is far more convenient to do so here.) Notice that the volume of water displaced and the weight of the object are similar (ideally the same). Record in a simple table:

If the object is fairly heavy yet compact it is easier to make the readings.

Type of ball	Weight of the ball	Volume of water displaced by the ball

Floating plasticine 100 g of plasticine	5	Try to float a ball of plasticine. This is impossible. Notice how much water the plasticine displaces as it sinks. Make the same piece into a boat shape. With care you can make it float. See how much water the boat shape displaces. Challenge the children in groups to make a boat out of 100 grams of plasticine that will carry the largest number of marbles. Ask the children to record what they did using diagrams and tables, and in writing.

Infants and lower junior children find it almost impossible to make plasticine boats. Use containers as boats.

Fresh and salt water	6	Find the mass of 1000 ml of fresh water and 1000 ml of salt water. Notice that 1 ml of fresh water has a mass of 1 gram. Colour one sample of water red and the other blue. If there is time set the children the task of weighing different amounts of each type of water.
Soap floats in salty water.	7	Demonstrate that soap will float in salt water but not in fresh. Ask the most able children to describe the forces at work, and less able children to write an illustrated description of what happened.

Light

Waves

Visible-light detectors

Umbra and penumbra

Light travels in straight lines.

What is light?

Light is an electromagnetic wave. Other waves in the same spectrum range from gamma rays, x-rays and ultraviolet waves through visible light to infra-red waves, microwaves and radiowaves. If we replaced our eyes, which are visible-light detectors, with ultraviolet or x-ray detectors, we would see ultraviolet or x-ray rays reflected off objects in the environment.

Radio telescopes like the one at Jodrell Bank look at objects which emit radio waves rather than light.

Shadows

Shadows are formed when an object blocks the path of light coming from a source. If the shadow is not completely sharp there is a dark region in the middle called the umbra with a less dark area around it called the penumbra.

Shadows are often used to demonstrate that light travels in straight lines, as are pinhole cameras. In the diagram of a pinhole camera below you can see how rays of light produced by or reflected off a candle pass through the tiny pinhole and continue travelling until they hit the greaseproof paper screen, where they form an image. The image is upside down because the light rays making it have travelled in a straight line.

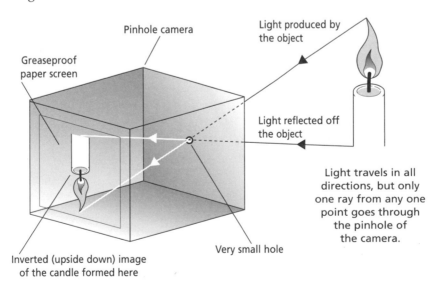

Pinhole camera

Light produced by the object

Greaseproof paper screen

Light reflected off the object

Light travels in all directions, but only one ray from any one point goes through the pinhole of the camera.

Inverted (upside down) image of the candle formed here

Very small hole

A pinhole camera

Reflection

All surfaces reflect light. Even bumpy and dull surfaces do so or we would not be able to see them. Only shiny surfaces like glass and polished metal reflect light in such a way that the reflected light forms images. To form an image light must be reflected from a surface at the same angle that it hits it. In other words the angle of incidence should equal the angle of reflection.

> Mirrors are made from a sheet of glass coated with a thin layer of silver.

Refraction

When light leaves one medium, such as air, and enters another, such as glass, it changes direction. It does this once, at the boundary between the two media; it does not change direction by gradually curving in the new medium. You can see this when looking at the way light travels through a triangular prism. Refraction is the reason why convex lenses focus light at a point.

> Refraction causes pencils in glasses of water to appear bent.

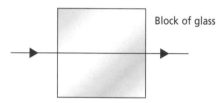

Block of glass

When light hits the boundary between two media at an angle of 90°, refraction does not affect its direction of travel.

Triangular prism

At any other angle, the direction of its travel is bent. This happens at both boundaries between two media.

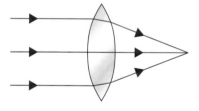

Almost all the light travelling through a lens is bent. Different parts of the lens bend it by differing amounts. In a convex lens this leads to light being focused.

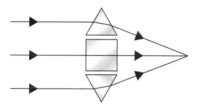

The direction of light passing through the centre of the lens is unaltered. Elsewhere it is bent, just as it would be if travelling through a triangular prism.

Convex lenses

Our eyes use a lens to focus light reflected from or produced by an object into an image on the retina. When an object is far away this lens needs to be thin to focus the light. When an object is close the lens must be fat to achieve focus.

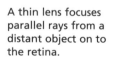

A thin lens focuses parallel rays from a distant object on to the retina.

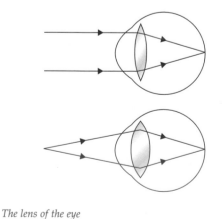

A fat lens focuses rays from an object close to the eye on to the retina.

> Small muscles in the eye change the shape of the lens, allowing it to focus in this way.

The lens of the eye

Common misconceptions

Beams from the eyes

How can light travel?

Correct language

Varied brightness

Active seeing

Children often think that seeing is an active process. They imagine that our eyes have beams that go out and see the environment, rather like radar and the way it 'sees' planes. The idea that seeing is a passive process in which light is reflected off objects into our eyes is not easily accepted by some children.

The concept that light travels can be problematic; light travels so quickly that it is impossible for us to see it set off from one point and arrive at another. To our senses light does not travel; it is instantly there. However, the concept that light travels is fundamental to understanding about light. The language you use when teaching about light is very important. For instance, refer to 'the light from the candle *travelling* to your eye' and discuss the way we see 'light from the lamp *hitting* the paper and *bouncing* into our eyes'.

The stars are in the sky all the time but we cannot see them by day because of the brilliance of the sun. You can help children understand this by talking about being dazzled by headlights or a bright torch.

> Superman is often shown as having active x-ray vision.

> Language can confuse. 'Cast your glance over this' implies that seeing is active.

List of resources

Resources for studying light

- torches
- small models
- colour filters
- kaleidoscopes
- a variety of transparent and translucent materials
- a very dark room or large cupboard
- mirrors
- mirror card
- glow stars
- equipment for a simple electrical circuit
- visual toys (including those from cereal boxes)

Summary of the programmes of study

Key Stage 1 Sc4: 3a–b

Key Stage 2 Sc4: 3a–d

Children should be taught about the following:
- light comes from a variety of sources
- darkness is the absence of light

- light travels from a source
- light cannot pass through some materials and this leads to the formation of shadows
- light is reflected from surfaces
- we see light sources because light from them enters our eyes

Key Stage 1 classroom activities

Light comes from many sources.

Light sources
- Discuss light sources and ask the children to list all the light sources they know.

> Sort these into natural and artificial sources.

Varied brightness	• Make three simple electrical circuits with a battery and bulb. Use a worn-out battery to make a dim light, an average battery to make a bright light and a new battery to make a very bright light. Ask the children to compare the brightness of these different light sources and rank them in order.
Darkness	• Find a place in the school that can be completely blacked out so the children can experience total darkness.
A glimmer of light	• Let the children try to see things in a completely dark place. Increase the light level by turning on a circuit with a weak battery and one bulb. Ask the children to try reading by its feeble light. They will be able to see remarkably well considering how dim the light is.
Sources of light	Light sources include the sun, other stars, light bulbs, light tubes, TV tubes, light-emitting diode displays such as in clocks, fire. The moon is not a light source as it reflects the sun's light.

> Children living in built-up areas may have little or no experience of complete darkness.

Colours

• Take the children on a colour walk. Talk about the significance of colours and their role in warning and informing. Look at the sequence of traffic lights and pedestrian-crossing lights if there are any nearby. Look at the colours of road signs and shop fronts. Which colours stand out and which blend in?

Traffic-light sequence

Red for danger

Red is traditionally the colour of danger and green the colour of safety. Yellow is used in nature to warn other animals that a creature is poisonous.

Key Stage 2a classroom activities

Shadows

Directional light

• Let the children use torches to make shadows. Go into the playground and make shadows using sunlight.

• Alter the size and shape of shadows by changing the distance between an object and its shadow or changing the direction of the light.

Sharp shadows

• Look at shadows that are sharp and distinct and shadows that are fuzzy.

Umbra and penumbra

Unless the light is highly directional and there is no other source of light, shadows are likely to be fuzzy, with umbra and penumbra areas.

As the distance increases between the surface where a shadow is formed and the object that casts the shadow, the size of the shadow increases.

> Draw silhouettes of the children in the class using an OHP as the light source. Find the best distance (a) from the child to the wall and (b) from the child to the projector.

Sun shadows

Shadows change during the day.

• Look at the shadow made by a skittle at different times of the day. Measure the shadow and note its shape on a piece of paper or use chalk to draw its outline.

> Look at the shadows made by objects in the playground at different times of day.

In Britain the sun is never overhead. Always, even in summer, it shines from the south at noon. The position of shadows is predictable and can be used to tell the time of day.

Opaque, translucent and transparent

Light passes through some materials.

- Give the children a range of materials. Ask them to classify the materials according to those they can see through as if not there, those they can just see through and those they cannot see through at all.

Using a standard light source and a computer datalogger, graph the amount of light that passes through the materials.

Sun block

- Give them different fabrics. Ask them to decide which would be best for curtains to stop the sun waking people up early in summer.

- Look at different sunglasses. Which are darkest?

Transparent, translucent and opaque

Light cannot pass through opaque materials. Some light can pass through translucent materials, but it is not possible to look through them and distinguish fine detail such as print. Light passes through transparent materials with ease. You can see details through transparent materials.

Key Stage 2b classroom activities

Speed of light

Light travels from a source.

- Ask the children to use secondary information sources to find out the speed of light and distances from the Earth to other celestial bodies.

- Let them use calculators to work out how long it takes light to travel from the moon to Earth, from the sun to Earth and from the nearest star, other than the sun, to Earth.

Light travels through the vacuum of space at 300 000 km per second. It is slower through transparent materials.

Speed of light

To travel to the Earth, light takes about eight minutes from the sun and four years from the next nearest star, Proxima Centauri.

Seeing

Light from light sources enters our eyes

- Ask the children to draw pictures with arrows showing how they think they see light sources. Ask them to tell you about their ideas.

This is an excellent way of finding out the children's existing ideas about the way light travels.

Reflected light enters our eyes

- Ask them to draw diagrams with arrows showing how they think they see objects that are not light sources.

Light from a source travels in many directions. Some of this light enters the eye.

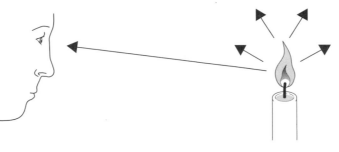

How light reaches the eye from a light source

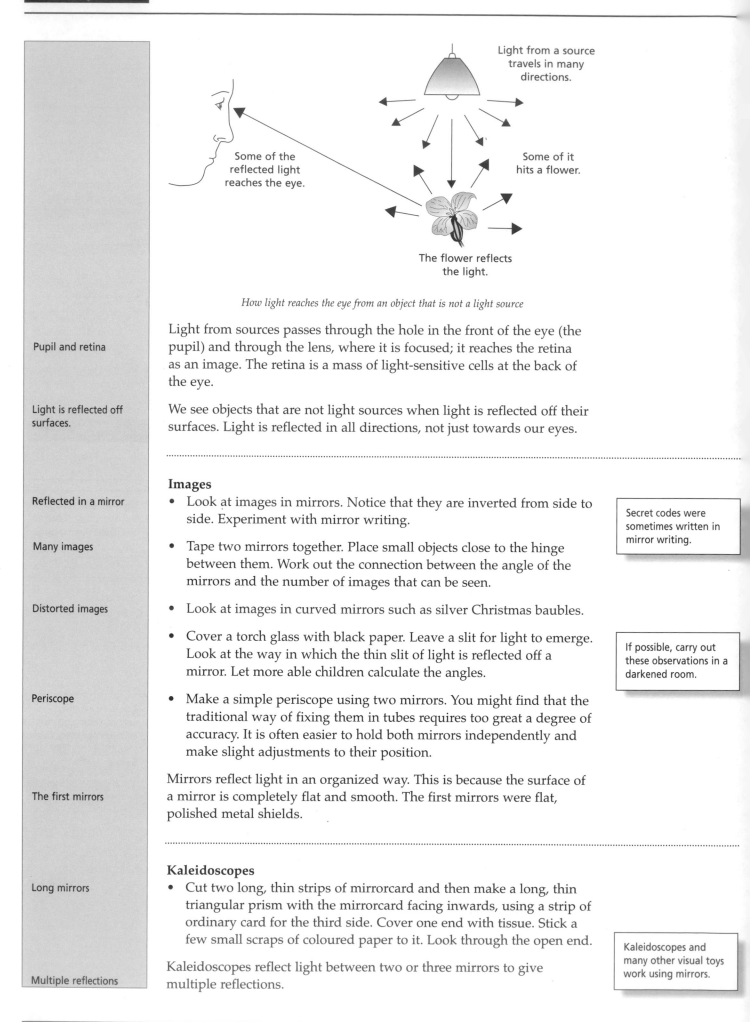

Light from a source travels in many directions.

Some of the reflected light reaches the eye.

Some of it hits a flower.

The flower reflects the light.

How light reaches the eye from an object that is not a light source

Pupil and retina

Light from sources passes through the hole in the front of the eye (the pupil) and through the lens, where it is focused; it reaches the retina as an image. The retina is a mass of light-sensitive cells at the back of the eye.

Light is reflected off surfaces.

We see objects that are not light sources when light is reflected off their surfaces. Light is reflected in all directions, not just towards our eyes.

Images

Reflected in a mirror

- Look at images in mirrors. Notice that they are inverted from side to side. Experiment with mirror writing.

Secret codes were sometimes written in mirror writing.

Many images

- Tape two mirrors together. Place small objects close to the hinge between them. Work out the connection between the angle of the mirrors and the number of images that can be seen.

Distorted images

- Look at images in curved mirrors such as silver Christmas baubles.

- Cover a torch glass with black paper. Leave a slit for light to emerge. Look at the way in which the thin slit of light is reflected off a mirror. Let more able children calculate the angles.

If possible, carry out these observations in a darkened room.

Periscope

- Make a simple periscope using two mirrors. You might find that the traditional way of fixing them in tubes requires too great a degree of accuracy. It is often easier to hold both mirrors independently and make slight adjustments to their position.

The first mirrors

Mirrors reflect light in an organized way. This is because the surface of a mirror is completely flat and smooth. The first mirrors were flat, polished metal shields.

Kaleidoscopes

Long mirrors

- Cut two long, thin strips of mirrorcard and then make a long, thin triangular prism with the mirrorcard facing inwards, using a strip of ordinary card for the third side. Cover one end with tissue. Stick a few small scraps of coloured paper to it. Look through the open end.

Kaleidoscopes and many other visual toys work using mirrors.

Multiple reflections

Kaleidoscopes reflect light between two or three mirrors to give multiple reflections.

Shoe boxes make good darkrooms.

Light is reflected off objects.

Overlapping filters

Safety reflections

*   Make a light box from a shoe box with a peep hole and other holes to let light in where necessary. Look at road-safety materials. Take them into a very dark cupboard or use the light box. Which road-safety material reflects light most effectively?

The reflective strips used by cyclists reflect a great deal of light straight back at car headlights using total internal reflection. Highly reflective materials absorb ultraviolet light and reflect it back in visible wavelengths.

Make a display of reflective and luminous materials.

Colours and colour filters

*   Look at objects through coloured filters.

A filter absorbs light of every colour other than its own. Two overlapping filters may block out all light.

Use the light box to look at objects in coloured light.

The way we see the colour of an object that is not a light source depends on light reflected from its surface.

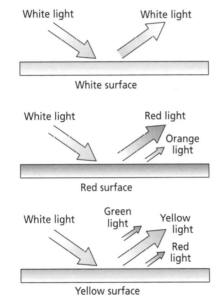

A white surface reflects white light and is seen as white.

The pigments in a red surface are mainly red, with some orange. The pigments reflect the red and orange parts of white light and absorb the rest. The surface is seen as red.

The pigments in a yellow surface are mainly yellow, with some green and red. The pigments reflect the yellow, green and red parts of white light and absorb the rest. The surface is seen as yellow.

If the light source has a colour, this affects how light is reflected from the surface of a coloured object.

Yellow light from street lamp

There are no pigments in blue that reflect yellow light. A blue car under a yellow street lamp absorbs all the yellow light. As a result the car looks black.

A white car under a yellow street lamp reflects the yellow light. As a result the car looks yellow.

Seeing colours

Teaching strategy: interactive displays

WHICH RED LINE IN EACH PAIR IS THE LONGEST?

Make movies

Use the flick book.

Try making one of your own using the pages of an old telephone directory.

Is it a face?

Look at the

What can yo

PUZZLE LINES

Coloured light

What colour is the object inside?

Change the filter on top of the bo

What colour is the object now?

Puzzle lines

Look at the lines A and B.

Which is the longest?

Are lines Z and Y straight?

ROAD SAFETY REFLECTIVE GEAR

Up periscope

Use the periscope to look over people's heads in the classroom.

How do you think it works?

Road-safety materials

Which is the most reflective material?

Look inside this box to see.

Laser patterns

Look at the patterns that are made when you spin this disc.

Make an interactive, stand-alone display for any age to enjoy. You will need to make instruction cards to accompany the display so that it is clear to users what they have to do.

Road-safety materials
Fluorescent materials absorb ultraviolet light then reflect it as visible light.

Puzzle lines/Is it a face?
We rely on many clues to make sense of the world. Our brains are constantly trying to interpret what we see.

Distorting mirror

Look at yourself in the curved mirror.

What do you look like?

Glow stars

Look at the glow stars in this box.

Leave the lid off for ten minutes.

What difference do you notice when you put the lid back on?

COLOURED FILTERS

Mirror patterns

Look at the patterns in this kaleidoscope.

There are two mirrors in the tube.

Use this simple model to see how kaleidoscopes work.

Many reflections

How many images of the doll can you see?

Move the mirrors to see more.

Bird in a cage

Spin the pencil around.

What happens to the bird?

Many reflections
There is a relationship between the angle of the mirrors and the number of images formed.

Glow stars
Luminous objects like this glow after they have been exposed to light.

Distorting mirror
Christmas baubles make excellent convex mirrors!

Bird in a cage/Make movies
These effects rely on the persistence of vision. The illusion of motion in film and television is achieved by a series of still frames shown in rapid succession.

Sound

Compression and decompression

Vibrations

Sound is produced by vibrations. A vibrating object causes the air surrounding it to compress and decompress, and this effect of air moving backwards and forwards spreads outwards from the object in a wave until the energy of the vibration is absorbed.

> A slinky spring shows this kind of wave extremely well. It even shows echoes.

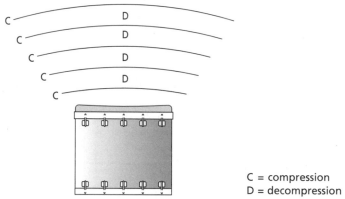

C = compression
D = decompression

Compression and decompression of air in sound waves

Speed of vibration

When the vibrations are very rapid the pitch of the sound is high. When the vibrations are slow the sound is low-pitched. Hertz (Hz) is the SI unit of measurement for frequency, and one Hertz is one vibration per second. The human ear can detect frequencies of between 20 and 20 000 Hz, and this is the range of frequencies we call sound. Unfortunately, our ability to detect high-pitched sounds declines rapidly and at a predictable rate as we get older. Ultrasound comprises those sounds that are at a higher frequency than we can hear. Infrasound is made when objects vibrate at a rate lower than 20 Hz.

Ultrasound
Infrasound

> Hertz is the measure of any frequency, not just the frequency of sound waves.
>
> For a list of the main SI units, see *Science for Primary Teachers* page 51.

Pitch

Strings

The pitch produced by a vibrating string depends on three factors:

thickness (mass) of the string	bass strings on a guitar are wound with wire to make them heavy
tightness of the string	to raise the pitch of a string you tighten it
length of the string	longer strings make a lower-pitched sound.

> Remove the front of a piano. Children will be fascinated to see how it works, and there are also many possibilities for artwork.

Pipes	Pipes such as organ pipes, recorders or bottles will, when blown into, produce a low-pitched note if they contain a long column of air. The note will be high-pitched if the column of air is short.
Bottles	Just to complicate matters, a bottle nearly full of water will produce a low-pitched sound when struck. However, in this case the glass and the water are vibrating, not the air.
Tuned percussion	A large xylophone bar or drum will produce a low-pitched sound when struck, whilst a small percussion instrument will produce a high-pitched sound. The loudness of a sound depends on the amount of energy in the vibrations.

Sound travels

Speed of sound

Thunder

Sound travels faster through solids and liquids but does not travel at all through space. This is because, unlike light, sound needs a medium to travel through. Sound travels at 350 metres per second in air. This explains why you hear the sound of thunder *after* you have seen lightning. Thunder is the sound of a lightning bolt heating up air.

> When air is heated by lightning it expands explosively.

Pitch and volume

The difference between pitch and volume is important. Teachers can unintentionally cause confusion by referring to 'high' and 'low' sounds when they mean loud and soft. Reserve high and low for pitch only.

Common misconceptions

Sound travels

Drawing sound

Many children find it difficult to believe that sound travels. Teachers can explore children's ideas about whether and how sound travels by asking them to draw pictures of how they think they hear sound. The way children visualize this can give an excellent idea of their thinking. Children's drawings are likely to fall into one of five groups:

No movement

No movement of sound is shown. The child might simply write something like 'We hear the bell'. Her picture suggests that she has no clear view that sound travels to her ear through the air. Sound is simply heard.

> It is useful to collect information about children's existing concepts before embarking on an episode of teaching.

No direction

No direction is shown and no idea of travelling is necessarily implied. A child drawing this picture is using some of the conventions of the comic or cartoon.

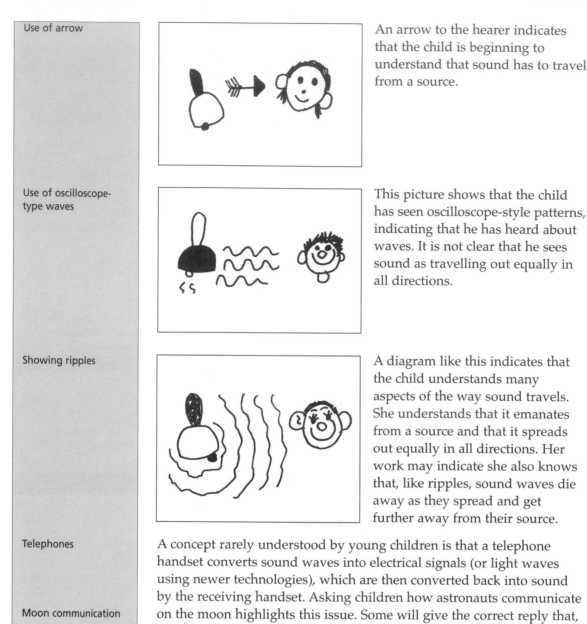

| Use of arrow | An arrow to the hearer indicates that the child is beginning to understand that sound has to travel from a source. |

| Use of oscilloscope-type waves | This picture shows that the child has seen oscilloscope-style patterns, indicating that he has heard about waves. It is not clear that he sees sound as travelling out equally in all directions. |

| Showing ripples | A diagram like this indicates that the child understands many aspects of the way sound travels. She understands that it emanates from a source and that it spreads out equally in all directions. Her work may indicate she also knows that, like ripples, sound waves die away as they spread and get further away from their source. |

Telephones

Moon communication

A concept rarely understood by young children is that a telephone handset converts sound waves into electrical signals (or light waves using newer technologies), which are then converted back into sound by the receiving handset. Asking children how astronauts communicate on the moon highlights this issue. Some will give the correct reply that, since there is no air on the moon, the astronauts need a radio to communicate with each other even if they are only inches apart.

List of resources

Resources for studying sound

- tuning forks (several sizes ideally)
- slinky spring
- guitar
- strings
- masses
- bottles
- instruments
- bottles with narrow necks
- balloons
- thin paper such as tissue or greaseproof
- a few grains of sugar
- thin plastic kitchen film
- rubber bands

Tuning forks are a valuable addition to science equipment. However, they need careful handling to stay in tune, so don't borrow any from the school's music specialist!

- bubble wrap
- cotton wool
- fabrics
- percussion instruments such as a drum, cymbal, triangle, chime bars, xylophone
- loud ticking clock or other sound source
- stethoscope (a good one – toy stethoscopes rarely work convincingly)
- three types of plastic or paper cups
- string, thread, wool

Summary of the programmes of study

Key Stage 1 Sc4: 3c–e
Key Stage 2 Sc4: 3e–g

Children should be taught about the following:
- there are many kinds of sound and many sources of sound
- sounds travel away from sources, getting fainter as they do so
- sounds are heard when they enter the ear
- sounds are made when objects vibrate
- the pitch and loudness of some vibrating objects can be changed
- vibrations from sound sources can travel through a variety of materials

Key Stage 1 classroom activities

Sources of sound

Listening
- Listen to sounds in and around the school. Draw a sound map during a walk around the school showing where the children heard particular sounds.

We can hear sounds when objects vibrate between 20 and 20 000 times per second. Dogs and bats can hear sounds with a much higher pitch. Children can hear higher-pitched sounds more acutely than adults.

Dog whistles

Instruments

- Ask the children to classify instruments into different groups. Record this classification using a piece of paper folded into four.

Musical instruments make vibrations as a result of being struck, scraped, plucked or blown, or through the use of electricity.

Sound travels

Sound travels.

- Discuss how sound reaches our ears from sound sources. Ask the children to draw a sequence of diagrams showing how sound reaches their ears.

> Asking children to draw their idea of how sound travels is a useful guide to misconceptions.

Sounds become fainter.

- Place six children in a line five metres apart in a quiet place outside. Stand at one end of the line and ask the children in it to face away from you. The rest of the class watches. Make a variety of quiet sounds. The children in line put up their hands if they hear anything. The watching children then tell the others what happened.

> This demonstrates that sounds get fainter as they travel further from their source.

Sound spreads out.

As a sound travels the energy in the sound wave spreads out. This means the sound becomes quieter. You can see in the diagram below that the proportion of a sound that enters the ear is less the further away from its source you are.

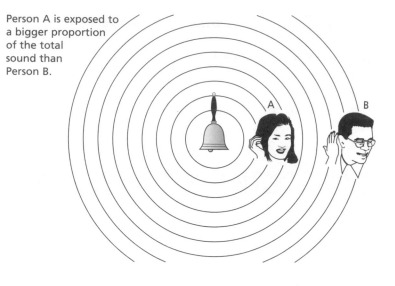

Person A is exposed to a bigger proportion of the total sound than Person B.

The closer the source, the louder the sound

Hearing

Sounds are heard when they enter the ear.

- Ask the children to compare what they hear when listening: normally; covering one ear; covering both ears; cupping their hands over their ears; using a very big funnel to listen through.

Ear drum

Large outer ears, such as those of dogs and rabbits, collect sound more efficiently than small ones. If we cup our hands over our ears or use an ear trumpet we capture more sound energy than our ears would do unaided.

Key Stage 2a classroom activities

Sound travels though different materials

Speaking tube

- Set up a long hosepipe with funnels at each end. Let the children talk into one funnel and listen with the other. Speaking tubes like this work very efficiently by containing sound and not allowing it to spread out.

> Set up these four simple activities as a small circus.

Hard materials transmit sound very effectively.

- Gently scratch one end of a long table or handrail. Ask the children to listen to this sound through the solid material. Note that it is much easier to hear the sound through the solid than it is to hear it through the air.

Some materials absorb sound

- Gently tap one end of a long table. Ask the children to listen to this sound through the solid material. Place several layers of books or thick scarves between the children's ears and the table. The sound will be difficult to hear. This is because some materials are soft and absorb sound energy.

String telephone

- Set up a string telephone. Make sure the string is taut and not touching anything. When someone is speaking into the telephone, gently touch the string for a moment to feel the vibrations. Make telephones with fairly short lengths of string as long strings are

> Vary the type of string and cup in different investigations of how a string telephone works.

cumbersome in a busy classroom. If two lines cross you can have a four-way telephone.

Sound travels by compressing and decompressing the material it passes through. Ability to conduct sound reflects the compressibility of different materials. Solids pass sound on efficiently, liquids do it fairly well and gases do this poorly. Gases are easily compressed and so are effectively quite squashy.

Vibrations

- Make a cooing sound with your mouth against a balloon. Feel the vibrations. Hold a thin piece of paper against your mouth and make a cooing sound. Feel the tingle as your lips vibrate.

- Feel the vibrations produced by a tuning fork. Hold it against your fingernail for maximum effect. But take care: tuning forks can chip tooth enamel.

The sound of our voices is caused by the vibration of two cords in our larynx or Adam's apple. Air forced out of our lungs makes these vocal cords vibrate.

- Look at how a ruler held firmly to the top of a table will vibrate when twanged. A twanged ruler vibrates and produces sound. By altering the length of the part of the ruler that is free to vibrate you can change the rate of vibration.

> You can see the vibrations in some objects.

- If a heavy blob of plasticine is attached to the free end of the ruler the rate of vibration is dramatically slowed. In a similar way, heavy strings vibrate more slowly than light strings.

- Place a few grains of sugar on a tight drumskin. Make a loud sound next to the drum and see the sugar grains move. Drum skins can be made to vibrate by loud sounds close by.

Loudness

- Devise ways to make very quiet sounds. How far away can these sounds be heard? Devise ways to make louder sounds. How far away can these sounds be heard?

> Exposure to loud sounds over a long period causes deafness. Most pop stars, understandably, wear ear plugs.

- Make simple, non-invasive ear protectors using a variety of different materials inside cups, which can be placed against the ear.

- Alternatively place a sound source inside a box and pack a material around it. Use a range of materials. Each time note how far away you can hear the sound, or use a sound detector plugged into a computer datalogger to make a record.

> For more information on datalogging, see page 24.

The volume of a sound increases as the size of the vibration gets bigger. The volume of sound is measured in decibels (dB).

Jet aircraft	140 dB
Walkman (mid volume)	130 dB
Thunder	110 dB
Train	90 dB
Talking	60 dB
Whispering	40 dB
Rustling paper	10 dB
Quietest audible sound	0 dB

> It is surprising that the quietest sound is 0 dB.

Margin terms
Crossed line

Sound travels as compression waves.

Balloon vibration

Tuning forks

Vocal chords

Rulers and vibration

Drum skins and sympathetic vibration

Volume

Ear protectors

Blocked and absorbed sound

Decibels

Key Stage 2b classroom activities

Pitch

Tuning forks

- Examine tuning forks. Suggest that the children use their fingernails to feel how high-pitched tuning forks vibrate more rapidly than low-pitched forks.

String pitch

- Use different weights of string and different masses to investigate the factors that influence the pitch of strings. Use strong spring balances to pull on the string; this will give the children practice in reading spring balances and reinforce the idea that stretch is a result of a pulling force.

> This is an interesting investigation but it does need a quiet classroom.

Bottle pitch

- Blow across the tops of bottles containing different amounts of water.

Tube pitch

- Blow across tubes which you move in and out of water (this has the effect of lengthening and shortening the column of air inside).

Vibrations per second (Hz)

The pitch of a sound depends on the number of vibrations per second produced at its source. Objects that make high-pitched sounds vibrate rapidly whilst those that make low-pitched sounds vibrate slowly.

The pitch of a string is influenced by three factors:

the *weight* of the string
the *length* of the string
the *tightness* of the string.

The pitch of a wind instrument is affected by the height of the column of air that vibrates. Air in long tubes vibrates more slowly (and has a lower pitch) than air in short tubes.

Wind chimes

- Collect several wind chimes and discuss the connection between the length of each tube and the pitch of its sound. Make your own chimes from lengths of scrap piping from a friendly plumber or use flowerpots, blocks of wood or tins.

> Large objects vibrate more slowly than small ones.

Teaching strategy: class lessons for Key Stage 2b

Class lesson 1

Delicate organs

Deafness

Theme:	TAKING CARE OF OUR EARS
Learning objective:	The children will learn that ears are delicate and must be looked after.
Organization:	Whole class
Resources:	Large, simple diagram of the ear
Lesson introduction:	*What things can we hear that we enjoy? What would you miss most if you were deaf? Do you know any deaf people?*

Ear diagram	**Theme:** TAKING CARE OF OUR EARS *(continued)*
	Lesson development: *Here is a diagram of the ear.*

Simplified diagram of the ear drum and its connection to the cochlea

Just the main features

Point out the main features:

The outer ear gathers sounds. What animals have very big ears to gather sounds?

The ear canal channels sounds to the drum.

The ear drum is a very thin skin that vibrates.

The inner ear is a series of bones and tiny organs that change vibrations into electricity. These impulses are sent to the brain along nerves.

> The design of the ear trumpet, an early hearing aid, was based on the principle of a big ear gathering and funnelling sounds.

Ear care

Talk about how we can damage our ears:

By poking things in the ear and making a hole in the drum, causing a perforated ear drum. Avoid doing this. Never push anything smaller than your elbow into your ear.

Loud sounds

By being exposed to very loud sounds. This damages the bones of the inner ear. Can you think of ways that you might be exposed to very loud sounds that could damage your hearing?

> Explosions can severely damage hearing.

By having a disease that destroys the nerve connections from the ear to the brain.

Talk about how our ears keep themselves clean:

Ear wax

They produce wax, which oozes out of the ear carrying any dirt with it. You don't need to dig wax out of your ear – leave that to the nurse who can wash out excess wax with water.

Ear health

Recording:	Children can write a simple pamphlet about 'how to look after your ears'.
Assessment:	*Criterion:* Do the children know some simple steps to protect their ears? *Mode:* Children write an ear health pamphlet.

Class lesson 2

Theme:	WHY DO WE HAVE TWO EARS?
Learning objective:	The children will learn how two ears can pinpoint sound.
Organization:	The whole class sitting in a circle in a very quiet room
Resources:	Blindfold

Quiet room

Theme:	WHY DO WE HAVE TWO EARS? *(continued)*
Lesson introduction:	Sit a blindfolded child in the centre of a circle of all the other children. Point randomly at children in the circle who then make a quiet click. The child in the centre has to point at the child making the noise. Try this again. Cover both ears of the child in the centre. Now try this again with one ear of the child covered. Make sure that some sounds are directly in front of and directly behind the child in the centre. These are the most difficult to pinpoint.
Lesson development:	Tell the children that: • *we pinpoint sounds because one ear will hear the sound a little before the other* • *it is tricky to tell whether a sound is coming from in front or behind because both ears will hear it at the same time* • *two ears pinpoint sound better than one* • *cats and owls move their heads slightly when hunting to pinpoint sound.*
Recording:	The children do a short piece of writing to explain what they understand.
Assessment:	*Criterion:* Do the children understand why two ears are better than one? *Mode:* The short piece of writing.

Margin notes (left): Spot the click. / Covered ears / In front and behind / Explain / Hunters

Margin note (right): The fractional difference in the time taken for the same sound to reach each ear is enough to tell us which direction it has come from.

Margin note (right): Owls use hearing more than sight when hunting in the dark.

Class lesson 3

Theme:	SOUNDS TRAVEL THROUGH SOLIDS
Learning objective:	The children will learn that sounds travel through solids.
Organization:	Whole class working in pairs
Resources:	For each pair of children, one metre of string with spoons or keys attached
Lesson introduction:	Ask the children how they can hear your voice. What is the sound travelling through? What else can sound travel through? Have they ever put their heads underwater in the swimming pool? Did they hear anything? *Everyone hum quietly. Now cover your ears. Hum again. What did you notice? What was the sound travelling through to reach your ears the second time?*
Lesson development:	Ask a child to hold one end of one of the pieces of string. Stretch it out. Ask the whole class what sorts of sounds they would expect to hear if they pressed the string to their ears. (Remember the children should not poke things into the ear canal, but it is not dangerous to press two fingers on to the outside of the ear.) The children will hear a sound like church bells through the string. Experiment with other objects on the string. One child puts an ear to one end of a table. Another child scratches the other end of it with a fingernail. All children press their ears to the wooden floor of a room and listen to sounds you make. Then they press their ears to the carpeted floor of another room and repeat the observation. Tell the children about native Americans who used to listen through the ground for the sounds of buffalo hooves.
Recording:	None. You will be doing more detailed work on this later.
Assessment:	None.

Margin notes (left): Pair work / Voices through the air / Sound travelling through bone / Church bells / Table scratch / Listening for buffalo

Margin note (right): Fish do not have external ears. They can detect sound very efficiently through the water and the bones of their heads.

The Earth and beyond

Solar system

Size of the Earth

Earth-centred system

Sun-centred system

In the beginning

Sun facts

Circling the sun

Key ideas

Earth

The Earth is a large piece of rock orbiting a ball of burning gas called the sun. The sun and the solar system came into being about five billion years ago.

The ancient Greek Eratosthenes was able, by careful observation, to determine the size and shape of the Earth to an astoundingly accurate degree. His countryman Aristarchus worked out that the sun was much larger than the Earth and correctly assumed that the smaller body (the Earth) must orbit the larger.

Before the middle of the sixteenth century it was widely believed that the sun, stars and planets revolved around the Earth on crystal spheres. It was the appearance of the Great Comet in 1572 that finally shattered the idea of crystal spheres.

However, it was not until 1543, when Copernicus published a book demonstrating that the sun, not the Earth, was at the centre of the solar system, that people began to accept the idea that the Earth was just one of several planets.

> This was during the European Reformation, when established ideas were being widely questioned.

Big Bang

The beginning of all time and space is supposed to be the event 15 billion years ago called the Big Bang. At that time all matter was created. The matter clumped together to form stars, and in those early stars new elements were created from the simple material of the Big Bang. In time these stars grew old and exploded, spreading their newly created elements across the universe. Our solar system was not born in the Big Bang; rather it was the result of material from exploded stars clumping together under the influence of gravity.

> Some stars now appear to be older than the theoretical age of the universe. Naturally, this is causing scientific debate.

The sun produces its energy by nuclear fusion. It is 150 million kilometres from the Earth and is 110 times the Earth's diameter. Its mass is 330 000 times that of the Earth's. The sun contains over 99.7% of all the material in the solar system. The temperatures in the middle of the sun are 14 million °C, but the surface temperature is a mere 6000 °C.

The planets

The planets in order from the sun are: Mercury, Venus, Earth, Mars, Jupiter, Saturn, Uranus, Neptune and Pluto. All circle the sun in

Anticlockwise

approximately the plane of the sun's equator. The major planets circle anticlockwise if looked at from the direction of the Pole Star (North), and most rotate anticlockwise on their own axes. All the planets except Pluto are spaced at increasing distances from the sun and have nearly circular orbits.

Pluto is thought to have been a large asteroid captured by the sun's gravity after the formation of the solar system.

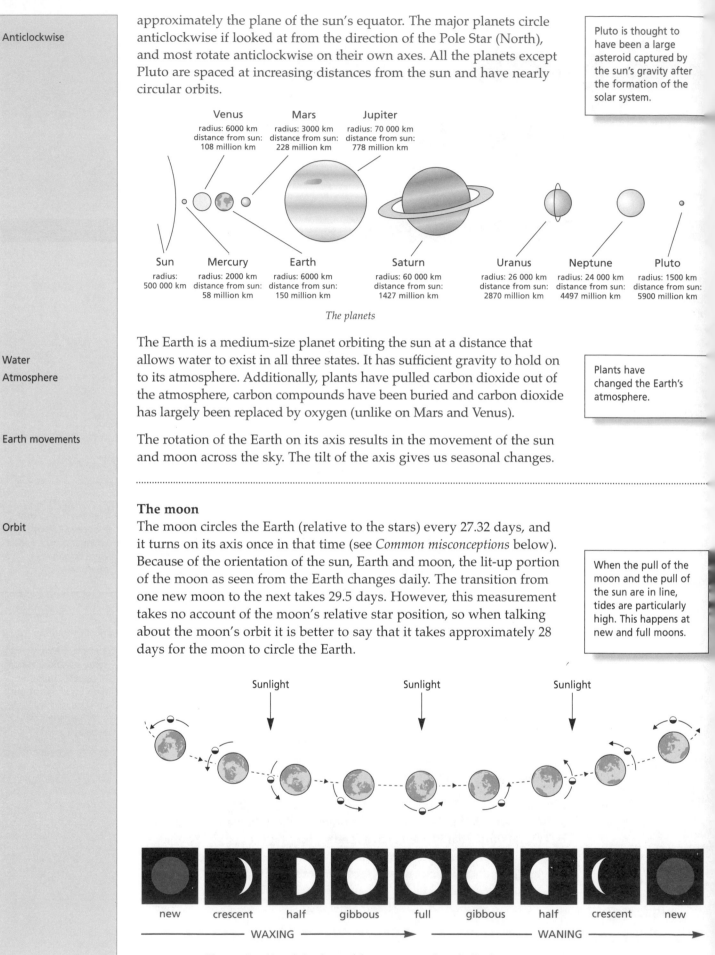

Venus
radius: 6000 km
distance from sun:
108 million km

Mars
radius: 3000 km
distance from sun:
228 million km

Jupiter
radius: 70 000 km
distance from sun:
778 million km

Sun
radius:
500 000 km

Mercury
radius: 2000 km
distance from sun:
58 million km

Earth
radius: 6000 km
distance from sun:
150 million km

Saturn
radius: 60 000 km
distance from sun:
1427 million km

Uranus
radius: 26 000 km
distance from sun:
2870 million km

Neptune
radius: 24 000 km
distance from sun:
4497 million km

Pluto
radius: 1500 km
distance from sun:
5900 million km

The planets

Water
Atmosphere

The Earth is a medium-size planet orbiting the sun at a distance that allows water to exist in all three states. It has sufficient gravity to hold on to its atmosphere. Additionally, plants have pulled carbon dioxide out of the atmosphere, carbon compounds have been buried and carbon dioxide has largely been replaced by oxygen (unlike on Mars and Venus).

Plants have changed the Earth's atmosphere.

Earth movements

The rotation of the Earth on its axis results in the movement of the sun and moon across the sky. The tilt of the axis gives us seasonal changes.

The moon

Orbit

The moon circles the Earth (relative to the stars) every 27.32 days, and it turns on its axis once in that time (see *Common misconceptions* below). Because of the orientation of the sun, Earth and moon, the lit-up portion of the moon as seen from the Earth changes daily. The transition from one new moon to the next takes 29.5 days. However, this measurement takes no account of the moon's relative star position, so when talking about the moon's orbit it is better to say that it takes approximately 28 days for the moon to circle the Earth.

When the pull of the moon and the pull of the sun are in line, tides are particularly high. This happens at new and full moons.

Sunlight   Sunlight   Sunlight

new   crescent   half   gibbous   full   gibbous   half   crescent   new

⟵ WAXING ⟶   ⟵ WANING ⟶

The moon's orbit and the phases of the moon as seen from the Earth

Tides

The moon has a profound effect on the Earth's oceans. Its gravitational pull draws up a bulge in the oceans that results in high tides. The pattern of tides on the Earth is related to the moon's orbit, the amount and location of ocean area directly affected by the moon's gravity at any one time, and the overall ocean movements that take place as a result.

Common misconceptions

Day and night

Moon in the way

Even when models of many kinds are used, the scientifically correct explanation of why we have day and night seems very unlikely to many children. They may talk about the moon getting in the way of the sun at night or simply say that at night the sun moves away.

> The Earth in space is a rich source of children's alternative concepts.

Seasons

We are not closer to the sun in summer.

Although seasons are not in the programmes of study for Key Stages 1 and 2, it is useful to be aware that many children think the Earth is closer to the sun in the summer. In fact, the Earth's orbit round the sun is nearly circular, so its distance from the sun varies little and certainly not enough to explain the seasons.

Rotation and orbit

The sun appears to move.

Has the Earth moved for you recently? We have no sense that tells us that the Earth is revolving. Observations of the sun, moon and stars moving across the sky could just as easily be explained by the possibility that these bodies are orbiting the Earth. It is no surprise to find that children are highly resistant to the idea that the Earth moves and the sun stays still.

Where does the sun go?

Many children do not use the idea of the Earth's rotation to explain day and night. Some believe that at night the sun:

goes behind the mountains   travels under the Earth
goes into the sea   moves away from the Earth
goes out   goes behind the moon.

> Ask the children where they think the sun goes at night.

The moon

Why does the moon glow?

The moon is thought by some children to glow because the sun shines through it, and not because it reflects the sun's light.

Orbit of the moon

The orbit and rotation of the moon is another source of difficulty. If the same side of the moon is always facing Earth, the moon cannot be spinning on its own axis, can it?

> Many adults initially find this a tricky idea to grasp.

Rotating moon

Try this for convincing proof:

Stand in the classroom facing a chair. Note what is behind it. Do a quarter turn round the chair, facing the chair. What is behind the chair now? Do another quarter turn. Are the same things always behind the chair? In relation to the room, as you orbit the chair you are also turning on your axis. You do one complete rotation with every full orbit.

List of resources

Resources for studying the Earth and beyond

- globes and atlases
- light sources including bright torches, projectors and desk lamps
- balls of different size
- masking tape
- Blu-Tack

- magnetic compass
- chalk
- metre rule
- card
- paper fasteners
- skittles or empty bottles

> The best resource is the sun, but in Britain it can't be relied on!

Summary of the programmes of study

Key Stage 2 Sc4: 4a–d

Children should be taught about the following:
- the sun, Earth and moon are approximately spherical
- the position of the sun appears to change during the day
- the Earth spins on its axis
- the Earth orbits the sun once each year and the moon takes approximately 28 days to orbit the Earth

Key Stage 2b classroom activities

Spheres

Balls of proportional size

Actual size

The sun's movement

Lines of latitude

Relative sizes
- Use balls to model the sun, Earth and moon. Show the children that to be at all realistic the balls need to be of dramatically different sizes.

Sun, Earth and moon are approximately spherical. Use balls that reflect their different sizes. The sun is roughly equivalent to a big beachball, the Earth a small pea and the moon a tiny spherical seed. Their actual sizes are:

	DIAMETER
sun	1 000 000 km
Earth	12 700 km
moon	3 600 km

- Take the children out early in the morning. Note the position of the sun relative to landmarks. Do the same at lunchtime and home time.

The position of the sun appears to change during the day because the Earth turns on its axis. This rotation is anticlockwise viewed looking down on the North Pole. This means that the sun always rises in the east and sets in the west.

> In Britain, the sun always shines from the south at midday.

The globe
- Ask the children to find these lines of latitude on the globe:

    equator
    Arctic and Antarctic circles
    tropics of Capricorn and Cancer

Looking closely at the globe

- Ask them to list the countries and oceans you would cross if you were to fly along each line.

Definitions of the lines of latitude are based on the way the sun's rays strike the Earth and are only indirectly related to climate. Sunlight strikes the tropic of Cancer from exactly overhead on midsummer's day. Sunlight strikes the equator from exactly overhead on two occasions a year: the March and September equinoxes. There is continuous daylight north of the Arctic circle on midsummer's day.

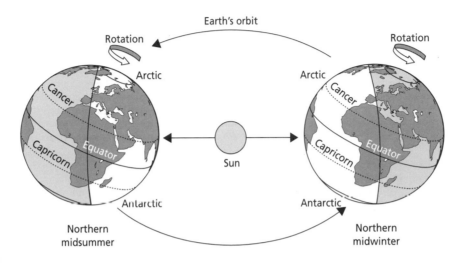

The Earth's lines of latitude

Time differences

- Ask the children to look at the globe. Work out the meals that people in other countries will be eating when it is midnight in Britain.

As the Earth turns on its axis different parts of it come into the light of the sun. Countries to the east of Britain, such as Russia and Poland, come into daylight before us. Countries to the west, such as the USA, come into daylight after us.

> The timing of live TV coverage of sports events from around the world provides useful opportunities to put this work into a real context.

Shadows
- Set up a shadow clock, either in the playground or on a sunny windowsill. As the Earth turns, the direction and shape of the shadows change.

Elevation of the sun

- Choose a convenient time of day. Look at shadows made by the sun at this time in March. Compare them with shadows made at this time in June. In the same way, compare the position of the sun relative to landmarks in March and June.

The tilt of the Earth remains constant throughout the year but the position of the tilt relative to the sun changes as we orbit.

> In winter we only see the top part of the arc made by the sun across the sky.

Earth orbits the sun.

- Discuss what a year is. Draw the orbit of the Earth on the board. Discuss how long it takes the Earth to do half an orbit. How far does the Earth orbit in one month? In one week?

The Earth completes an orbit of the sun every 365 and a quarter days.

Teaching strategy: class lessons

Class lesson 1

Theme:	THE EARTH, SUN AND MOON
Learning objective:	The children will know about the shape, size and characteristics of the Earth, sun and moon.
Organization:	Whole class
Resources:	• beachball • pea • tiny seed • books showing pictures of the Earth, moon and sun
Lesson introduction:	Find out what the children know about the shape and size of the moon, Earth and sun. Ask simple questions to stimulate discussion: *Where do you live? What is your planet called? What is the source of light and heat on Earth?*
Lesson development:	*How big is the Earth compared with the moon? How was the Earth created?* Show the children balls of different sizes. Discuss the relative size of the Earth and the sun. *How far away is the sun? What would happen to you if you went close to the sun? What do the sun and the moon look like? What colours are the spheres? Is there life on the sun and moon?* Ask one child to be the sun, another the Earth and another the moon. *The sun is one million kilometres in diameter, so on this scale the Earth should be 150 metres away from the sun! The moon should be about 40 cm away from the Earth.* Discuss how long it might take a rocket to reach the moon from the Earth (about three days). *So how long would it take to get to the sun by rocket?* The speed of the rocket is roughly 30 000 km per hour and the distance is about 150 million kilometres.
Recording:	See assessment. Give out a duplicated sheet or ask the children to copy from the board.
Assessment:	*Criteria:* Do the children know about the three bodies? *Mode:* Give the children the sheet below, which shows the characteristics of each body. Ask them to fill it in. **Join the bodies to the correct descriptions** It is silver coloured. It is mainly blue. It is yellow. It is a star. It is a planet. It is a satellite. It has lots of water on it. It has no water at all. It is very hot indeed. It is very cold. It is the right temperature for living things. We live here. It is the source of heat and light. moon Earth sun

Margin notes (left):
Some facts

Acting the sun, Earth and moon

Speed of a rocket

Use an assessment sheet.

What is it like?

Margin notes (right):
See page 174 for the sizes of Earth, sun and moon in kilometres.

There are many wonderful stories about the creation of the Earth, including Norse myths, Genesis and Hindu stories.

Use a calculator to work it out.

An assessment activity

Class lesson 2

The movement of the sun

Theme:	THE SPINNING EARTH
Learning objective:	The children will know that the Earth rotates on its axis.
Organization:	Whole class split into pairs. Preferably use a large room such as the school hall.
Resources:	Globes
Lesson introduction:	*The sun appears to move across the sky. What do you think causes this? Which room at home is sunny in the morning? Which is sunny in the evening?*
Development:	Ask one of the children to be the sun and one to be the Earth. Tell the Earth-child slowly to orbit (circle) the sun-child. *This takes one year to complete.*
	Talk about the seasons but do not try to explain them at this stage. Concentrate on the orbit and ignore the rotation of the Earth.
	Stand still. Now we are going to look at the rotation of the Earth and ignore the orbit. The Earth-child should imagine there is a person living on her nose. Is it day or night for your nose? Turn half a turn slowly anticlockwise. (You will have to imagine that you are looking down on the Earth's head.) Is it day or night for your nose now? The Earth turns anticlockwise so the sun appears from the left hand side (east). Compare this activity with how the sun appears to move across the sky. Remember to think about the tiny person living on your nose.
	Now demonstrate the same rotation idea using a globe. Mark the position of Britain with a blob of Blu-Tack.
Assessment:	*Criterion:* Can the child tell you about the reason why there is day and night?
	Mode: A week after the lesson ask the children to jot down what causes day and night. Ask them to include a few drawings.

Modelling the rotation

The sun rises on the left.

Day and night

Acting out the motion of Earth and sun is a powerful way of visualizing an otherwise highly abstract idea.

Carrying out a focused assessment like this is fairly quick and easy.

Further reading

Children's alternative constructs

Russell, T. *et al* (1990–present) *Primary SPACE Reports* (on a variety of subjects including: *Rocks, Soil and Weather, Growth, Processes of Life, Evaporation and Condensation, Sound, Materials, Electricity, Light* and *Forces*), Liverpool: Liverpool University Press.

These reports, which are published regularly, describe research conducted collaboratively with class teachers with the aim of developing young children's scientific ideas. Children's alternative constructs in a number of domains are documented and insights into how teaching can affect their ideas offered.

See also:

Driver, R. (1983) *The Pupil as Scientist,* Milton Keynes: Open University Press.

Keogh, B. and Naylor, S. (1997) *Starting Points for Science*, Millgate House.

Nuffield Primary Science (1995) *Nuffield Primary Science,* London: Collins.

This major series includes eleven useful Teacher's Guides for Key Stages 1 and 2.

Osborne, R. and Freyberg, P. (1985) *Learning in Science: The Implications of Children's Science*, Oxford: Heinemann.

Science education

Bentley, D. and Watts, M. (1994) *Primary Science and Technology*, Buckingham: Open University Press.

Bentley and Watts describe a constructivist approach to conceptual change and development. They discuss issues such as planning, management, organization, and teaching and learning, and consider effective questioning techniques and problem solving. Case studies are used as supportive evidence for the advice given and suggestions made.

Cross, A. and Peet, G. (1998) *Teaching Science in the Primary School: Book 1 A Practical Sourcebook*, Plymouth: Northcote House.

Department for Education and Employment (1998), *Science: A Scheme of Work*, London: DfEE.

Glauert, E. (1996) *Tracking Significant Achievement in Primary Science*, London: Hodder and Stoughton.

A useful source of practical advice about on-going teacher assessment, this book defines assessment and covers planning and record-keeping. Significant achievement is discussed, and examples of children's work are given, together with practical advice, to help teachers recognize what achievement is and how it can be used to aid teaching and learning.

Harlen, W. (1996) *The Teaching of Science in Primary Schools* (second edition), London: David Fulton Publishers.

Practical guidance, with examples, about developing children's scientific ideas, process skills and attitudes is the focus of this book. Harlen discusses planning, provision, assessment and evaluation of learning in primary science, drawing on available research evidence and learning theory to describe how children learn science and develop their understanding through enquiry. The book considers a constructivist approach to teaching and learning, using and handling questions and covers a range of assessment and recording methods.

Hodson, D., and Hodson, J. (1998) 'From Constructivism to Social Constructivism: A Vygotskian Perspective on Teaching and Learning Science', *Social Science Review* 79 (289), pp.33–41.

An accessible introduction to Vygotsky's work and its relationship to constructivism.

National Curriculum Council (1993) *Teaching Science at Key Stages 1 and 2*, York: NCC.

Concerned with the teaching and learning of science, this book offers activities and guidance to enable teachers to implement National Curriculum science more effectively. Issues covered include planning for learning, continuity and progression, differentiation, how children learn science, managing investigations and practical activities, and linking Attainment Target 1 with the other attainment targets.

Ollerenshaw, C. and Ritchie, R. (1997) *Primary Science: Making it Work*, London: David Fulton Publishers.

This practical working guide for teaching primary science, aimed at both established teachers and trainees, combines constructivist learning theory with constructivist teaching methods. Children's recording, assessment and record-keeping and professional development are dealt with in specific chapters.

Osborne and Simon (1996) 'Primary Science Past and Future' in *Studies in Science Education* 26, 99–147.

A very readable journal article reviewing the history of primary science.

Qualter, A. (1996) *Differentiated Primary Science*, Buckingham: Open University Press.

In this practical approach to differentiation in science, Qualter discusses links with learning theory, definition of ability, process and planning, and grouping strategies, and combines starting points with children's ideas. Detailed examples of differentiated learning models are given.

Science background for teachers

Farrow, S. (1996) *The Really Useful Science Book: A Framework of Knowledge for Primary Teachers*, London: Falmer Press.

Farrow gives detailed background information in support of the National Curriculum's programmes of study for science (Attainment Targets 2–4). Key ideas in the various areas are developed into science concepts specifically aimed at Key Stages 1 or 2.

Kennedy, (1996) *Primary Science: Knowledge and Understanding*, London: Routledge.

Peacock, G. and Smith, R. (1992) *Teaching and Understanding Science*, London: Hodder and Stoughton.

Also covering Attainment Targets 2–4 of the National Curriculum for science, this book provides primary teachers with the scientific background to help them develop their own understanding. It suggests practical activities linked to specific scientific ideas drawn from the relevant programmes of study.

Smith, R. and Peacock, G. (1995) *Investigations and Progression in Science*, London: Hodder and Stoughton.

Focusing on Attainment Target 1 of the National Curriculum for science, Smith and Peacock offer support and advice on developing children's investigative skills. They define progression and give detailed examples for the different levels of attainment showing how progression can be achieved. Planning for progression throughout a school is also discussed and practical advice given.

Wenham, M. (1995) *Understanding Primary Science: Ideas, Concepts and Explanations*, London: Paul Chapman Publishing.

Based on the requirements of the National Curriculum, this book offers primary teachers key background information. Practical examples and demonstrations that can be adapted for use in the classroom support the facts, concepts and theories given.

Periodicals

Primary Science Review, Hatford: Association for Science Education.

A quarterly journal containing research findings, articles and classroom ideas relating to primary science.

Junior Focus Magazine, Leamington Spa: Scholastic.
Infant Projects Magazine, Leamington Spa: Scholastic.

Monthly magazines about infant and junior practice, with many science themes.

Questions Magazine, Birmingham: Questions Magazine.

A monthly magazine devoted to science and technology.

School Science Review, Hatfield: Association for Science Education.

A quarterly journal for primary and secondary teachers containing slightly weightier articles than those published in *PSR*.

Science classroom schemes

Hopkins, S. and Hunter, A. (1990) *Teacher's Classroom Manual: Key Stage 1*, Lincoln: Thomas Nelson.

A manual providing practical advice for planning and implementing science in a cross-curricular context. It suggests methods for the organization, implementation and evaluation of different themes and gives examples of ways of questioning, experimenting and investigating.

Peacock G., Coltman O.P. and Richardson R. (1997) *Science Connections*, London: Longman.

A highly structured scheme with a useful Teacher's Book.

Phipps, R., Feasey, R., Stringer, J. and Goldsworthy, A. (1997) *Star Science*, Aylesbury: Ginn.

A comprehensive scheme with a range of big books and references.

Information technology

Computers in primary science
Frost R. (1995) *IT in Primary Science*, Hatfield: Association for Science Education.

Department for Education and Employment (1998) *Information Technology: A Scheme of Work*, London: DfEE.

Doherty, G. (1998) *101 Things To Do With Your Computer*, London, Usborne.

Kalbag, A. (1998) *World Wide Web for Beginners*, London: Usborne.

Resources available from the Internet
Schools Online Science Project
http://www.shu.ac.uk/schools/sci/sol/contents.htm

Understanding Electricity
http://ds.dial.pipex.com/understanding

Centre for Alternative Technology
http://www.foe.co.uk/CA

Science Line
http://www.sciencenet.org.uk

You can also use the standard site of the DfEE to find a range of current information from government. The address is:
http://www.standards.dfee.gov.uk

CD-ROM resources

These can provide useful support to science teaching and be a valuable source of background information for teachers.

The *Interfact* series from Two Can is easy-to-use and makes an excellent starting point when using this type of resource. Titles include:

Electricity and Magnetism
Polar Lands
The Senses

Amongst other useful CD-ROMS are:

Dangerous Creatures (Microsoft)
Garden Wildlife (Anglia)
Magic Bus Explores the Human Body (Microsoft)
The Ultimate Human Body (Dorling Kindersley)

The Earth and beyond

Many organizations are able to provide ideas and information that can enrich teaching and learning about a topic. Here are some to which you could turn for support in planning work on The Earth and Beyond:

NASA Education and Awareness Branch, John F. Kennedy Space Centre, Florida 32899, USA. (Multiple copies of resources not supplied.)

European Space Agency, Educational Affairs, Noordwijk, The Netherlands.

British National Space Centre, Polaris House, North Star Avenue, Swindon SN2 1ET, UK.

Armagh Planetarium, College Hill, Armagh, BT61 9DB, UK.

Jodrell Bank Space Centre, Macclesfield, Cheshire, UK.

Dennis Ashton (operator of mobile planetarium), 64 Muskoka Drive, Sheffield S11 7RJ, UK.